Brief Christian Histories

Brief Christian Histories

Getting A Sense of Our Long Story

JAMES W. WHITE

Foreword by
Brian McLaren

Icons by
Melissa White Addington

WIPF & STOCK · Eugene, Oregon

BRIEF CHRISTIAN HISTORIES
Getting A Sense of Our Long Story

Copyright © 2014 James W. White. All rights reserved. Except for brief quotations in critical publications or reviews, no part of this book may be reproduced in any manner without prior written permission from the publisher. Write: Permissions. Wipf and Stock Publishers, 199 W. 8th Ave., Suite 3, Eugene, OR 97401.

Wipf & Stock
An Imprint of Wipf and Stock Publishers
199 W. 8th Ave., Suite 3
Eugene, OR 97401

www.wipfandstock.com

ISBN 13: 978-1-55635-243-0

Manufactured in the U.S.A.

In Loving Memory of

LOREE ELIZABETH WHITE
Disciple of Christ — Woman of Prayer
March 5, 1912 — March 9, 2013

Contents

Acknowledgments | ix
Foreword by Brian McLaren | xiii

Introduction | 1

Chapter 1
The People of God:
The Main Characters of Our Faith Story and Their Roles | 7

People Timeline | 51

Chapter 2
Christians' Ethics:
Historical Trajectory on Relating to God and Neighbor | 65

Chapter 3
Practices and Pieties of The Pilgrimage:
With Matching Quizzes for Historical Periods | 104

Chapter 4
Christ and Culture Interacting:
Societal Settings, Dynamics, and Formations of the Faith | 148

Conclusion: Looking Back, Looking Forward | 197

APPENDIX A: A Listing of Some Biblical and Ecclesial Roles, Offices, Titles, and Functions | 201
APPENDIX B: Christian Practices and Pieties through the Years | 205
APPENDIX C: Author's History with These Histories | 209

Bibliography | 215
People Index | 219
Subject Index | 223
Bible and Literature Index | 229

Acknowledgments

BLANCHE DUBOIS OF TENNESSEE Williams's *Streetcar Named Desire* famously said, "I get by on the kindness of strangers." Me, I've made it through by the "competence of acquaintances"—steady friends, thoughtful students, princely scholars, empathetic colleagues, helpful writers, and loving family. These acquaintances generously critiqued the classes I taught, read the trial balloon manuscripts I generated, and suggested better big ideas and little words for this book. I am off-the-charts grateful for their wise words and red ink. By location here are the names of folk *I remember* contributing to historical-theological-ethical thought in these pages:

In **Norman** at the University of Oklahoma: Dean Lizsey, John Raines, Leslie Smith, and J. Clayton Feaver

In **New Haven** at Yale Divinity School: Harry Adams, Sydney Alstrom, Roland Bainton, James Gustafson, Paul Holmer, B. Davie Napier, and H. Richard Niebuhr

In **Ft. Collins** and at Colorado State University: Louise Cordsen, Bob Essig, Bob Geller, John Hallsten, George Purvis, and Harry Rosenburg

In **Berkeley** and at the Pacific School of Religion/GTU and the University of California: Robert Bellah, Dale Heckman, John Hsu, Charles McCoy, Wayne Rood, and Nevitt Sanford

In **Denver** at First Plymouth Congregational Church (UCC) and the University of Denver/Iliff School of Theology: Dick Anderson, Howard Brand, Allen Breck, Theodore Crane, Jim Davis, Linda Glenn (especially), Will Gravely, Dave Harmon, Stuart Haskins, Sally Italiano, Jim Kirk, Alan Pfnister, Sherry Sargent, Jan Skein, Pat Schroeder, Roy Smith, Bob and Bobbye Tucker, Jim Vandermiller, Anita McCullough White, Dana Wilbanks, Ray Zwerin, and many class participants

Acknowledgments

In **Moline**: Kate Bastion-Feeney, Beverly Carl, Al McCune, Sunny and Jim Moorhusen, Carol Smith, Bob and Mary Tallitsch, Barb and Eric Trimble, and Jim and Joan Winship

In **Edinburgh**: Andrew Wall and Lamin Sanneh

In **Westfield**: Betsy Chance, Nancy Donny, Linda Kreil, Freia Mitarai, Sandra Rooney, Barbara Thompson, and "The Thursday Class"

In **Colorado Springs** at First Congregational UCC Church and Colorado College: Hays Alexander, Fawn Bell, Lucy Bell, Jim Bramwell, Kay Branine, Benjamin Broadbent, Janet and Paul Carpenter, Flo Carris, Jim Clamp, Jim Diers, Don Dunn, Kathryn Eastburn, Steve Ferguson, Gail Finlay, David Gardiner, Jerusha Goebel, Steve Handen, Joe Henjum, RoMa Johnson, Virginia Lee, Linda Lemieux, Kathy Lindeman, Sharon Littrell, Carol Malkin, Jim Matson, Carol Neel, Joe Pickle, Howard Ray, Chris Reimer, Eric Ridings, Debbie and John Saxon, Alan Severn, Dave Seyfert, Paul Schwotzer, Robbie Limpert and Sid Shelton, Pam Shockley-Zalabak, Peter Sprunger-Froese, Tom Stella, Anthony Surage, Paul Tatter, Bill Taylor, Jerry Trigg, Jane and Bruce Warren, Sara Weatherman, David Weddell, Cathy and Jerry White, and "101/102 Participants," class-after-class-after-class. (Also in passing-through Colorado Springs, speaking at Colorado College and/or our church's James W. White Endowed Lectures: Marcus Borg, Gil Bailie, Walter Brueggemann, Joan Chittister, John Dominic Crossan, Amy-Jill Levine, Bernard McGinn, Brian McLaren, Robin Meyers, John Selby Spong, and Susan Thistlethwaite.)

In **Decatur** at Columbia and Candler Theological Schools: Walter Brueggemann, Roberta and Richard Bondy, Oliver Daley of Jamaica, Mark Douglas, Catherine and Justo González, Jet Harper, Thomas Long, Jaroslav Pelikan, Don Saliers, Stan Saunders, and Jan Vales from the Czech Republic

On **El Camino de Santiago de Compostela**: Toby and Deanne Eccles of Australia

In **Wichita**: Leigh and Mike Aaron-Leary, William Browning, Michelle Davidson, Ann Dorrah, and participants in the Sunday Forum

In **Seattle**: Jane and Mike Emerson, Catherine Foote, Paul Forman, Peter Ilgenfritz, Kathy Kripps, Michelle Kuster, David McCracken,

Acknowledgments

Mark Miller, Kathy and Greg Turner, Gary Waffle, Nancy Wiesner, and participants in the ongoing Jesus Seminar

In **Bali**: Shirley Cruthers, Emily Evans, Annegret Hoerrmann, Kade Mastra, Susan Setiawan, Tio Sagari, Jeanne Tuttle, and participants in the Vestry Class

In **Russia**: Bruce Rigdon, Father Vladimir, our Moscow and St. Petersburg guides, and "The Twenty-Five Pilgrims"

In **Eugene**: Christian Amondson and Matthew Wimer, editors

From Minneapolis: content editor nonpareil Hermann Weinlick

Exactly when-where-how the above colleagues assisted is suggested in Appendix C of this book, "Author's History with These Histories."

Most especially, from **Phoenix**, my thanks to Melissa Marie White Addington, iconographer for the chapter sections, from **Florida**, Brian McLaren, fly-fisherman and author of the fertile Foreword* to this book, AND, **on every road and stop of the way**: Patti Limpert White, encouraging wife/careful proofreader, and Bruce Kuster, fishing partner/indulgent listener.

And, I know, I'm forgetting . . . many.

That said, the closing lines to *The Paradiso* in Dante's *The Divine Comedy* sum things up well:

> Here my powers rest from their high fantasy,
>   but already I could feel my being turned—
>   instinct and intellect balanced equally
>   as in a wheel whose motion nothing jars—
>   by the Love that moves the Sun and the other stars.

For that Love, thanks be to God!

*Brian writes so ingeniously, it makes me want to read the book myself.

Foreword

BY BRIAN MCCLAREN

JIM WHITE AND I share four passionate commitments, and they serve as helpful introductions to the important book you now hold in your hands.

First, we love fly-fishing. That might be a strange place to begin, since this is a book about Christianity and history. But fly-fishers are students of trout, and trout live in streams, and streams are beautiful, complex, dynamic systems. In any stretch of stream, there is a current, a flow, a direction in which water runs. There are also eddies, places where the current encounters an obstacle that creates an anomaly in the flow—maybe a slow space, a backflow, an upwelling. There are edges, bends, and channels where the currents move at varying rates. There are seams, where different subcurrents meet. To add complexity and dynamism to this already complex and dynamic system, life in the stream adapts to seasons and weather conditions and times of day.

Now many people wonder—especially the spouses of fly-fishers—what is the difference between (a) fishing and (b) standing on the shore, waving a stick, looking stupid. But for those who have come to appreciate the beauty and complexity of nearly every stretch of nearly every stream, there is a big difference indeed. Jim White is a master angler who has developed a profound sensitivity to beauty, dynamism, and complexity, and that sensitivity has served him well in writing this book.

Like a stream, the Christian faith has a flow to it, and it has encountered any number of obstacles that have created any number of anomalies and eddies. It has edges, bends, and channels aplenty, and is constantly interacting with times, seasons, and changing conditions. People without sensitivity to beautiful, complex, dynamic systems would miss so much of this, but not Jim White.

Foreword

Along with fly-fishing, Jim and I share a passion for story. We sense that stories are more comprehensive and adaptable than lists of dates and doctrines or organizational charts of hierarchical institutions. So for us, Christian faith is best understood as a story, a story that, like a stream, has a flow or current. And just as a great stream teems with many fish and other forms of life, the Christian story teems with any number of doctrines and personalities and formations, which are interesting and worth studying . . . as part of the larger narrative flow.

Besides trout streams and stories, we also share a great love for teaching. We believe that the best teaching strives to be comprehensive rather than sectarian, irenic rather than polemic, and iterative rather than linear. Each of those characteristics deserves a bit of explanation, because each tells you something about this book and what makes it special.

Comprehensive rather than sectarian: Jim wants to help readers get the largest vision of Christian faith possible, so he presents a comprehensive vision of Christianity that includes many versions, or Christianities, within it.

Irenic rather than polemic: His aim isn't to argue why one version of Christian faith is better than all others; his goal is to help readers get a sense of how all the versions are interrelated and how all share commonalities that make their differences all the more interesting.

Iterative rather than linear: Imagine walking down a streamside trail and having a naturalist point out the trees around you. Then the next day you walk the same path, learning about the birds in the trees. Then the next day you focus on geology—land features, rocks, and earth processes that shaped that stream valley. Then the next day you learn about the role of that steam and surrounding forest in human history. At the end of those four walks, you'll know that forest far better than if you had walked it only once and been deluged with all the information at once. As you read this book, you'll have the sense that you're being taken on successive guided tours of the same territory, but shown different things on each tour.

Many teachers—especially of religious matters—prefer to teach with sectarian and polemic ends, using strictly linear means, which helps explain, I think, why so many people have been turned off to religion. Jim has an approach that is better suited, I think, both to most of us students and especially to his subject matter.

And that subject matter is the fourth passionate commitment that we share. You sense in Jim's writing not the detached objectivity of an outsider,

Foreword

but the devoted wisdom of someone who loves the Christian faith, loves its essence, loves its past, and loves its potential.

Once you've read this book, you'll share that love, and you'll be better equipped to be part of fulfilling our common faith's potential.

So it's time for you to wade in. You'll soon be hooked!

Introduction

And when in time to come your son asks you, "What does this mean?" You shall say to him, "By strength of hand the Lord brought us out of Egypt, from the house of bondage."

—Exodus 13:14 (RSV)

In order to be at peace, it is necessary to feel a sense of history—that you are both part of what has come before and part of what is yet to come. Being thus surrounded, you are not alone; and the sense of urgency that pervades the present is put in perspective.

—Elisabeth Kübler Ross

It's in vain, Trot, to recall the past, unless it works some influence upon the present.

—Betsey Trotwood, in Charles Dickens's *David Copperfield*

How to undergird Christian enthusiasm with Christian substance? That is the question. It's the question the clergyperson, ordained as "pastor and teacher," confronts in the call to equip the saints for faithful living. It's a tough problem. America, according to cultural analyst Stephen Prothero, has become a nation that is at once "deeply religious and profoundly ignorant about religion."[1] Most American adults cannot name one of the four

---

1. Prothero, *Religious Literacy*, 1.

Brief Christian Histories

Gospels, and one high school senior wrote, "Sodom and Gomorrah were husband and wife"! The average Christian knows even less about post-Bible history—nothing, for example, about gifts to us from Benedict of Nursia or the Anabaptist Conrad Grebel. On a medieval history exam, I'm told, a college student penned, "Joan of Ark, wife of Noah, was burnt as a steak"!

Lament and humor about our religious illiteracy notwithstanding, thoughtful folk suspect that, beyond sermons and Sunday school *as usual*, and certainly beyond devotional-rack literature, there is significant faith-enriching grist yet to be ground for our nourishment. We especially need a grasp of our venerable narrative. Laypeople know this but have a hard time gaining a satisfactory feel for the length, width, and depth of historic Christianity.

The book the reader has in hand addresses the problem.

As a pastor, I've always wanted people in the congregation to have a feel for the *whole* Christian story; and, by "whole" I mean both our biblical *and* our ecclesial—that is, "church"—history. So I have taught . . . and so this book.

Here, though, the reader may ask, as have many students. "But, Reverend White, how can what happened *before* Jesus be *Christian* history?" The answer is that the Hebrew Bible—which I like to call the Old*er* Testament—is *our* story just as much as it is the story of Jews. Jesus in the Gospel of Matthew, for example, is clearly cast in the likeness of Moses; said another way, the Word, Spirit, and Wisdom of God, spoken of so regularly in the Older Testament, are attributes also ascribed to Christ Jesus. For the Christian narrative to be complete, all the dots in our long story need to be connected.

Why? So that all of us might better understand "from whence" we have come.

Then it is just possible we might go forward, perhaps not making so many mistakes—like believing that a king's or czar's or president's "customary way" of doing things is actually our Sovereign's.

Though the scope of this book is wide, it wants to be *brief* and is so named. In fact, it is **four brief histories**. The long story of our biblical and ecclesial history comes in concise—roughly fifty-page—iterations. My intention is for the reader to quickly and easily grasp the whole narrative.

These whole-cloth renderings of our history create a unique book, distinct from all the brief Christianity books I know about. To be sure, there are many "Intros to Christianity" on the market. Their focus is often on

Introduction

how to become a Christian or what Christians believe. Such is not the focus here. My focus is our religion's long history and how that history is influencing us. In this regard, the available shorter faith-history books in the market are of two types: overviews of the Bible and short church histories. Amazingly enough, no one book joins biblical and church stories in a single volume. This one does.

Of course, *Brief Christian Histories* cannot cover everything in our faith narrative, but it goes the way of enabling the interested reader to begin to get the big picture. It can happen even in a single evening's read at the kitchen table! What I commend is quickly going through any one of the four narratives, just to *sense* what the whole may be. The chapter with which one starts does not matter. Each tells the same basic narrative. If the reader gets "lost" at some point, he or she may check out the People Timeline located after chapter 1.

This book narrates faith-history by taking a *theme* and running it through Christianity's four-thousand-year story. Let me share how I developed the theme approach to doing religious history. While teaching Bible history or church history in the usual church educational setting, I learned that sharing something fully is, at best, difficult. Most educational offerings in the church are hit-and-miss affairs. If you offer a seven-Sundays-in-Lent course on a topic—say, the parables of Jesus—many class members miss some sessions, thus not learning the parables well. If you do a *history* course, it is more troublesome, for to miss a session creates a continuity gap, and to understand history, one needs the sequences. My solution to the missed-classes problem has been to tell our story complete every session. This way even a one-time attendee gets the big picture, albeit along a narrow track. Persons who attend two, three, or all the sessions have a fuller grasp of the long narrative. Learning our history by taking a manageable-but-important-themes approach is, I am convinced, a good way to get our hoary story communicated. So, this book.

The four themes followed in *Brief Christian Histories* are as follows:

- People—"who" has done what in which roles
- Ethics—"how" we've construed the moral life through the centuries
- Practices—"what" we've done to demonstrate loyalty to God and one another
- Cultural Interaction—"where" our religion engaged . . . and to what effect

My earlier book, *Christianity 101: Tracing Basic Beliefs*, followed a similar theme approach. That book dealt with (1) the *central events* that formed us, (2) the *history of God*, as we've appropriated it, (3) *Christ* before-during-and-after his earthly time, and (4) life in/with the *Holy Spirit*(uality). Those themes highlighted basic beliefs, that is, what we hold to be "true" about God as Creator, Redeemer, and Sustainer. However, believing, the concern of that book, is only *part* of Christian faith. Part.

An equal portion of our religion has to do with who we are and how we act in the world. This dimension to Christianity concerns behaving and belonging. Said another way, half of the Ten Commandments have to do with relationship with God, and the other half with life in community. *Brief Christian Histories* turns to work with themes that trace our history in terms of the Good, more than via the True (beliefs) or the Beautiful (the arts). If my earlier book had to do with interpretation, this one concentrates on implementation of the faith.

This book is going to be most helpful for learners-about-Christianity generally and Christian laypeople in particular. *Brief Christian Histories* comes as a resource for individual readers, learners in parish study groups, college students in intro-to-religion classes, seminarians, and resource librarians.

Let me say more about the four themes actively traced.

Chapter 1, "The People of God—The Main Characters of Our Faith Story and Their Roles," is a broad overview of our biblical and ecclesial past in terms of men and women. We know our story, our "play," through the players. Those players gave, used, and altered church roles, many of which are operative today. The role of church musician, for example, has a history from Miriam, the 1250-BCE tambourine-playing prophetess, to Mahalia Jackson, a twentieth-century-CE gospel singer.

Chapter 2 is "Christians' Ethics—Historical Trajectory on Relating to God and Neighbor." Our actions through the years have been guided by (1) command, (2) call, (3) response, and (4) virtue—four major modalities of living morally. These modalities are described by H. Richard Niebuhr and Robin Lovin. We'll see how and where these various ways of construing the moral life operated in the past—so that we might be guided in the present.

Chapter 3, "Practices and Pieties of the Pilgrimage," shows that through the centuries we have nodded to God differently and similarly, and we've observed, forgotten, and kept innumerable rituals. We have been ascetic and indulgent, venerated certain objects and eschewed others. Some practices and pieties, the reader will discover, are timeless, others fleeting. This chapter comes with matching quizzes at the end of each section.

Chapter 4 is "Christ and Culture Interacting—Societal Settings, Dynamics, and Formations of the Faith." Belief and behavior have consequences. They affect our relations with others. Relationships over the millennia are traced in these pages. Christianity has been shaped by its physical, social, and cultural environments . . . *and* there have been countershapings of the world by the faith. It is helpful to recall these dynamics, even as we struggle with "the culture" today, a matter addressed in the chapter's closing pages.

What each chapter does is give readers a *sense of the whole* Christian story. Necessarily, there will be repeating of events, incidents, people, things. Repeated, they serve as guideposts for the long journey. Each theme works to overlay, thicken, or, if you will, *decoupage* the narrative.

Feel for our whole faith history, then, is the goal of this book. To help in that development, each chapter is offered with nine repeated subdivisions or time periods. The nine intervals with their icons—appearing in the chapters—are

Pre-Monarchic Millennium (2000–1000 BCE)	Moses' Staff
Time of the Kings and Prophets (1000–550 BCE)	Star of David
Second Temple Period (550–20 BCE)	Torah Scroll
Newer Testament Times (20 BCE–110 CE)	Resurrection Lamb
Struggling Centuries of the Church (110–500 CE)	Constantine's Chi Rho
The Age of Monasticism (500–1100 CE)	Celtic Wild Goose
High Christendom Years (1100–1450 CE)	Three-tier Miter
Reformations/New Worlds Era (1450–1650 CE)	Open Bible
Ecumenical/Global Age (1650 CE to the Present)	Oikoumene Boat

In the dating shown above, and throughout the book, I use BCE/Before the Common Era and CE/Common Era.

At the end of each chapter are Questions for Reflection and Discussion, for individual readers and for use in the classroom. Footnotes, intentionally, have been kept to a minimum throughout, only occasionally inserted when better documentation is called for or when a relevant or interesting aside seemed in order. At book's end is a bibliography, a strong one. Church historian Robert Bruce Mullin says about his *A Short World History of Christianity*, "If readers finish this book hungering for more

Brief Christian Histories

in-depth knowledge, it will be the author's dream come true. There are many fine encyclopedic histories they can consult."[2]

To which dream I add a hearty "Amen!"

James W. White,
Colorado Springs, Colorado

---

2. Mullin, *Short World Christianity*, xiii.

Chapter 1

The People of God
The Main Characters of Our Faith Story and Their Roles

Let us now sing the praises of famous men [and women], our ancestors in their generations. The Lord apportioned to them great glory, his majesty from the beginning.

—Sirach 44:1–2

*I sing a song of the saints of God / Patient and brave and true,
Who toiled and fought and lived and died / For the Lord they loved and knew.
And one was a doctor, and one was a queen, / And one was a shepherdess on the green:
They were all of them saints of God, and I mean, / God helping, to be one too.
And one was a soldier, and one was a priest, / And one was slain by a fierce wild beast:
And there's not any reason, no, not the least, / Why I shouldn't be one too.*

—Lesbia Scott, Lyricist

Brief Christian Histories

. . . to lose respect for the great lights along with the lesser ones, to forget Elizabeth of Hungary or Thomas More, Catherine of Siena or Martin of Tours, leaves us alone on the edges of life, lacking both models and guides.

—Sister Joan Chittister, *In Search of Belief*

I say more: the just man justices;
Keeps gráce: thát keeps all his goings graces;
Acts in God's eye what in God's eye he is—
Christ—For Christ plays in ten thousand places,
Lovely in limbs, and lovely in eyes not his
To the Father through the features of men's faces.

—Gerard Manley Hopkins, "As Kingfishers Catch Fire"

More than most religions, Christianity emphasizes relation to God through people. Ask a gathering of Christians how they came to the faith, and the number one reason will involve people: "The influence of my sainted grandmother," "Because a neighbor invited me to services," or simply "My daughter." Only occasionally in Christian decision is it religious doctrine, ritual, stance on an issue, or program that counts. Mostly it's people.

When world religions are symbolically depicted, we may see a Star of David for Judaism, a yin and yang circle for Taoism, a crescent for Islam, and so on. A cross usually shows Christianity. Such representation notwithstanding, our main symbol, finally, is *not* a cross, nor a three-in-one geometric figure, nor a book or place or story or season or attitude. It is a human being, the man **Jesus of Nazareth**,[1] the one we call the Christ. On either side of Jesus-as-the-Christ stand witnesses. In this chapter, I want to remember some of these men and women before and after Jesus, he being for us the fulcrum of history—an understanding suggested by theologian

---

1. In these pages, as I talk about the main characters and the roles they fulfill in the Christian story, I boldface names. The reader is referred to Appendix A for an extensive listing of roles mentioned in this chapter and existing in the wider world of historic Christianity.

The People of God

Robert McAfee Brown.[2] Our faith flows to Jesus and from Jesus with people. The fulcrum can be seen in the following overreaching but illustrative graphic:

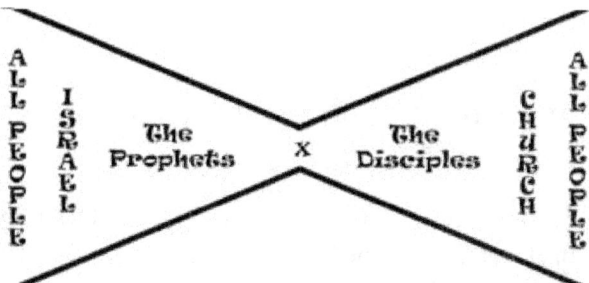

The idea here is that, in creation, **all people** were in close relation to God, called to be part of God's realm. But, as a whole, humanity let God down. So God focused attention on a particular people, the people of **Israel**, to be the Divine's representatives on earth. They/we could not do/be, however, what was needed. So hope came to reside in **prophets** directing us into right relationship. The prophets, though, also could not bring about the restorative work. It was then thought, *perhaps an individual might be adequate*. "Yes," our faith says: the individual was Jesus of Nazareth, whom we call the Christ, here shown with an **X**. By/in/through Christ the relationship with God was righted.[3]

Now, for the flow out of the fulcrum.

Jesus chose a small band of **disciples** to carry on after him; they are comparable to the prophets. The disciples, in their time, helped constitute the **church** of Jesus Christ (in the fulcrum, comparable to Israel), with a mission to relay word of reconciliation with God in love to **all people**.

That is the "really, really big" picture, albeit oversimplified, overstated.

In this picture, we of the Christian church find ourselves *surrounded by so great a cloud of witnesses . . .* [that we should] *run with perseverance the*

---

2. Brown, *Bible Speaks*, 15. The diagram was tendered by Brown at a National Student Conference in the 1960s held in Portland, Oregon, which I attended. I have revised it slightly.

3. Another way to picture this is to make the Tanakh (Older Testament/Hebrew Bible) the fulcrum of history, leading us and all people into right relationship with God. If I were a Jew, that is what I would say. As will be seen in this book, I contend that rabbinic Judaism and Christianity (or, Christian Judaism) began at the same time, 70 CE, when our faith ancestors were expelled from Jerusalem. I don't want to forward supersessionist ideology, saying Christianity trumps Judaism. No. Both arose together at the same time, out of the same struggling history.

race that is set before us, looking to Jesus, the pioneer and perfecter of our faith* (Hebrews 12:1, 2). Let us then consider some of our foremothers and forefathers in the faith, to see what they did and stood for, considering how they might inform us and what we do and are in this world.

PRE-MONARCHIC MILLENNIUM (2000–1000 BCE)

The assemblers of the Bible, who gave the Older Testament its final form, began the book of Genesis by saying, "In beginning, **God** . . ." God, the Holy One, is both **the main character** *and* the highest office holder.

God is the first actor and the creator of all, including

The man **Adam**

"from the ground/*adamah*"

and

The woman **Eve**

"from a chop of the man"

"mother of all living/*hawwâ*"

These two are symbols of humanity, the **all people** of the fulcrum above. To borrow a current image, "The Wo/Men 'R Us!" We humans are considered *imago Dei*, made in the image of God. We are given God's original blessing . . . *and* we experience separation from God. The story of Adam and Eve is accurate description of the human condition. Likewise, the early stories show how we are given to violence, as in the Genesis 4 account of two brothers, **Cain** and **Abel**, one of whom murdered the other.

In the book of Genesis, there also is **Noah** of ark and flood fame, along with Noah's descendants, leading to the ancestors who built the tower of Babel, the purpose of which was *to make a name* for themselves (Genesis 11:4). All these notable mythic characters—who "never were but always are," as Thomas Mann says—lead toward the legendary patriarch and matriarch of our religion, **Abram and Sarai**. We are told that, *by faith*, this couple left their home in Chaldea (southern Iraq), traveled into and out of Haran (northern Iraq) to a land God would show them, namely, Canaan/Palestine. Renamed **Abraham and Sarah**, the pair was succeeded by **Isaac and Rebekah**, and they by **Jacob**, also known as **Israel**, and his wives-plus-maids, the best known woman being **Rachel.** Jacob and his consorts' twelve sons constituted the twelve tribes of Israel. In the last chapters of Genesis, we meet coat-of-many-colors-or-with-long-sleeves **Joseph,** who saved the tribal families from famine and facilitated their move from Canaan down to Egypt. There, the Genesis story suggests, our ancestors dwelt from around 1700 until 1250 BCE.

In time, a new king/pharaoh arose in Egypt, a king *who knew not Joseph.* This new king enslaved the people of Israel and began to oppress them. So, our narrative says, "we cried out to God for deliverance."

God answered. God called **Moses,** without question the person of greatest importance in the Older Testament. Faith history runs to and from him in much the same way it goes to and from Jesus in the fulcrum above. Hundreds of years after the time of Moses, writers of the scripture generate stories that set the stage for Moses' arrival, then tell of his time and doings, and, finally, cast subsequent history in his shadow.

There is as yet no hard archaeological evidence for Moses. Still, we consider him to be a historical figure. Certainly the People of Israel considered creation of themselves *as a people* to be related to Moses. Moses is the liberator, the lawgiver, and the everything-man. In his person he embodied four primary ministerial roles that are ever so important in our subsequent religious history. They are the ministerial roles of being...

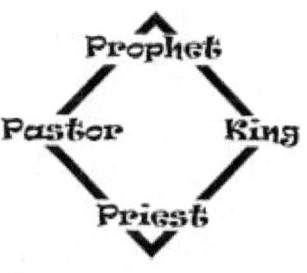

The reader may consult Exodus 3:1-14, Moses' burning-bush encounter with **YHWH** or **Yahweh**—the Bible's best name for God—for demonstration of these roles. Moses is king or leader, the one who is responsible for the governance of the people, just as later there will be judges, kings, popes, abbesses, ruling elders, and so on, people responsible for running things. "King" is one of the major roles Moses established for all time, his rod or staff (see icon above) carried by those in authority yet. A second role is that of pastor. Moses was literally a shepherd, one who tended sheep, and also one who shepherded the People of Israel out of slavery and cared for them in their wilderness wandering. The caring, counseling, healing, serving ministries of today's church may, in this sense, be traced to Moses. Thirdly, consider the role of priest. This role is that of being an intermediary between God and people, especially in the sacramental life at the altar, but also in the many ways that worship has been conducted through the centuries. A contemporary clergyperson celebrating Holy Communion is very much a priest. Finally, note prophet. Prophet suggests presenting *the Word of the Lord*, as in the Ten Commandments, which Moses did, but also teaching the faithful and proclaiming the righteous God's ethical demands, which many a preacher still does.

So we have the four historic roles of ministry. *More* rather than less, they function today.

In time the roles passed from Moses to his successors. Specifically, the kingly role went to **Joshua,** who was first of the judges, later to include **Gideon, Deborah,** and **Samson.** Moses' brother **Aaron** assumed the priestly role, and the tribe of Levi carried this function forward. Unnamed persons became the pastors responsible for *thousands, hundreds, fifties, and tens* described in Exodus 18:25. Moses' sister **Miriam** was the first person after Moses to take on the role of prophet. She is called "the prophetess" and also, with her tambourine and song, the first musician.

In the eleventh century BCE, the title of prophet landed solidly on **Samuel,** son of **Hannah,** a petitioner of God. Samuel initiated a process that moves the people of Israel toward governance by monarchy.

TIME OF THE KINGS AND PROPHETS (1000–550 BCE)

First of all, Samuel anointed a man named **Saul** to be king of Israel. Saul began to pull the several tribes of Israel together in resistance to their coastal enemies, the Philistines. In his struggles Saul was aided by a young captain, **David of Bethlehem**. This David was the one Samuel also anointed to be king—in place of Saul.

In biblical stature, David stands right there with Moses. He was multitalented: a musician playing a soothing harp, a poet with the Psalms attributed to him, a brave soldier who slew the Philistine giant Goliath, and the faith's chief mourner, weeping at the death of his friend Jonathan. David was a totally capable leader, remembered as Israel's greatest king, the model of what a messiah/anointed leader should be, including penitent, confessing his sin of adultery and murder . . . and receiving forgiveness.

One mark of David's genius is shown in his establishing a new capital city for the competitive tribes of Israel. It was Jerusalem. He was its founder, and he brought into Jerusalem the Ark—read "chest"—of the Covenant

The People of God

with the tablets of the Ten Commandments in it. Thus Jerusalem became the symbolic religious center of a united empire.

David's son **Solomon** reigned next and is remembered in the role of builder. On a locale known as the Mount of Abraham or Zion, Solomon built a temple, one named after him. In it the **sons of Zadok** and the **Levites** functioned as priests. According to the Bible, under Solomon's leadership, the Israelites' empire expanded to its fullest extent. The whole Jordan rift valley from Damascus in the north to Ezion-geber on the Gulf of Aqaba became his. Seven hundred years after his time, Solomon, revered for his sagacity, had "wisdom" literature attributed to him.

In passing, it should be noted that during the tenth and ninth centuries BCE, writers of some of the basic documents of the Bible were putting Israel's narrative story onto scrolls. The J or **Yahwist** writer and the E or **Elohist** writer are two of these authors. They generated material that will go into the first five books of the Older Testament. Another writer, called D or the **Deuteronomist**, created most of the material for a book that would bear his name, plus the books of Joshua, Judges, Samuel, and Kings. The Deuteronomist's book of 2 Samuel focuses on David and his dysfunctional family. First Kings is an account of Solomon's reign.

Following the death of Solomon, the kingdom broke into two parts, south and north, to be known respectively as Judah and Israel. King **Rehoboam** with two tribes in the south ruled at Jerusalem. King **Jeroboam I** with ten tribes in the north ruled at Samaria. Others followed them in subsequent generations, persons such as

King **Asa**, who reigned successfully for forty-one years

King **Ahab** and Queen **Jezebel**, who were in conflict with the prophet Elijah

King **Hezekiah**, who got locked up in Jerusalem "like a bird in a cage" by the Assyrians

According to the Bible, the best monarch after David was King **Josiah**, whose priests found the Deuteronomist's writings in the temple. Upon hearing the "Second Law," Josiah instituted reforms, especially in the worship of Yahweh, meaning worship *only* in Jerusalem. He was, we might say, an early reformer.

Alongside the kings, often in opposition to them, were the prophets. Greatest of the prophets, as a symbol for all the prophets, was **Elijah**. He had a dramatic contest on Mount Carmel with the prophets of Ba'al. In the contest, his offering, a water-soaked bull, was consumed by fire, while the Ba'al prophets' dry bull was not. Elijah is also remembered for hearing *the still small voice of God* outside a cave to which he had fled. So, in addition to being a prophet, he is honored as a mystic. Elijah and his successor, **Elisha**, were also considered wonder workers, as they both restored life to children thought dead.

Besides Elijah and Elisha, there were other prophets in the eighth century BCE. Some of them wrote down what they said. **Amos, Hosea, First Isaiah,**[4] **Jeremiah,** and their disciples were writers of God's "word." They proclaimed a radical monotheism, thundered for justice and righteousness in the land, and pronounced judgment in God's name. Below is a strong sample from Amos, speaking for God. The passage also reveals how a prophet differs from a priest.

> I hate, I despise your feasts,
>   and I take no delight in your solemn assemblies.
> Even though you offer me your burnt offerings and grain offerings,
>   I will not accept them;
> and the offerings of well-being of your fatted beasts,
>   I will not look upon.
> Take away from me the noise of your songs;
>   I will not listen to the melody of your harps.
> But let justice roll down like waters,
>   and righteousness like an ever-flowing stream. (Amos 5:21–24)

While there is judgment, at the same time, most of the prophets hold out hope for redemption in the face of destruction. Hosea, for example, asks, on behalf of Yahweh, "How can I give you up, Ephraim? . . . My heart recoils within me . . . I will not execute my fierce anger . . . for I am God and no mortal, the Holy One in your midst, and I will not come in wrath" (Hosea 11:8–9).

Yet destruction came. This is a huge part of our people's story. There were enemies. **Sennacherib** of Assyria obliterated the northern kingdom of Israel, even as recorded in a famous poem by Lord Byron:

> The Assyrian came down like the wolf on the fold,

---

4. The book of Isaiah is thought to have had three major contributors: First Isaiah, who composed chapters 1–39; Second Isaiah, of the mid-sixth century BCE, who penned chapters 40–55; and Third Isaiah, of the late sixth or early fifth centuries, to whom chapters 56–66 are attributed.

And his cohorts were gleaming in purple and gold;
And the sheen of their spears was like stars on the sea,
When the blue wave rolls nightly on deep Galilee.

Then the ten tribes of the north were no more, as the people were carried off into slavery. Non-Israelite, non-Yahwist-believing people were brought in to repopulate the region. This destruction took place in 722 BCE.

The southern kingdom of Judah barely withstood Sennacherib's onslaught and later Assyrian attacks. Finally, though, Jerusalem fell. It fell to King **Nebuchadnezzar** of Babylon, who carried the leading citizens of Jerusalem into exile. This deportation was in 586 BCE, "a year to live in infamy." Now one-in-exile became a veritable role for many, including the person who wrote Psalm 137, verse 1: "By the rivers of Babylon—there we sat down and there we wept, when we remembered Zion, which was no more"—not for the exiles.

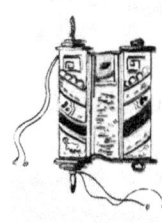

SECOND TEMPLE PERIOD (550–20 BCE)

Zion/Jerusalem, though, was to be home again for the exiles. Why? How? Because King **Cyrus the Persian** defeated the Babylonians. He then said to the captive Judeans, "You may go home." In 538 BCE groups of them started the 600-mile trek back to their Holy Land. They said of Cyrus that he was a messiah, one anointed of God, chosen to give them a new lease on life.

Back in their country of origin, the remnant people began anew. **Nehemiah**, former cupbearer to a Persian king, became the repairer of the wall around Jerusalem, thus securing the Holy City. By the year 515 BCE, **Zerubbabel** the builder erected a new temple on the Holy Mount. And, finally, there was **Ezra**, priest and purist for the Law, who began a process of making Jews more scrupulous about their religion. For one thing, he counseled that orthodox Jewish men should divorce their foreign wives.

Other leaders in Israel, however, took a more open stance in interpreting the Law than did Ezra. They said, in essence, that instead of narrow nationalism, the will of God is for inclusion of a wider slice of the nations, including Gentiles/non-Jews. So a story is told of **Jonah,** a reluctant prophet, who tried to escape delivering Yahweh's warning for people in the hated city of Nineveh. He fled by boat but was thrown overboard and brought back to land—by a great fish—to give a message, "Repent," to the Ninevites . . . and the Ninevites did repent. They were *non*-Israelites experiencing the generosity of God. Similarly, the author of the book of Ruth notes that **Ruth**, grandmother of David and a heroine in her own right, was from a *foreign* country, Moab. As for a role title, Ruth was a kind of mother to the nation.

For the most part, we do not have names for the people in this period who made the greatest long-term contributions to our religion. These were the anonymous authors and editors of the Bible, some called redactors. They assembled the Older Testament. Written materials generated by people previously mentioned—the Yahwist, Elohist, and Deuteronomist writers—were integrated. So the Torah or first five books of the scripture came to be. Last of the contributors to the Torah is the P or **Priestly** writer, who gave the book of Genesis its strong beginning and enriched the corpus with emphases on ritual and holy-day observances.

The writing prophets, discussed above, seem to have had disciples, who put their words on scrolls. These were assembled in such a way as to create the second major classification of biblical books, the Prophets. So, "the Law and the Prophets" were generated as written documents during the fifth and fourth centuries BCE.

"Other Writings" for the Bible came later, more slowly. Most notably, Psalms and Proverbs emerged, with Psalms attributed to David and Proverbs to Solomon. In truth, these poems and wisdom sayings were mostly done by anonymous writers. To them we may also be grateful for

- the narrative of **Esther**, "the queen who saved her people"
- Ecclesiastes' **Koheleth**, the preacher who knew about "vanity of vanities"
- an **unknown** poet who gave us Song of Songs, with its beautiful love verses

Song of Songs would be especially revered by Christian mystics two thousand years later.

Some of the written-last-in-time books, notably Ezekiel, Daniel, and Third Isaiah, speak their hope that perhaps a single person, a new Moses, someone like David or Elijah or a "Son of Man" would come as Messiah to redeem God's people, as the opening fulcrum depicts. Malachi, the last book in the Older Testament, sets the stage for the coming again, at least, of Elijah.

For Christians—and this is *our* telling of the salvation story—things happened like this: In the late fourth century BCE, Alexander the Great of Macedonia came as conqueror of the Middle Eastern world, toppling the Persians. In time his Greek-controlled empire was divided, the land of Judah coming under the control first of Ptolemaic/Egyptian Greeks and later of Seleucid/Syrian Greeks. One of the Seleucid kings, **Antiochus IV Epiphanes**, during the mid-second century BCE, desecrated the temple in Jerusalem. He placed a statue of the Greek god Zeus on the altar! This "abomination" is told of in the book of Daniel. Opposition arose in the persons of three brothers, one of whom was **Judas Maccabee**, "the Hammerer." The brothers were essentially freedom fighters. Fighting, they succeeded in ousting the Greeks from Judah, giving their successors a hundred-year reign of relative autonomy. In 63 BCE, however, the Roman general Pompey took control of the region for Rome. Eventually the Romans installed **Herod**, called "the Great," as king. Late in his reign (37–4 BCE), a baby boy was born in "David's royal city," Bethlehem. The boy's name was **Jesus** or **Joshua,** which means "God saves." He is the long-awaited Messiah, our center for the fulcrum of history.

NEWER TESTAMENT TIMES (20 BCE–110 CE)

The advent of Jesus was heralded by **John** the baptizer and prophet, who was cast in the image of Elijah. He entered the scene with a message of repentance, proclaiming that God was about to break into human history. All the Gospel writers (**Matthew, Mark, Luke,** and **John**) tell us that the Baptizer looked for one who would come after him, yet who would be mightier than he. John the Baptist found "that one" to be the man **Jesus from Nazareth in Galilee**, whom he immersed in the River Jordan. At his baptism Jesus received a sense that he and God were in a unique and eternally important relationship. Jesus' followers would say of that relationship that he was the Son of God and Emmanuel ("God with us").

What Jesus did was launch a ministry in which he was, variously, healer, exorcist, miracle worker, rabbi/teacher, preacher, activist, contemplative, and much more, including the historic four roles of priest-prophet-pastor-king originating with Moses. In all his roles and activities, what Jesus seemed to be most focused upon was proclamation of the *Basileia/*

Kingdom/Reign of God on earth. That reign is one, he said, in which men and women are deeply related to God and living in right relationship with one another. Such was Jesus' passion, and that passion brought him into conflict with authorities not sharing his great vision. In particular, he was opposed by Pharisees (religious purists) and later, in Jerusalem, by Sadducees (temple-connected, Roman-collaborating conservatives). These two *religious* opposition groups ultimately joined with *political* elites, Herodians and Romans, to have him crucified.

Standing with Jesus, all but to the end, was a close coterie of at least a dozen men and women: **Peter, James,** and **John,** as well as **Mary Magdalene** and **Mary and Martha of Bethany.** They were Jesus' disciples (see the fulcrum), often called apostles—the men, anyway. Beyond the closest circle of friends were others: fishermen, tax collectors, his own mother **Mary,** his blood brother **James,** "the seventy" whom he sent on an errand of peace telling, a Roman soldier whose daughter he healed, some Greeks, children, lepers, a woman taken in adultery, a woman at a well, blind **Bartimaeus,** the prominent lawyer **Nicodemus,** and on and on.

When Jesus' words and action provoked the religious and governmental authorities to come down on him, his followers either melted away into betrayal (**Judas Iscariot**) or denial (**Simon Peter**) or hiding (**Thomas**). Jesus overturned the tables of money changers at Herod's temple, crying out that God's house, which was intended as a "house of prayer for all people," had become a "den of robbers" (Mark 11:17). Such action and words provoked the powers that be. **Caiaphas,** the high priest of the Sanhedrin court, and **Pilate,** Roman governor of the province, conspired together to be rid of Jesus. They arrested him, put him on trial for blasphemy, a religious offense, and for sedition, a political crime. They obtained his conviction and had him scourged. He was crucified and died on that cross. In dying he was alone, sensing God might also have abandoned him. With the writer of Psalm 22:1 he cried out, "My God, my God, why have you forsaken me?"

But was he forsaken? **Mary Magdalene,** coming to his grave early of a Sunday morning, the third day after his crucifixion, said Jesus was *not* forsaken, for she found the tomb empty. With angelic counsel she concluded about Jesus, "He is risen!" God had raised him. She thus became the first witness to the resurrection.

With the experience and testimony of Mary and others, **Jesus,** the God-centered, all-loving, crucified human one, now became the Risen Christ. His resurrection and renewed presence ignited the "Christian" faith per se. The followers of Christ now looked back to remember "all that came before"—trying to grasp its meaning—and they looked forward to "all that shall be," trying to establish direction for themselves.

The apostle **Paul**, writing fifteen to twenty years after Jesus' death, contended that with the crucifixion and resurrection, the axis of the world changed. Paul lifted up—and the Gospel writers echoed—that Jesus, "a man without sin," in whom God dwelt, died an innocent victim. His death, Paul contended, was a sufficient sacrifice, so great as to effect reconciliation between God and all people (again, see the fulcrum) for all time. It is a huge claim, of course, with the implication that Jesus is "the Savior of the world." With historian René Girard, I would make the same assertion for Christ, but for a somewhat different reason, namely, that Jesus' perfect model of self-giving love is what saves and will save the world.[5] In either interpretation—or other explanations, for there have been many—Jesus the Christ is pivotal.

Moving forward, Jesus' followers came to believe that the Risen Christ was active in the world, especially through the **Paraclete** or Comforter, whom our Lord said would come after him. We know the Paraclete best in terms of God's **Holy Spirit**.[6]

The Bible says that the Holy Spirit comes fully at work in the world with the disciples/apostles as they spread the word of the life, death, and resurrection of Jesus Christ. In the book of the Acts, one person we learn about is the young man **Stephen**, who is stoned to death for his testimony. He becomes the first Christian martyr, meaning "witness." Acts also describes other people engaged in the spread of the Good News: **Peter, Philip, Silas, Barnabas, Bartholomew** and, pivotally, the apostle **Paul**. Paul becomes the missionary par excellence. He establishes churches in the Gentile/Greek world, ever encouraging those churches by his letters or

---

5. French historian René Girard contends that in Jesus' total identification with the victim and in his nonblaming of anyone while on the cross, he rejects "mimetic violence"—the way societies and cultures have always done things. From time immemorial, oppressed people in their revolution have "mimicked" the violent ways of their oppressors, calling any new violence on their part "God's just will." Girard, though, says that Christ opened a new nonblaming, nonvictimizing way to believe and be in the world, a way that does not permit "sacral counterviolence." *That* understanding is what will save the world! As such, then, Jesus is truly The Savior of the World. Jesus' nonviolent "virus," Girard suggests, is still active in the world, working to change the way all people, societies, and cultures operate—"in time," of course. See Girard, *Reader*, 186, and Bailie, *Violence Unveiled*, 217.

6. See the fourth section of White, *Christianity 101*, 115–50.

"epistles." His letters actually are the earliest-written materials of the emerging Newer Testament, in which more than half the material is by him or attributed to him.

Paul was a missionary in Asia Minor/Turkey and Greece. Other missionaries went elsewhere. By tradition, **Mark** brought Christianity to Egypt, **Mary Magdalene** to France, **Andrew** to Scythia in today's Turkey, and **Thecla**, another woman, to Seleucia of modern-day Iraq. Christianity thus spread throughout the Roman Empire . . . and beyond. Tradition holds that "Doubting" **Thomas** took the Gospel to India, though it is more likely that later-in-time Syriac Christians took it there, as well as south to Arabia and across the Red Sea to Ethiopia.

By the early second century, all the books of the Newer Testament were written. In the earliest-written books (those by Paul), we hear about teachers, administrators, charismatics, and healers. Later-to-the-canon books, such as 1 Timothy, describe new roles in the church: deacons, presbyters/elders, and bishops. The later-developing roles indicate that church-as-institution was coming into being. In all of these, we discern Moses' fourfold offices of prophet-priest-pastor-king being enacted. These leaders, along with the *laos*/laity (ordinary faithful persons), lived in what is first called the Way. Later they took the name "Christian," meaning that they were both *followers* of our Lord and persons trying to be *Christlike*.

STRUGGLING CENTURIES OF THE CHURCH (110–500 CE)

In the earliest years of the Christian movement, **women**, mostly unnamed, played a prominent part, often as celebrants/worship leaders in house churches or in catacomb settings. One ancient fresco shows a communion table presided over by a woman surrounded by women. However, this feminist authority was lost over the early centuries as, more and more, the church conformed to Greco-Roman social protocols in which women were constrained and men alone empowered in leadership.

So this period of church history is often called the time of the church fathers. Here is a listing of some of the prominent fathers (showing when they died), with a brief indication of role and doings:

- **Ignatius** (–117 CE), bishop of Antioch, who organized the church along Roman government lines and was an early martyr

- **Polycarp** (–154 CE), aged bishop of Smyrna (today's Izmir, Turkey), a man of faith, who was burned at the stake under Emperor Marcus Aurelius
- **Justin Martyr** (–164 CE, beheaded in Rome), first Christian apologist, who wrote to explain the faith to the Romans and to build bridges to Greek thought
- **Marcion** (–165 CE), heretic rejecting the Older Testament, who set up a circumscribed canon for the Newer Testament, causing a crisis about what constitutes scripture
- **Irenaeus** (–202 CE), bishop of Lyon, France, who wrote *Against the Heretics* (Gnostic Christians) and was the first great theologian in the Western church
- **Tertullian** (–230 CE) of North Africa, Latin theologian who wrote *Apology* and first used the term "Trinity" in talking about God
- **Hippolytus** (–235 CE), priest in Rome, known for his learning, who created a communion liturgy that is in use yet today
- **Origen** (–254 CE) of Alexandria and Caesarea, Bible scholar, who emphasized the Bible's allegories, wrote *On Prayer*, and was a mystic

By these sketches of a few leaders, one can also pick up some of the roles and titles developing during the early centuries of the church.

The most important role was that of bishop. Bishops, especially those of the important "sees"/cities—Alexandria, Antioch, Constantinople, Jerusalem, and Rome—were the ones who thought and acted most significantly for the church during its first five hundred years.

Secondly, many of the bishops were also martyrs, persons slain for their faith. These witnesses are a reminder that there was periodic and regional persecution of Christians. The title martyr was one that women wore too. **Blandina** of Lyon was martyred in 177 CE, along with forty-seven other Christians. Two female martyrs especially remembered are **Perpetua** and **Felicitas**, killed by animals in the Roman coliseum of Carthage in 203 CE. While Perpetua was in prison, her father came pleading with her to recant her faith. She asked him, "Do you see this vessel lying on the table as a little pitcher or as something else?"

He replied, "I see it as a little pitcher."

"Then, can it be called by any other name than what it is?"

"No."

"Nor can I call myself anything else than what I am . . . 'a Christian.'" So Perpetua.

One of the highest categories of saint was that of virgin martyr, as was the legendary **Cecilia** of third-century-CE Rome. Her story is that she died singing, thus becoming patron saint of musicians. These women and men constitute a few of the many who died as witnesses during this period.

In time, many of the martyrs—wrapped in legend, to be sure—were given the title saint, and that is the third thing to note about our early faith-parents. "Saints" include the first followers of Jesus, major players in the Newer Testament, and subsequent others. One could be designated a saint if he or she had

- done an heroic deed, like **St. George** who, the story goes, slew a dragon
- performed a miracle, as did **St. Genevieve**, saving Paris from attack by her prayers
- been a giving person, like **St. Martin of Tours**, who cut his cloak in two for a beggar

Such things might lead to "beatification" and eventual canonization as a saint in the church. In the mid-eighteenth century CE, Father Alban Butler listed 2,565 persons in his *Lives of the Saints*. Over the years, in the Roman Catholic tradition 4,500 men and women have been canonized. If local venerations and stories are included, the count of saints is well over ten thousand.

From the names above, one can see that some of the church fathers were apologists; that is, they were thinker-writers who wanted to make our religion understood and appreciated both by fellow Christians *and* by those in the wider world of Greek, Roman, Jewish, Gnostic, and pagan thought. They were our early theologians and scholars. Certainly **St. Jerome** of Jerusalem (–420 CE) would be considered a scholar, translating the Older Testament from Hebrew and the Newer Testament from Greek into a Vulgate/Latin version. Working alongside him was the wealthy Roman widow, **St. Paula** (–404 CE), who, with her daughter, built churches, a hospice, a monastery, and a convent for women religious. She was the convent's prioress or abbess. Both mother and daughter were Hebrew scholars.

Another noteworthy woman is **St. Catherine** of Alexandria, who, legend has it, argued the faith with philosophers of that city and, finally, was sentenced to death on a spiked wheel. She is considered one of fourteen female "holy helpers," hers a "voice" heard by Joan of Arc a millennium later! This is the Catherine for whom the famous St. Catherine's Monastery in the Sinai Desert is named. The monastery is on the site where Moses, by tradition, received the Ten Commandments. In recent centuries, some of the best preserved and most ancient manuscripts of scripture were found there.

Early in the fourth century CE, persecution of Christians ended. **Constantine**, a Roman general and son of a Christian mother, **Helena**, defeated a throne-contending adversary in the West. Then in 313 CE, with the ruling general of the East, he issued an Edict of Toleration. That ended persecution. Beyond this, Constantine wanted to unify things. So, upon becoming sole ruler of the Roman Empire in 324 CE, he facilitated a gathering of bishops in Nicaea, near his new capital city of Constantinople. Among other things, the bishops put together a *credo* or statement of faith. The Nicene Creed begins to define *right* or orthodox belief.

None of this should suggest that there was easy agreement about matters of faith. Bishop **Athanasius** (–373 CE) of Alexandria argued in Nicaea against the followers of a deacon **Arius** (–336 CE), also of Alexandria. The issue before them was with regard to the nature and work of Jesus Christ: Was he *from the beginning* with God the Father? The Arians said no. In the end, Arius was designated a heretic, while the mantle of orthodox/"right believer" was given to Athanasius. Centuries of conflict on this matter would come to the church. Chief among the orthodox defenders of the faith were the Cappadocian Four: **Basil the Great, Gregory of Nazianzus, Gregory of Nyssa,** and, sister to two of these, **Macrina.** The Cappadocians were of what would be soon be known as the Eastern or Greek or Orthodox Church.

In the Western or Roman or Latin or what would be called the Catholic Church were two important figures of the late three hundreds CE. One is **Ambrose** (–397 CE), bishop of Milan, who is also honored as a hymnist. Ambrose is best remembered, though, as the preacher who influenced the greatest of the Western thinkers, **Augustine of Hippo** (–430 CE). After Augustine's dramatic conversion (described in his tell-all book *Confessions*), he became a bishop in North Africa and the theologian who contributed to our understanding of the Trinity, saying it is dynamic relationship in love. He also wrote the *Enchiridion,* a catechism, and the *City of God.* The latter gave perspective on Alaric the Arian Visigoth's sack of Rome in 410. Augustine contended there is but one Eternal City . . . and that is with God in heaven, not on earth.

The awareness of one's home being in heaven was early in the consciousness of some Christians. One question was how to get there. In the late third century, Egyptian believers took to the deserts and other solitary places to be anchorites or hermit/eremite monks. **St. Antony** (–350 CE), who lived to be 106, is best remembered in this role. The solitary monk style, practiced by Antony, was also the way of **Simeon Stylites,** who lived atop a column in Syria for forty years. These "athletes for Christ" had their case for *voluntary* suffering strengthened in the early fourth century CE, when toleration was granted to Christians, and then even more so in 381 CE, when Christianity became the *favored* religion of the realm. Essentially the Emperor **Theodosius** made Christianity the empire's official religion. Tolerance and such favor, however, convinced wanting-to-suffer-like-Christ souls that they ought *not* be comfortable in the world but more ascetic. Many became monks and nuns.

Solitary monks like Antony were complemented early on by communal or cloistered monks called cenobites. The founder of an early cenobitic monastery was Abba **Pachomius** (–346 CE). He wrote a *Rule* for the gathered communities of men and women in Egypt, which *Rule* was further developed by **Basil the Great** in Asia Minor/Turkey during the late fourth century.

By the year 500 CE, the Christianity that subscribed to the creed of Nicaea—that creed reasserted even more strongly at Chalcedon in 451—was spread out to the limits of the Roman Empire. Christianities with variant takes on those "right belief"/orthodox creeds were often beyond the Roman borders, in northern/barbarian Europe, in eastern Syria and Persia, and in Ethiopia. Of whatever theological persuasion, leadership in the several Christianities was provided by their bishops, as with Basil the Great of Caesarea and Ambrose of Milan. Miaphysite ("Christ is of *one* nature, not dyophysite/two natures) Christians in Ethiopia looked to the Miaphysite Coptic bishop or patriarch of Alexandria to appoint a bishop or abum for them, which the Alexandrian patriarch did—and did for fifteen hundred years! Inside the Roman Empire, bishops aided Christians in surviving persecution and in making Christianity intellectually acceptable in that world. The faith of the carpenter from Nazareth was en route to becoming a world religion.

New challenges were ahead, met less by bishops and more by monks and nuns.

THE AGE OF MONASTICISM (500-1100 CE)

The chief cenobitic monk in the West and for Catholicism was **Benedict of Nursia** (-550 CE). For his monastic community, he too drew up a self-governance *Rule*. His community lived by it, as have hundreds of thousands of monks ever since. Benedict's sister, **Scholastica** (-543 CE), adapted the *Rule* for women religious (a noun). Scholastica's convent was in Plombariola, near Benedict's at Monte Cassino, Italy. What leaders of monasteries and convents were called to do in the second half of the first millennium was to keep Christianity alive in the face of three major onslaughts coming on the Greco-Roman world.

The first onslaught was that of the so-called barbarians (meaning "bearded ones"), tribes of people from northern and eastern Europe who flooded into western Europe. Alaric the Visigoth, who sacked Rome in 410 CE, has already been mentioned. Attila the Hun, aka "the scourge of God," is another invader whose name is remembered. Even without designating all their leaders, the tribal names suggest the blitzkrieg of the fourth, fifth, and sixth centuries: Vandals, Suevi, Franks, Angles, Saxons, Jutes, Heruli, Goths, Lombards, Burgundians, and, late in the millennium, the Magyars/Hungarians. Interestingly enough, some of the invaders were Christian, albeit *Arian* Christians. Most, though, were pagan, little interested in Christianity. Converting them was difficult but not impossible. **Clovis** (-511 CE), king of the Franks, was brought to the faith by efforts of his wife, Queen **Clotilde** (-545 CE), a Christian woman, a title of no small dimension.

As the pagan invaders established themselves in western Europe, a new start for Christianity and "civilization" had to be made. That restart happened because of intact monasteries about Europe, especially those in Ireland. In the early four hundreds Saint **Patrick** introduced Christianity to the Emerald Isle, one land *not* overrun by barbarians. Christianity took hold there and a century later the faith went *east* under the leadership of **Columba** (-596 CE), Celtic abbot and missionary. His name means "dove," and the Celtic wild goose (see icon) suggests his flying for the faith. Columba won over the Picts of Scotland. His immediate followers made converts in northern England and Wales. In time, another Celtic monk,

Columbanus, went across the English Channel to France and points east and south in Europe.

Meanwhile, for England proper, Pope **Gregory I the Great** (–604 CE) in Rome commissioned a Benedictine monk named **Augustine of Canterbury** (–605 CE) to begin work anew among de-Christianized Anglo-Saxons. Gregory was moved to do this when he saw a beautiful child on the slave block in Rome and was told that lad was a barbarian Angle. "Not Angle," Gregory said, "but an angel." So he sent Augustine to the land of the Angles. Augustine had remarkable success, establishing Canterbury as the ongoing—to this date—center for British/Anglican Christianity. A century and a half later, *English* Anglo-Saxon monks were commissioned by French kings to take the faith to kinsfolk *German* Anglo-Saxons across the Rhine. **Boniface** (–754 CE), aka **Wynfrith** or **Winfrid**, was one such missionary. The story is that, in Germany among the pagans, he cut down the sacred oak tree of the god Thor and used the wood to build the first Christian church. Boniface eventually became a martyr.

Monks of the *Eastern* Church also played a key role as missionaries. Two brothers, **Cyril** and **Methodius**, went to Bohemia with the Christian message in the ninth century. They are now known as the apostles to the Slavs. A century later, the church at Constantinople, upon request by Prince **Vladimir** and his Greek-Christian wife, **Anne**, sent monks to Kiev. Vladimir was baptized in 988 CE. From Kiev the faith spread among "the Rus" (Vikings in Slavic lands). They became—with Slavic intermarriage—the Russians of Muscovy, the Ruthenians, Lithuanians, and, ultimately, the Ukrainians. In the 1000s a monk by the name of **Antony from Mt. Athos** in Greece came to the Caves of Kiev, founding a monastery. He began a Russian tradition of holy men known as hesychasts, solitaries oft wandering the forests of northern Russia seeking "stillness" and endlessly reciting the Jesus Prayer, "Lord Jesus Christ, Son of God, have mercy on me, a sinner".

So, by offering our religion to invaders and taking it to northern lands, the missionary monks expanded the frontiers of Christianity.

Outside the Byzantine Empire, Nestorian or Church of the East missionaries from Babylon carried Christianity out to China, where monasteries were started. In the 780s **Timothy I**, katholikos or patriarch of the Church of the East consecrated a bishop for Tibet. On the Silk Road the Nestorians made converts among the Mongols, so that their brand of Christianity was strongly present during the rise of the Mongols in the

The People of God

thirteenth century. Notably, the wives of the Mongol khans (rulers) were avowedly Christian.

About the monks and nuns of this time, we should note that they took upon themselves the fourfold work of ministry that we first spoke of as vested in Moses. They were the prophet-teachers, in that they kept scholarship and learning alive. They were the pastors in the world, feeding people, offering hospitality and medicine, founding schools, and providing for orphans and unwed mothers. With their *ora et labora* ("pray and work") ethic, they modeled a rhythm for life that included the priestly role of meaningful worship, punctuated by enriched vocal music, especially Gregorian chants—named after Gregory the Great. The kingly role was exercised in monasteries by abbots and abbesses. Such leaders were active in church political affairs as well as missions. Monasticism was the main character of Christianity in these centuries, from Ireland in the west to China in the east.

The second major onslaught of non-Christians in this period came from the south and east. During the seventh century, Arabs rode out of the Saudi desert to conquer in the name of Allah. Inspired by the teaching of the prophet **Muhammad** (–632 CE), Islamic armies conquered Persia, moved into eastern Mediterranean lands, across North Africa, and eventually into Europe through Spain. Many Christians in these areas welcomed the Arabs, as they disliked the Byzantines—that is, their imperial rule from Constantinople—so much. Muslim advance in the West was checked at Tours, France, in 732 by **Charles Martel**, chamberlain of the Merovingian Franks. In the Muslim-conquered lands, Christianity hung on—and hangs on—through the continuing faithfulness of priests, monks, and believers of Orthodox and off-Orthodox (e.g., Armenian, Coptic, Abyssinian, Church of the East/Nestorian, and Uniate Catholic) tradition. Even so, over the centuries Christianities in the Middle East have been adversely affected by the rise of Islam, losing thousands of churches and millions of adherents.

As the Arabs gained control of North Africa and the Middle East, commerce with Europe lessened, causing enormous difficulties for Europeans, such as loss of grain, spices, and goods formally supplied from the east. Trade curtailed, the European economy was reduced, coinage disappeared, and cities shrunk. Any sense of a coherent empire vanished. These were in many ways "dark ages" for the Christian church as well, with clergy often illiterate. Records are lost on some of the popes—one of whom *might* have been a woman, Pope **Joan**. Meanwhile, Islam became a major religion of the world... growing to have more than one billion adherents worldwide today.

The third major onslaught on Christian Europe was that made by tribes from Scandinavia who went "a-viking," plundering down the Atlantic coast and up various rivers in their shallow-draft longboats. These attacks began in the late ninth century and continued into the eleventh. Norse/*North*men ventured into the Mediterranean, occupying the island of Sicily and establishing a kingdom in Italy. Their reach to the east took them along the Baltic-Volga waterway, down to the Black Sea. These Swedes gave themselves the name "Rus," as previously noted. They extended trade routes to Baghdad. One contingent of Norsemen became personal guards for the Christian Byzantine emperor. They were a fierce people with their Norse gods.

The Carolingian kingdom of what would become France was severely threatened by the Norse who settled in *Nor*mandy. Over time these Danes (mostly) came to Christianity by the witness of laypersons and by monks who modeled alternative ways of being in the world. One monk, **Anskar** (–865 CE) became "apostle to the North." He went *to* the Scandinavians. In England, Christian Anglo-Saxon King **Alfred the Great** fought the invading and occupying Danes to a draw, ceding them the eastern half of the British isle—called "Danelaw"—but in the process persuaded them to accept Christianity.

*

As there were these three major *external* attacks—Germanic, Muslim, and Norse—on European Christianity, there was also an *internal* splitting. Differences in the one church were in

Geography	West vs. East
Culture	Roman vs. Byzantine
Capital city	Rome vs. Constantinople
Language	Definitive Latin vs. Subtle Greek
Political leadership	European kings vs. Eastern emperors
Church leadership	Pope vs. Patriarch

Misunderstandings leading to conflict arose, as over a clause in a creed: the Roman Church concluded, via a Western council, that "the Holy Spirit proceeds from the Father *and the Son* [Latin *filioque*]." The Greeks would not accept the *filioque* insertion, contending this interpretation was contrary to earlier, binding decisions of church councils. Relations worsened when **Otto the Great** (–973), Frankish-German king, took on the title of "Emperor of the [new] Holy Roman Empire," a title that Byzantine emperors thought belonged to them. The bishops in the East stayed loyal to the Byzantine emperors, while the Western church leaders looked more and more to the monarch who reigned from Aachen on the French-German border. By comparison, the Byzantine church in Constantinople was relatively affluent, whereas the church in Rome, connected to the Western kings, was much poorer.

In the year 1054, Pope **Leo IX** of "the First Rome" and Patriarch **Michael Cerularius** of "the Second Rome" in Constantinople issued mutual anathemas or curses. Hereafter, European Christian believers were either Orthodox (Eastern) or Catholic (Western).

Something of the east-west difference can be told in instances of church-state relations. Emperor **Leo III** (–740 CE) in Constantinople tried to abolish icons in the church, convinced they were a violation of the commandment to *make no graven images* (Exodus 20:4). By his power, he got an Eastern Church council to rule against icons. Others, though—especially monks and the pope in Rome—resisted Leo's program. The result was the iconoclastic controversy. **St. John of Damascus** (–750 CE), theologian, wrote a treatise, *Against the Iconoclasts*. The controversy lasted for over a century, concluding in 843 CE, when regent Empress **Theodora** (–867) helped bring icons back. A compromise was struck regarding Christian art: only gold, stylized, flat-surface paintings, frescoes, and mosaics, would be permitted among the Orthodox. The Roman Church could keep all these, plus statues. The return of icons to worship is celebrated today in the Eastern Church as the Triumph of Orthodoxy.

We see then how the church was branching east and west.

If the Western Church was deeper in the Dark Ages, light came to it in the late eighth century via the Carolingian/Frankish King **Charlemagne**. In what is known as the Carolingian Renaissance, he began to undo centuries of harm brought on by what one professor of mine called "destruction by the Goths and the moths." Scholarship began anew in Charlemagne's palace school at Aachen. Because he believed that God understood only Latin, Charlemagne wanted prayers in the liturgy to be rightly prayed—in Latin. **Alcuin of York** (–804), a Celtic monk, was brought in to help; among other things, Alcuin translated the Bible into better Latin. Meanwhile,

Charlemagne showed himself to be a church reformer. The first *parish* churches were set up during his reign. Tithing also was implemented and missionaries sent—Boniface, for example, into Germany. A close alliance developed with **Leo III** (-816 CE), pontiff in Rome. In a surprise action during mass on Christmas Eve 800 CE, Leo snuck up behind praying Charlemagne and crowned him monarch. By that action he was asserting the right of the church to do king making. Eventually an equestrian statue of Charles the Great (Charlemagne) was set up in St. Peter's Basilica, right alongside that of Constantine the Great. They ride together into the present.

Pope Leo's "crowning" achievement, with implicit assertion of church primacy over that of the state, was not necessarily welcomed by later French kings. The secular nobility thought, for example, that they, in their domains, should be able to appoint bishops and other church officeholders. The popes disagreed. In one Middle Ages round, Pope **Gregory VII** (-1085) excommunicated King **Henry IV** (-1106) and put the Franco-German people under an interdict, which meant they could not receive the sacraments of the church. To make things right for his people, Henry crossed the Alps barefooted in the winter of 1077, seeking the pope's forgiveness. Later he acted much less penitently, setting up an anti- (or alternative) pope!

Basically, though, French emperors supported the church in Rome. Monasticism was also a beneficiary of royal largesse, especially the monastery in Cluny, located in east central France. Begun in 910 CE, Cluny was blessed by several great abbots. One was **Saint Odo** (-942). Cluny became a reform model for other monasteries and a "sending station" for Christianity. One of the places to which Cluniacs were sent was England, especially after 1066, when, **William the Conqueror** (-1087), aka "the Bastard," ceded one-fourth of the land there to the church. Over time, in England, in France, and, more broadly across Europe, one thousand Cluniac houses came to be. In the twelfth century the Cluniac order faded in favor of the Cistercians, a stricter Benedictine order, whose numbers included the monk-abbot-mystic-reformer **Bernard of Clairvaux** (-1153). St. Bernard dogs are named for him—or at least for a rescue hospice in the Alps named after him.

HIGH CHRISTENDOM YEARS (1100-1450 CE)

Though the churches East and West after 1094 CE were not in communion, the Byzantine Emperor **Alexius I Comnenos**

(−1118) issued a plea to powerful Pope **Urban II** (−1099) in Rome, to "come help" him/them in the struggle with invading Seljuk Turks. The Seljuks were Muslims who had wrested much of the Middle East from the Byzantines, and they were threatening to take more. Pope Urban responded positively, calling for a crusade, a holy war, against both the Seljuk Turks and Arab Muslims; the latter had held Jerusalem for centuries. **Peter the Hermit** (−1115) helped recruit for the First Crusade, generating thousands of pilgrims headed for the Levant or *Outremer* (land over the sea). His efforts were joined militarily when nobility, such as **Robert I of Normandy** (−1035), marched and/or sailed eastward. In the First Crusade, crusaders captured Jerusalem, slaughtering its citizens mercilessly, many of them Christians—albeit *Arab* Christians. In control of Palestine, **Baldwin of Bouillon** (−1118), conqueror, established a Latin kingdom of Jerusalem. So began two centuries of war involving many Western crowned heads, such as **Richard the Lionheart** (−1199) of England and Saint **Louis IX** (−1270) of France. The Knights Templar were a new militant order of monks safeguarding crusaders, and the Hospitallers an order to care for pilgrims.

The most effective warrior *against* the crusaders was **Saladin**, the Kurdish Muslim who defeated the crusaders at the Battle of Hattin in 1187. By the end of the twelve hundreds, the Crusades were over, and Constantinople, initially wanting to be helped, was weakened considerably, sacked by a Western Christian army! (It was so weakened that in 1453 the Second Rome was captured by Ottoman Turks and renamed Istanbul, not Constantinople, as the song says.)

During one of the Crusades, an Italian named **Francis of Assisi** (−1226), wearing the title of friar or brother, came to Egypt to see if he might be an "instrument of peace" there. He had no known effect on the war, but he did have lasting impact on Europe and subsequent history through his religious order, the Order of Friars Minor or Little Brothers. Obtaining endorsement in 1209 from Pope **Innocent III** (−1216) to be a new community in the church, the Franciscans lived lives of "chastity, poverty, and obedience," but *not* in cloistered communities, as did most other monastic orders. The Franciscans went out into the world as preachers to the common people, mendicants begging for their daily bread, and servants to lepers. Their lifestyle was one of simplicity and joy. Thousands joined them, and today the Franciscans are the largest of all the orders in the Catholic Church.

In addition to the Franciscans, a second group of brothers came into being, the Dominicans. Their founder was a **Dominic** (–1221) of Spain. The *Ordo Praedicatorum*/Order of Preachers received papal approval in 1216. They were mendicant preachers, whose first assignment was to proclaim the Catholic faith to a group judged as heretical, the Albigenses or Cathari in southern France. Concerned for truth in religion, the Dominicans ultimately channeled their energies into teaching and learning. They attached themselves to cathedral or major-church schools, which eventually became universities. From their ranks came scholars **Albertus Magnus** (–1280) and his pupil **Thomas Aquinas** (–1274). Both Albert and Thomas are recognized as doctors of the church, Aquinas being Christianity's most significant theologian since Augustine. He did much to take the rediscovered work of the ancient Greek philosopher Aristotle and integrate it into Christian thought. His *Summa Theologiae* explores what faith pushing the mind might discover, namely, proofs for the existence of God.

Besides the Franciscans and Dominicans were the Norbertines or Premonstratensians, coming from the previous century. **St. Norbert** of Germany-France (–1134), an eloquent preacher and miracle worker, was their founder and first abbot general. The Norbertines were known as the White Canons, for the color of their habits. As canons, they were religious persons, somewhere between monks and secular clergy, taking the lead as reformers and as pastors throughout Europe.

The Franciscans, Dominicans, and Norbertines had counterpart orders for women, whose members called themselves sisters. **Clare** was the Sister Moon to Brother Sun Francis, she founding the Order of Poor Clares. Clare was first abbess in the order, starting in the year 1215 and functioning in that capacity until her death in 1254. Another prominent female religious, from a century earlier, was **Hildegard of Bingen** (–1179). Hildegard not only exercised influence as prioress but was a visionary, mystic, hymnist, and prophetess, a person about whom there is a considerable revival of interest today. Not a prioress, but an anchoress, meaning a solitary, was **Julian of Norwich** (–1432). Thousands came from all over Europe to be near her cell and receive her words. Some of her words went into an English-language book, *Showings of Divine Love*. Like Hildegard, Julian had ecstatic visions and composed songs.

The likes of Clare, Hildegard, and Julian in the Middle Ages, like Paula and Scholastica in the previous millennium, will appear again with **Teresa**

The People of God

of Avila (–1582), **Teresa of Lisieux** (–1897), and Mother **Teresa of Calcutta** (–1997).

Three other—but variant—Christian formations happened during these high-Christendom years. These were not given papal recognition, for they were perceived as *against* correct Catholic theology and practice. Such was the case with the Poor Men of Lyon, a movement started by **Peter Waldo** (–1218). When Peter's Waldensians did not respond to Dominican sermons for their repentance, they were subject to bloody repression. During the early fifteenth century, Professor **John Hus** of Bohemia—with ideas on change such as offering the cup to the faithful during communion—was not accepted. Neither were the reform notions of **Savonarola** in Florence, Italy, in the late fourteen hundreds. Popes and councils condemned such reformers as Waldo, Hus, and Savonarola, calling them heretics. Hus and Savonarola were burned at the stake, as many Waldensians had been before them.

Though intolerant in matters of doctrine and practice, the Catholic Church did encourage the arts. This was the age of *the* Renaissance. Here are the names of a few of the more prominent contributors who dealt with Christian themes:

- **Dante Alighieri** (–1321), poet of *The Divine Comedy*
- **Giotto** (–1337), painter of the piece *Flight into Egypt*
- **Guillaume de Machaut** (–1377), composer of *Messe de Notre Dame*
- **Geoffrey Chaucer** (–1400), poet of *Canterbury Tales*
- **Thomas à Kempis** (–1471), author of *The Imitation of Christ*[7]
- **Leonardo da Vinci** (–1519), artist of *The Last Supper*

Art and architecture, interestingly enough, may be what did in European unity in the Catholic Church. In order to raise money for buildings, such as St. Peter's Basilica in Rome, and to pay an artist like **Michelangelo** (–1564), Popes **Julius II** (–1513) and **Leo X** (–1521) sold "indulgences," that is, "chits" that they said could release souls from purgatory. Such a claim seemed unbiblical and unjustifiable to an Augustinian monk and professor living in Wittenberg, Germany.

---

7. Other than the Bible itself, *The Imitation of Christ* is the most widely read book of all Christian literature.

REFORMATIONS/NEW WORLDS ERA (1450-1650 CE)

Martin Luther (-1546) is the first reformer among several in the Protestant movement. Luther did not set out to start a new branch of the Christian Church, but to question questionable practices in the Catholicism of his day. Using the Bible as primary guide (see icon) and emphasizing the idea of "salvation by faith alone" rather than by works—including purchase of indulgences, noted above—Luther *protested against* corruptions and *testified for*

- the Bible (the Newer Testament, in particular) as authoritative
- faith as the only proper stance toward God
- the priesthood of the laity
- use of the vernacular, rather than Latin, in worship
- communion "in both kinds" (bread *and* wine)
- marriage for clergy
- preaching

Luther was aided politically in his struggles against church and state hierarchy by Prince **Frederick III** of Saxony (-1525), his protector, and in systematic thinking by theologian **Philipp Melanchthon** (-1560). Melanchthon produced the Augsburg Confession, so important for Lutheran doctrine. Fittingly, Melanchthon was buried next to Luther, along with **Katherine von Bora Luther**, the first "PW," pastor's wife.

Close behind Luther in time was the priest-reformer **Huldrych Zwingli** (-1531) of Switzerland. While broadly agreeing with Luther, Zwingli argued that Christ was present in the communion elements only insofar as Christ is first in the *heart* of the believer. Zwingli's start in Zurich was taken up in Geneva by a brilliant young French lawyer, **John Calvin** (-1561). Essentially, Calvin established the Reformed branch of the Protestant church. His *Institutes of the Christian Religion* stressed the sovereignty of God, which, among other things, makes a case for predestination, that is, that God predetermines who is saved. In Geneva Calvin's followers tried to set up a theocratic government. As much as anything, though, it was Calvin's theological "school" that made the greatest impact. It attracted students from other countries and then sent those students back to reform churches in their own countries. **John Knox** (–1572), founder of the Presbyterian Church of Scotland, is the foremost example.

The Church of England was created by the political machinations of King **Henry VIII** (–1547). Henry wanted an annulment of his marriage, which had produced no male heir, but the pope in Rome would not grant it. In addition, the monarch desired properties belonging to the monastic orders. So he disestablished monasticism. Henry was aided in these efforts by clergy such as cardinal **Thomas Wolsey** (–1531) and the archbishop of Canterbury, **Thomas Cranmer** (–1556). The latter is largely responsible for *The Book of Common Prayer*, so central in the Church of England's self-identity. From it springs the worship tradition known as evensong. A Reformed Protestant voice was added to the Englishmen's conversation by **Anne Boleyn** (–1536), the second wife of Henry VIII, whom he greatly desired—until he beheaded her. Before decapitation, however, Anne birthed the girl child known to us as **Queen Elizabeth I,** who was sovereign from 1558 till 1603. Early on in her reign, Elizabeth established the English Protestant Church, of which she became the Supreme Governor. Whoever is monarch in England yet today bears this title.

Some thought that King Henry, Cranmer, and Elizabeth did not go far enough in reshaping the church. They were Englishmen who had gone to Geneva, drunk of Calvin's Reformed theology, and returned to England with hopes to purify the church. Hence they were called Puritans. Agitating for reform in the sixteenth century, the Puritans made their boldest mark in the seventeenth with **Oliver Cromwell** (–1658). He led a rebellion in 1641 that eventuated in the beheading of the English monarch, **Charles I**. When Cromwell became Lord Protector of the English church, he tried to expunge all trace of high church "bell, book, and candle." The rule of Cromwell and his son lasted until 1660, when Restoration of the monarchy occurred. In the Restoration, the Church of England was reestablished as England's official religion.

There is yet a fourth Protestant branch that arose in the fifteen hundreds. Some Christians in England, Germany, Switzerland, the Lowlands, and elsewhere called for reform more radical than the three above. The names of **Thomas Münzer, Menno Simons, Conrad Grebel, Robert Browne,** and **John Smythe** come forward. They wanted closer adherence to the Bible, less hierarchy, and purer, congregational governance. They were Anabaptists, advocating adult believers' baptism—and by the Newer Testament's way, by immersion. Swiss **Conrad Grebel** is considered father of the Anabaptist movement because he did the first baptism by immersion, that of a married former priest, **George Blaurock**. The Baptist of greatest name recognition is, of course, **John Bunyan** (–1688), author of *Pilgrim's Progress*, an allegorical story about a man named Christian who travels from "the City of Destruction" to "the Heavenly City." In the free-church tradition, later in time came the pacifist **George Fox** (–1691). He was jailed many times for his radical notions of God as "Divine Spark" within people, so that, being so guided, they had less need for scriptural restriction, much less church hierarchy. Fox's followers came to be called Quakers.

Protestantism was met by a Counter-Reformation. Early on, the Capuchin and Theatine Fathers of the Catholic Church sought (1) to refute the Protestants and (2) to renew the Catholic Church from within. An even stronger effort at counterreformation came with the Jesuits or Society of Jesus, founded by Spaniard **Ignatius Loyola** (–1556). Loyola is remembered as author of the *Spiritual Exercises*. The work of the counter-reformers was helped by the Council of Trent, which concluded in 1563. That council instituted important internal reforms, such as doing away with the sale of indulgences, *and* by adopting Thomas Aquinas's natural-law theology for the church. Catholic doctrine and practice were in some places, notably Spain, enforced by continuation of the medieval institution of the Inquisition, established in the previous century to root out heresy. Dominican friar **Tomás de Torquemada** (–1498) was one inquisitor general who put a number of people to death—usually after torturing them.

As might be expected, religious difference, combined with political and economic interests, led to bloodshed. The worst conflict was the Thirty Years' War of the early seventeenth century; hundreds of thousands were killed, wounded, and made homeless. From one-third to one-half the population of Bohemia were murdered. Among the many parties in the conflict were King **Gustavus Adolphus** (–1635) of Sweden, who won battles for Protestants, and Cardinal **Richelieu** (–1642), who gained ground for Catholics and France. The interventions of these two figures, fighting for religious *and* political purpose, effectively consigned the Holy Roman Empire to a Vienna-based eastern European domain.

Some resolution of conflict came in 1648 with the Peace of Westphalia. There various warring parties agreed to the principle of *cuius regio, eius religio* ("the religion of the region shall be that of the ruler"), first put forth in the Peace of Augsburg in 1555. So there came to be in Europe what historian Diarmaid MacCulloch calls "magisterial" Christianity, the religion

The People of God

of people determined by the preference of the magistrate/prince/king/city council of an area. Central Europe became a patchwork of Catholic, Lutheran, and Reform principalities—with little space for nonconformists. Anabaptists continued to be hounded by all parties, exceptions being in Moravia and Poland.

Concerning the Thirty Years' War, one commentator on all the bloodshed said, "The people in general were determined never again to fight another war in the name of religion."[8]

They would, though, fight or faith—and for other things as well: gold, power, country, race, fame, and so on. Why? Because, in part, there were new regions in which to find such things, especially in the New World.

*

The *first* new world to be sought was the world of the Far East, long cut off by Islamic caliphs and countries. **Henry the Navigator**, king of Portugal, starting in the 1430s sought to find a way to the Orient by sending ships of exploration down the West African coast. As much as for trade, his captains went in search of **Prester John**, a legendary Christian ruler, rich and powerful, they had heard of. Prester John was rumored to dwell in sub-Sahara Africa—or somewhere south and east. Henry's thought was to make alliance with Prester John and, in a pincer military strategy, defeat the Muslims. Since there was no Prester John, nothing like that happened. What did happen, though, was that **Alfonso IV**, king of the Congo (–1542) became a devoted Catholic Christian and in 1526 started an indigenous program of evangelization in his sub-Sahara country. Fast-forward to the twenty-first century, and Christianity is now "the majority religion in most countries south of the Sahara."[9]

In 1498, Portuguese explorer **Vasco da Gama** made his way around the African Cape of Good Hope and, in short years of further travel, discovered the St. Thomas Christians of India, forgotten-to-Christians-of-the-West. In 1542 Jesuit **Francis Xavier, missionary,** arrived the west coast of India and organized the Church of the Fisher Caste. Then he went on to Indonesia and Japan. Over time, Xavier's efforts in the Orient were extended to China in the person of Jesuit **Matteo Ricci** (–1621) and others.

---

8 *Westminster Dictionary of Church History*, 820.
9. Baur, *Christianity in Africa*, 18.

Brief Christian Histories

These earliest ventures to the global South and East established footholds and presences that in time would make Southern or Third-World adherents greater in number than in Europe.

The main *new* world for European navigators was the world of the Americas, opened in 1492 when **Christopher Columbus** (-1506), explorer, planted the Spanish flag in the Bahamas on the island he named San Salvador/Holy Savior.

Seeing in 1493 that the Portuguese were exploring east and that Spain was searching for passage to the Orient by going west, Pope **Alexander VI** (-1503) ruled that lands in the Atlantic Ocean east of the 100th meridian would be for the Portuguese to explore, while everything west of the mid-Atlantic would be for the Spanish. Thus Brazil in South America came into the Portuguese orbit of influence. The rest of the Americas, for the time being, went to Spain.

At first in search of a trade route to India, the Spanish soon launched essentially *invasions* of the Americas to find gold, slaves, spices, and, in the case of one conquistador, **Ponce de León** (-1521), the fountain of youth. Queen **Isabella** and King **Ferdinand** of Spain directed persons sent to New Spain with these words: "Diligently seek to encourage and attract the natives of said Indies to all peace and quiet, that they may willingly serve us and be under our dominion and government and above all that they may be converted to our holy catholic faith."[10]

So missionaries, especially of the Franciscan and Dominican orders, accompanied the conquistadors into the Americas. Because the religious had taken vows of poverty and because they were accustomed to simple lifestyles, the padres were able to live among the native people and influence conversions. They also witnessed the disastrous results of colonial policies. One of the most famous of the early missionaries seeing the devastation was the Dominican padre **Bartolomé de Las Casas** (-1566). He defended Native American people from conquistador and slave plantation abuses. In 1768 Dominican fray **Junípero Serra**, in Baja California, took over missions from the Jesuits and began establishing the now-famous "mission jewel" churches of California. Having traveled 24,000 miles in his lifetime, mostly on foot, Serra died in 1784.

In the sixteen hundreds, "Black Robe" French Jesuits were active among First Nations peoples of Canada. They accompanied explorers into the North American interior. Father **Jacques Marquette** (-1675), for

---

10. González, *Story of Christianity*, 1:379.

example, accompanied explorer **Louis Jolliet** down the Mississippi waterway. Women religious were also involved. Ursaline nun **Mary of the Incarnation,** with other sisters, came to Montreal in 1639 to work among Indian people. A Belgium-born Jesuit, Father **Pierre Jean de Smet** (–1873), was with the French trappers in the Rocky Mountains.

Also during the sixteen hundreds Protestant groups began to arrive on the eastern seaboard of North America. The first were Anglican colonists in Virginia, who mostly came to plant *themselves* in the New World and prosper economically. Others came specifically for religious freedom, to wit, English dissenters, now remembered as the Pilgrims. They traveled under the leadership of Governor **William Bradford** (–1657), arriving off "the stern rock coast" of New England in 1620. Inspiring words of their Old-World pastor, **John Robinson,** still sounded in their ears: "God has yet more light and truth to break forth from his Holy Word." The Pilgrims were quickly followed by larger numbers of Puritans. These folk came to build houses and live. In the process, of course, they displaced Native Americans, whose conversion, education, and welfare they sometimes sought—but only sometimes.

So we have start of the opening of the New World.

To follow events in New England just a little further, disagreement arose among the Puritans. So dissenter **Roger Williams** in 1635 left—or was expelled from—Massachusetts and went to live with the Indians in Rhode Island, establishing a Baptist church there. He was among the earliest to develop ideas of religious tolerance. Williams welcomed **Anne Hutchinson** (–1643), female preacher and teacher, who offended too many divines in Boston and so also was sent into exile.

Other leaders in Colonial America include

- The Reverend **John Livingston** (–1672) in New Amsterdam/New York City, who broke from his Dutch/Holland roots in 1628 to create the first denomination in America, the Reformed Church of America
- Lord **Baltimore** (–1675), who made Maryland a home for fellow Catholic settlers and a welcome place for Jews
- Governor **William Penn** (–1718), who in 1681 brought the Society of Friends/Quakers into his *sylvania*/woods

- Elder **Francis Makemie** (–1708), who came into New Jersey and the middle colonies with Scottish and Irish Presbyterians in 1706 and organized the first American presbytery

All, essentially, were founders of their faith communities in America. There would be other denominations started in America later, most strongly the Methodist Church.

THE ECUMENICAL/GLOBAL AGE (1650 CE–PRESENT)

The Church of England was repurified/enriched/nuanced in the eighteenth century by **John Wesley** (–1791), evangelist. Early in his ministry, Wesley had an appointment in the American colony of Georgia as a priest. Onboard a ship back to England among fervent Moravians, Wesley experienced a religious deepening. It led to his own heartfelt spiritual conversion later. This, in turn, birthed a significant movement, Methodism, which was enthused through singing power by John Wesley's brother, **Charles Wesley** (–1788), hymnist. Having been on the American frontier, Wesley encouraged church planting and nurturing of converts by saddleback preachers in America. **Francis Asbury** (–1816) and **Thomas Coke** (–1814) were two such riders. They became Methodist bishops. During the Revolutionary War they sided with the colonists, whereas the Wesleys did not—primarily because the brothers opposed the slavery in the colonies, then on its way out in England.

The creation of the United States made for a major change in the way church and state related. Religiously, many of this nation's founders were deists, notably **Thomas Jefferson** (–1826) and **James Madison** (–1836). They helped put a provision into the new republic's Constitution that there would be "no establishment of religion" and no prevention "of the free exercise thereof." So religious institutions—almost for the first time since the days of Constantine in the fourth century CE—were disestablished, that is, separated from government!

Disestablishment meant a couple of things. One was that recruitment was needed to build and maintain churches. Following in the footsteps of evangelists **Jonathan Edwards** and **George Whitefield** of the seventeen hundreds, who presided over the Great Awakening, **Timothy Dwight** (–1817) and **Charles Grandison Finney** (–1875), were divines who guided the Second Great Awakening. These revivalists were followed in time by **Dwight Moody** (–1899) and **Billy Sunday** (–1935). Today's television evangelists share in this tradition. But almost all American religious groups—Protestants, Catholics, Jews, Muslims—have been market driven in the American climate of disestablishment.

Disestablishment also allowed for the proliferation of sects, aka denominations. Restorationist **Alexander Campbell** (–1866) and evangelist **Barton Stone** (–1844) began a movement known as the Christian Church (Disciples of Christ). These founders saw themselves as opening an umbrella under which all Christians might be shaded, but the irony is that more churches split away, notably the Church of Christ (noninstrumental) and the Independent Christian Churches. The Disciples and their progeny are American-born-and-bred denominations. So is the Church of Jesus Christ of Latter-Day Saints, aka the Mormons. Its founder was **Joseph Smith** (–1844), followed by president **Brigham Young** (–1877). Young led the Saints west to Utah.

Consider too the following founders and their churches:

- **William Ellery Channing** (–1842)—The Unitarian Church
- **William Miller** (–1849)—Seventh-Day Adventists; he was a millennialist
- **Daniel S. Warner** (–1894)—Church of God (Anderson, IN), a Holiness denomination
- **Mary Baker Eddy** (–1910)—Christian Science; she was a healer
- **Charles Taze Russell** (–1916)—Jehovah's Witnesses
- **Aimee Semple McPherson** (–1944)—Foursquare Gospel; she was a charismatic

The list goes on and on. American Protestantism is certainly a "many-splintered thing." Lutherans and Orthodox believers in this country divided along Old-Country nationality and ethnic lines.

Catholicism in America was less vulnerable to major fracture, but a number of new orders were born. America's first canonized saint, Mother **Elizabeth Seton**, founded the Sisters of Charity in 1852. Seton's order had new branches: the Sisters of Charity of Cincinnati, Ohio; of New Jersey; of Greensburg, Pennsylvania—seven in all, each with its own "charism" and president.

Brief Christian Histories

The divide-and-multiply character of American Christianity repeated itself around the world, so that today, according to the *World Christian Encyclopedia*, there are 33,800 distinguishable denominations! More come almost every day.

The disestablishment policy itself was made possible by change in social and political thought. A new philosophy emerged that emphasized human reason without divine revelation as the way to understand the world. The post-Reformation era entered into the Age of Reason or the Enlightenment. **Descartes, Voltaire,** and **Rousseau** in France; **John Locke** and **Edmund Burke** in England; and **Gotthold Lessing** in Germany are associated with this new rationalism. In America, **Ben Franklin** was drawn to Enlightenment thinking, as were the previously noted Thomas Jefferson and James Madison. To say the least, the rationalists' and/or deists' thinking did not harmonize easily with traditional Christianity.

In time, creative Christians gave theological answer to the challenges of the Enlightenment and of dry Protestant scholasticism, which had come to dominate Lutheran thought. Theologian **Friedrich Daniel Ernst Schleiermacher** (–1834) delivered a modern answer. He described religion as "the *feeling* of absolute dependence on God." Thus religious authority was moved toward individual subjectivity. The Danish theologian **Søren Kierkegaard**, in the same nineteenth century, and **Paul Tillich, Evelyn Underhill,** and **Thomas Merton**, in the twentieth, continued to focus on interiority as the realm of the Holy. In fact, religion generally, Orthodox to Pentecostal, has stayed with subjectivity, testifying to a "triumph of the therapeutic," recognized in such roles as that of the pastoral counselor and the spiritual director. Franciscan **Richard Rohr** on his audiotapes says that Christians today simply cannot think except in psychologized spiritual categories.

*

The last three hundred years also include the rise of science and technology. In mathematics and physics, scientist **Sir Isaac Newton** (–1727) led the way into the modern world. Michael Hart, author of the book *The 100: A Ranking of the Most Influential Persons in the World*, puts Newton as second most influential—after Muhammad and before Jesus! Newton said he was "thinking God's thoughts after him." Later scientific thinkers were not always so God-conscious, and some of their work contradicted both the Bible and church teaching. Most especially we point to **Charles Darwin**

(–1882). He formulated a theory of evolution on the origin of animal species that did not harmonize with the seven-day creation story of Genesis 1. While most Christians have *not* found Darwin's work a threat to faith, others have, as the ongoing creationism vs. evolution controversies in the United States bear witness.

Pioneers in other fields did work eliciting Christian response, much of it negative. **Karl Marx** (–1883), influenced by atheist **Ludwig Feuerbach** (–1872), developed a economic and social theory that defined religion as "opiate for the people," administered on behalf of the ruling classes. **Sigmund Freud** (–1939), psychoanalyst, spoke about God as a projection of human wishes. Much of what these men said has been acknowledged as important and then rethought or incorporated into Christian understanding. For example:

- Brazilian Bishop **Dom Helder Camara** (–1999), who appreciated Marx's insights into social sin *and* also recognized religion as a source of revolutionary hope for oppressed people
- **Carl Jung** (–1961), who took Freud's ideas about the unconscious and spoke about a collective and unconscious realm that is *very holy*, having with it an archetypal Wise Old Man, Great Mother Figure, and Divine Child—a near Trinitarian formula

Other scientists offered perspectives that *complemented* Christian understandings. Mathematician-philosopher **Alfred North Whitehead** (–1947) rejected the static worldview of Newtonian science, with its distant God, in favor of a dynamic world and a God ever in process. Following Whitehead's lead, theologian **Norman Pittenger** (–1997) came to understand God as Dynamic Becoming. Such a God works with/alongside people and the world and therefore is more limited—that is, *not* all-powerful or all-knowing—although everywhere present. Jesuit paleontologist **Teilhard de Chardin** (–1955) told Christians that the world is evolving to an Omega Point of fulfillment in God.

The conflict between religion and science is much less extreme at the start of the twenty-first century than it was one hundred years ago.

The Enlightenment and Age of Science affected the culture generally and contributed to disbelief with subsequent losses in church membership, especially in Europe. At the same time, there continued to be witnessing to Christ and growth of the church elsewhere in the world, a reaching out to all people, as suggested in the opening fulcrum of Christian history. There have been missionaries:

- **William Carey** (–1834) in India ("Expect great things from God and attempt them")
- **David Livingstone** (–1873), "I presume" missionary-explorer in Africa's interior
- **Robert Moffat** (–1883), translator of the Bible for the peoples of South Africa
- **John Mott** (–1955), author of *Evangelization of the World in This Generation*
- **Frank Laubach** (–1970) in the Philippines, "apostle of literacy"

As a result of the work of these leaders, along with tens of thousands others, the number of Christians living in the Southern Hemisphere now is greater than the number of believers north of the equator! Of the six billion people on the earth today, more than two billion accept the name "Christian."

As there has been significant growth in numbers, so has there been considerable social witness and action. There were abolitionists. The work of Anglican evangelical **William Wilberforce** (–1833) eventuated in the abolition of slavery in the British Empire. In the United States abolition was a major concern of brother and sister **Henry Ward Beecher** (–1887) and **Harriet Beecher Stowe** (–1896), the latter the author of *Uncle Tom's Cabin*, a powerfully influential book. Issues finally were taken to Civil War battlefields with the Bible-literate President **Abraham Lincoln** noting that "both sides pray to the same God."

Beginning in the mid-eighteen hundreds there was increased lobbying by women in the United States for the right to vote. Some Christian suffragettes were

- **Sojourner Truth**, black abolitionist, who *also* asked, "Ain't I a woman?"
- **Antoinette Brown**, in 1853 the first woman ordained to ministry in America
- **Susan B. Anthony**, a founder of the suffragette movement in 1869
- **Elizabeth Cady Stanton**, author of *The Woman's Bible*, published in 1895

The People of God

These women were part of a larger social gospel movement, which at the start of the twentieth century was in full bloom. Among its leaders was **Washington Gladden**, Congregational minister and hymnist, who wrote "Once to Every Man and Nation." The hymn has the following wonderful verse concerning God:

> Though the cause of evil prosper, / Yet 'tis truth alone is strong,
> Truth forever on the scaffold, / Wrong forever on the throne.
> Yet that scaffold sways the future, / And, behind the dim unknown,
> Standeth God within the shadow / Keeping watch above his own.

The name of **Walter Rauschenbusch** registers on the social gospel ledger too, as author of *Christianity and the Social Crisis*. Gladden and Rauschenbusch sought to change not just individual hearts, but the very structures of society. They both died in 1918 at the close of World War I.

More than just two American social gospelers died about then too. A fifteen-hundred-year connection between church and state also passed away, a connection established in 313 CE by Emperor Constantine. In 1914, at the start of that war, Catholic **Archduke Francis Ferdinand**, heir to the Austro-Hungarian Empire, was assassinated. By the end of the war, there was no trace of a Holy Roman Empire to affiliate with Rome via an emperor.[11] During the war, the Bolshevik Communists took over in Russia and executed **Czar Nicholas II**, ending centuries of a monarch being in control of the Russian Orthodox Church. Defeated in war, Kaiser **Wilhelm II,** head of the German state *and* the supreme bishop of the Prussian Evangelical Church, was gone, eliminating that Protestant monarchic alliance. There simply would be no more kaisers-czars-caesars. Historic Caesaropapism was coming to its end. Not unrelated, in 1922 **Sultan Mehmed VI** of the Ottoman Empire, who had joined the war on the side of the Germans and Austrians, had to abdicate. The sultanate was abolished, and with the abolition, ties to/with Islam were severed. Turkey became a quite secular state.

The only major European power left with an officially established religion was England. There **King George V,** officially "defender of the [Anglican] faith," kept the state-church connection alive, but mostly as titular head of the country and titular head of the church—with little real authority in either. Such too was/is the case in places like the Netherlands and Sweden and, more or less, in Spain since 1931. In France and the United

---

11. The death knell for the Holy Roman Empire is usually considered as rung in 1806 by Napoleon.

States, disestablishment of religion happened more than a century earlier. Thus a millennium and a half of kings and bishops joined at the hip in a love affair ended. Let it be said, though, that nations and their politicians always seem to find ways to connect with religion—or, should we say, to use religion? Every American president *directs* God to "Bless the U.S.A.," for example.

Meanwhile, back in 1918, a Swiss-German Reformed theologian by the name of **Karl Barth** (–1968), disillusioned with the naive optimism of Enlightenment religion (so popular in Germany up till then), published his *Commentary on Romans*. This blast of a book revived Pauline, Augustinian, and Reformation theological themes that had been muted or omitted in liberal theology. He took the sovereignty of God, the sinfulness of humans, the saving work of Christ, and the importance of faith more seriously than previous generations of Christians. So began the theological movement called neo-orthodoxy.

It was not a movement, however, without social or political dimension. In the 1930s, as Adolf Hitler and Nazism came to power in Germany, Barth was part of the Confessing Church of that country, which proclaimed on the basis of its theology that "Jesus alone is *der Führer!*" One German Lutheran pastor, **Dietrich Bonhoeffer,** went to prison for participation in an assassination attempt on Hitler's life and was executed as World War II came to an end in 1945, making Bonhoeffer a martyr. Another martyr was Franciscan friar **Maximilian Kolbe** of Poland, who volunteered to die in place of a stranger at the Auschwitz concentration camp. In 1982 he was designated a saint by the Catholic Church. For many Christians—not to mention six million Jews of the Nazi Holocaust—**Hitler** could only receive the title of Antichrist.

As part of the neo-orthodox reconfiguration in the United States, theologian and ethicist **Reinhold Niebuhr** (–1971) wrote *Moral Man and Immoral Society,* in which he keenly observed that sin is not just within individuals but also inherent in collectivities, such as Ford Motor Company. As a pastor in Detroit he saw firsthand how management abused its workers, though those executives personally were decent, tithing family men.

There is a long list of neo-orthodox-influenced theologians or activists who have focused on social justice issues. Especially we remember **Martin Luther King Jr.** (–1968), who led the struggle to win civil rights for black Americans. He must be designated a prophet. A spokesperson for peace and disarmament was **William Sloane Coffin** (–2006), chaplain at Yale

The People of God

University and senior minister of the Riverside Church in New York. In Central and South America, great justice work was initiated by Peruvian Father **Gustavo Gutiérrez,** who in his book *Liberation Theology* contended that God has a "preferential option for the poor." Standing with the poor in El Salvador, Catholic Bishop **Oscar Romero** was murdered and so became a twentieth-century martyr. **Sally McFague,** former professor at Vanderbilt University, has called for eco-justice, speaking about "the earth as God's body." However uncomfortable these five might be with the label, they belong to the more liberal wing of recent Christianity—some would say radical.

More conservative takes on our religion were offered by **A. A. Hodge** (–1886) and **Benjamin Warfield** (–1921), professors at Princeton Seminary. In the second decade of the nineteen hundreds, Warfield set forth the tenets of what is now called fundamentalism, a prime thesis being that the Bible is inerrant, that is, without errors. Fundamentalism segued into evangelicalism in the course of the century, with evangelicals responsible for growth in Christian numbers and churches. A foremost figure in conservative evangelicalism has been the evangelist **Billy Graham** (still living in 2014). **Carl Henry** (–2003), editor of *Christianity Today,* stood on the intellectual, theological side of the movement.

In the billion-member worldwide Catholic Church, a similar liberal-conservative tension exists, signaled by the presence of German theologian **Hans Küng,** a modern spirit, who was opposed by Cardinal **Joseph Ratzinger,** traditionalist voice in the Vatican Congregation on Doctrine. Ratzinger seems to have prevailed, for he became Pope **Benedict XVI** in 2005, hewing to a more traditional way of thinking; he silenced women religious who spoke of the possibility that their kind might become priests.

*

During the last several centuries, the second largest church in the world, the Russian Orthodox Church, continued to continue. Always the Russian Church, in Byzantine tradition, was intertwined with the state, controlled by the czars, but likewise protected. As noted, such protection disappeared in 1918 when the Bolsheviks took over the country, murdered the monarch, and started dealing with the 1917-reinstalled Patriarch of All Russia, **Tikhon** (–1925). Starting in 1922 and continuing for seventy years, Tikhon and his successors witnessed the confiscation of church property, the closing of monasteries and seminaries, and the mass murder of Russian and Ukrainian priests. Under the Communists in the Soviet Union—but also via the Nazis in World War II—perhaps as many as fifty million Russian Orthodox believers were massacred in the twentieth century. Only after ouster of the Communists from political power in Russia and other eastern European countries, beginning in 1989, did the Russian Orthodox Church—and other churches, such as Baptist and Uniate-Catholic—begin to function with greater freedom, doing much rebuilding.

Though the Christian church experienced persecution and hardship during the last century, vitality and growth also happened, especially in Southern-Hemisphere Christianity with charismatic or Pentecostal Christianity. One date of beginning for contemporary Pentecostalism is 1906, with the Azusa Street revival in California, led by a black Holiness-preacher-become-charismatic, **William Seymour** (–1922). Speaking in tongues (*glossolalia*) is the major feature in this movement, with faith healings, miracles, and other Spirit-led manifestations. The American denomination best exemplifying Pentecostal vitality is the Assemblies of God, begun in 1914. No one person stands as the Assemblies' founder, but many prominent persons have been on its roll: televangelists **Jim and Tammy Bakker,** faith healer **Benny Hine**, singer **Elvis Presley**, and 2008 vice presidential candidate **Sarah Palin**. Pentecostalism went viral, more or less influencing all churches, Baptist to Catholic, in the world. It swept through/is sweeping through much of Africa, Latin America, and Pacifica. The largest-membership church in the world, the Yoido Full Gospel Church in Seoul, South Korea, with 1,000,000 members, is Pentecostal, with **David Yonggi Cho** its senior pastor.

Worldwide, in addition to Pentecostalism, a second major global Christian phenomenon came along in the twentieth century: ecumenism. In Edinburgh, Scotland, there was the World Missionary Conference in 1910, over which YMCA Secretary **John Mott** (–1955), mentioned earlier, presided. The conference led in time to the creation of the World Council of Churches. Officially organized in 1948, it has continued ever since. In it many Protestant and Orthodox branches of the wider church started cooperating. Besides Mott, two of the World Council's great spokespersons were the Dutch **Willem Visser 't Hooft** (–1985) and Czech **Joseph Hromadka** (–1969), who were, let us say, ecumenists. So was layman **John D. Rockefeller Jr.** (–1960), who brought his organizational skills and financial resources to the movement and helped establish the World Council of Churches headquarters in Geneva, Switzerland, and the U.S. National Council of Churches offices in New York City.

The People of God

The sine qua non symbol of ecumenism, though, is the 1960s Roman Catholic ecumenical council, known as Vatican II. Vatican II was called together by a thought-to-be-interim pope, **John XXIII** (–1963). The called-to-Rome cardinals and bishops met for three years and came out with recommendations for change in Catholic practices. They dropped Latin as the only language for worship services and offered the cup of the Eucharist to laity. Most importantly, Vatican II opened up Catholicism for conversation with long-separated Orthodox and Protestant communions. Slowed sometimes (see above) and sometimes on track, the conversation has continued. One historic and symbolic moment transpired in 1987. Then Pope **John Paul II** (–2006) met with Ecumenical Patriarch **Dimitrios I** (–1991) in Rome, and together in Greek they recited the Nicene-Constantinople Creed of the church as originally articulated, that is, without the *filioque* clause! Roman Catholic and Eastern Orthodox prelates had not been so together in almost a thousand years!

*

There are many **women and men** today taking various roles, titles, functions, and offices in the church, almost all of which have been assumed previously by our ancestors in the faith.[12] If you hear a preacher today—your own pastor or someone like **Barbara Lundblad**—be assured she/he stands with **Hosea, Koheleth, Peter, Ambrose, Dominic, Luther, Hutchinson,** and **Finney.** If there is a musician in the house—singer **Sandi Patty** or a soprano from your choir—her song is sung with **Miriam, David, Cecilia, Gregory, Bach, Wesley,** and **Gladden.** Consider your favorite Sunday school teacher or a seminary professor like **Sally McFague.** Both are rabbis/teachers beside **Moses, Josiah, Jesus, Jerome, Augustine, Aquinas, Calvin,** and **Whitehead.** A Christian martyr such as **Oscar Romero** in El Salvador shares "witness" with **Jeremiah, Polycarp, Boniface, Becket, Hus,** and **Bonhoeffer.** Pray-ers today, whether in a Baptist church's Priscilla Circle or **Henri Nouwen**'s chapel, kneel with **Isaiah, Daniel, Silas, Antony, Julian, Wesley,** and **Underhill.** Priests are at the table with **Aaron, Ezra, Paul, Anselm, Cranmer,** and **John XXIII.** A mystic, whether **Thomas Keating** or a weekend contemplative-wannabe, keeps tradition with **Elijah, John of Patmos, the Cappadocians, Dionysius the Pseudo-Areopagite, Hildegard,** and **John of the Cross.** Today's social activists revoice utterances of the prophets **Amos, Judas Maccabee, St. James the Greater, Chrysostom,**

---

12. For a fuller list of these roles-titles-functions-offices, see Appendix A.

Brief Christian Histories

Francis of Assisi, Münzer, and **Rauschenbusch.** If there are administrators around—perhaps called senior ministers—let them be assured they have kingly predecessors: **Solomon, Nehemiah, Peter, Benedict, Leo, Ignatius, Bradford,** and **Visser 't Hooft.** Missionaries go out with **Jonah, Thomas, Thecla, Columba, Anskar, Xavier,** and **Carey.**

And on and on. Faithful people of God may sing,

> If I could, I surely would
> Stand on the rock where Moses stood.

And they do. The holy ground is extended to where they are and what they/we do in Christ's name.

Questions for Reflection and Discussion

1. List who you think are the twelve most influential persons in the history of our faith. If Jesus is #1 and Moses comes in #2, who's after them? Are #3 and #4 biblical or postbiblical people? Any women on the list? Who?

2. Consider—and, if in a group, share—the name and influence of an individual from childhood and one from adult years who particularly influenced your spiritual journey. Any common characteristics among these significant others? Do any look like a man or woman of the historic Christian journey?

3. In your local church's history, who were—or are—the people who have made a major difference in the body? Were they clergy, laypeople, elected leaders, outside consultants/agitators?

4. What is your role in the church? Is your office related to the four major roles that Moses filled? Are there some positions that just don't seem to go back so far?

5. Discuss the difference between belonging and believing or between fellowship and faith. In your estimation, is one more important than the other? (This is a huge sociology-of-religion issue between Max Weber and Emile Durkheim.)

6. If now you were to christen a child, which name/person would you choose from among the many "saints" met in this chapter? Why?

People Timeline

THE TIMELINE PRESENTED BELOW is built in conjunction with chapter 1, The People of God, but works with and for the three other brief histories that follow. It is date-helpful and worth keeping a sticky tab or other marker in, for ease of era-reference. Admittedly, the time line information "hops around" from country to country and culture to culture with sundry people. In so doing, it provides a wider view of our faith. The reader will note, for example, that in the mid-five hundreds CE, as St. Benedict in Italy was writing rules for Western monks, Patriarch Jacob Baradeus in Mesopotamia was organizing the Church of the East.

In truth, our timeline is a brief Christian history in itself, a fifth narrative, if you will. While emphasizing the names of men and women so involved in our story, there is also indication of what they did, what they stood for, what was going on around them. The reader also will discover names of a few people who do not appear in any chapter—artists and philosophers, for example. They figure in our story, only more obliquely. King John of England in 1215 CE is illustrative; he may *not* be among the saints, but the Magna Carta, which he signed, becomes a document in time shaping Christianity along with the nations.

Because of some historical uncertainties, dates may vary or include decades; in such cases they are shown with a ± (plus or minus) symbol. For the premonarchic period (1800–1000 BCE) in particular, considerable scholarly uncertainty exists about dates, people, and events (e.g., Abram's journey), but we will work more with the *Bible's internal accounting* than hard archeological evidence in some cases. It's our story, and we're sticking with it.

For the sake of keeping bio-data notation to a single line, abbreviations are used, such as c for century, K/k for king, Sn/sn for Southern, NT for Newer Testament, P/p for pope, Bp/bp for bishop, Pt/pt for prophet,

51

Brief Christian Histories

HRE for Holy Roman Empire, Xn for Christian, Xnty for Christianity, Patr/patr for patriarch, mya for million years ago, and others. To the right on this timeline, influential cultures are indicated.

Key Characters in Our Faith Story *Influential Cultures*

TIME BEFORE BIBLICAL HISTORY

13 mya	GOD creates universe in the Big Bang	CELESTIAL
6 mya	GOD brings earth/Gaia—and evolution—into being	
4004	GOD, says 17th-c-CE Anglican Bp Ussher, forms Adam and Eve	

PRE-MONARCHIC MILLENNIUM (2000–1000 BCE)

2000±	Ur-nammi builds ziggurat in Ur (cf. tower of Babel)	SUMERIAN
1850±	Akkadian scribes set down ancient *Epic of Gilgamesh*	AKKADIAN
1850±	Abram/Sarai in Mesopotamia move to Haran, then Canaan	NOMADIC
1800±	Isaac, Jacob, their wives and children live in Canaan	
1750	Babylonian K Hammurabi puts down his *Law Code*	
1700±	Joseph is taken to Egypt, to be followed by his brothers	EGYPTIAN
1377	Akhenaten reigns in Egypt	
1250±	Moses leads exodus from Egypt, gets Decalogue	
1200	Joshua "fit" the battle of Jericho	
1184	Achilles defeats Hector in Trojan War (*Iliad*, ca.700)	
1100s	Gideon, Deborah, Samson, others are judges	PHILISTINE

TIME OF THE KINGS AND PROPHETS (1000–550 BCE)

1025	The pt Samuel anoints Saul, later David, to be k in Israel
1000	K David unites tribes, founds Jerusalem
954	K Solomon builds temple in Jerusalem
926	Rehoboam and Jeroboam split kgdm into Judah (south) and Israel (north)

People Timeline

860	Pt Elijah wins contest with pts of Ba'al	
800±	Pts Amos, Hosea, Micah speak/act/write	
753	Romulus and Remus found Rome	
742	First Isaiah begins his priestly/prophetic career	
722	Assyrians obliterate nn kgdm, deport people	ASSYRIAN
628	Pt Jeremiah begins long career	
621	K Josiah institutes Deuteronomic reforms	
612	Babylonians defeat Assyrians at Nineveh	BABYLONIAN
586	Nebuchadnezzar destroys Jerusalem, deports leading inhabitants	
550	Second Isaiah gives oracles of hope to exiles	

SECOND TEMPLE PERIOD (550–20 BCE)

538	Cyrus the Persian defeats Babylonians, ends Jews' exile	PERSIAN
515	Zerubbabel finishes rebuilding the temple in Jerusalem	
490	Greeks defeat Persians at Marathon	
475	Esther, if historical, is queen in Persia	
444	Nehemiah the governor builds wall around Jerusalem	
440	Ezra the scribe institutes reforms/practices for his people	
4th c	Scribes assemble the Bible's *Law,* then *the Prophets*	
469–322	Socrates, Plato, Aristotle live in Greece	
332	Alexander the Great of Macedonia conquers Jerusalem	GREEK
250	LXX scholars translate Hebrew Bible into Greek	
150	Judas Maccabeus leads successful revolt against Seleucid Greeks	
125±	Scribes complete the Bible's *Other Writings* for Tanakh (OT)	
63	Roman general Pompey takes Jerusalem	ROMAN
37	Herod the Great made ruler of Judea by Romans	
31	Octavian defeats Mark Antony/Cleopatra at sea battle of Actium	

NEWER TESTAMENT TIMES (20 BCE-110 CE)

20 BCE	K Herod rebuilds temple in Jerusalem
06/04 BCE	Jesus of Nazareth born in Bethlehem
20 CE	Philo of Alexandria adopts idea of the *Logos* for God
29	Jesus of Nazareth teaches-heals-acts re the Kgdm of God
30	Jesus the Christ crucified by the Romans and raised by God
30	Holy Spirit at Pentecost propels Jesus' disciples into mission
33	Stephen becomes the first martyr
40s	Paul the missionary, also Thecla, make their journeys
50s	Paul writes various epistles to the churches, e.g., *Romans*
62	Mark founds Alexandrian ch, and other apostles do so elsewhere
64	Nero in Rome persecutes Xns; Peter and Paul are martyred
70	Roman General Titus destroys Jerusalem and temple there
75±	Mark the evangelist writes the first Gospel
85±	Matthew and Luke write their Gospels
90±	John writes the Fourth Gospel
90	Rabbis at Council of Jamnia affirm *Older Testament* canon
95±	John of Patmos writes *Revelation*
108	Bp Ignatius of Antioch opposes heretics, is martyred
110±	Unknown author completes NT with *2 Peter*

STRUGGLING CENTURIES OF THE CHURCH (110-500 CE)

135	Bar Kokhba's rebellion fails; Jews and Xns banned from Jerusalem
150	Xns in Rome are reciting *the Apostles' Creed*
155	Bp Polycarp of Smyrna dies a martyr
180s	Clement of Alexandria and Irenaeus of Lyon write *Apologies*
203	Perpetua and Felicity are martyred in Carthage
210	Apologist Tertullian offers first formulation of the Trinity

People Timeline

230	Hippolytus in *Apostolic Tradition* instructs on the Xn life	
240	Origen of Alexandria is reconciling Greek and Xn thought	
250	Roman Emperor Decius attempts empirewide persecution	
270	St Antony goes to desert of Egypt as a solitary monk	
301	K Tiridates III makes Armenia the first Xn nation	
303	Emp Diocletian initiates "the Great Persecution"	
313	Emp Constantine issues Edict of Toleration for Xns	
320	Abbot Pachomius starts communal monasticism in Egypt	
323	Constantine's mother, Helena, identifies sacred sites in Palestine	
324	Bps come to First Ecumenical Council in Nicaea	
325	Athanasian vs. Arian theological struggle begins	
325±	Frumentius brings Syriac Xnty to Ethiopia's K Ezana	
330	Constantine makes Constantinople the imperial capital	BYZANTINE
358	Basil the Great founds monastery in East, has *Rule*	
361	Martin of Gaul gathers monks, builds first *capellae/* chapels	
367	Athanasius lists 27 books for *Newer Testament*	
375±	Cappadocian Fathers and one Mother define orthodox theology	
380	Emp Theodosius's Edict makes Xnty the religion of Roman Empire	
381	Bps hold 2nd Ecumenical Council in Constantinople	
385±	Evagrius Ponticus in Egypt writes of imageless spirituality	
400	Ninian establishes *Casa Candida* beyond Hadrian's Wall in Scotland	
405	Jerome completes Vulgate (Latin) translation of Bible	
406	Barbarians cross over the frozen Rhine, enter Roman Empire	GERMANIC
410	Alaric the Arian Visigoth sacks Rome, hence, its "fall"	
415	John Cassian founds Marseilles monastery, supports mystic contemplation	
426	Augustine of Hippo completes *City of God*	

Brief Christian Histories

431	Council at Ephesus declares Mary *Theotokos*; Nestorius objects
435	St Patrick goes to Ireland
451	W & E bps adopt Chalcedon Creed, leading to separating out of various Xntys
	Miaphysite (Coptic, W Syriac, Ethiopian, Armenian) and Dyophysite (Nestorian/Ch of East, E Syriac, Indian)
452	Pope Leo I's diplomacy saves Rome from Attila the Hun
476	Odoacer deposes last wn emp, Romulus Augustus
496	K Clovis receives baptism, and all the Franks follow

AGE OF MONASTICISM (500–1100 CE)

500±	Pseudo-Dionysius the Areopagite writes on purging-illumination-union	
500±	K Arthur (an historical Xn king?) defeats Saxons at Mt Baden	
527	Dionysius Exiguus creates BC-AD (BCE-CE) dating scheme	
530	Brendan the Navigator of Ireland takes seven-year sea voyage by the Spirit	
537	Justinian and Theodora rule Byzantia, build Hagia Sophia	
550	Benedict finishes *Rule* for Wn monks; Scholastica adapts it for nuns	
553	Jacob(ite) Baradeus becomes metropolitan in Edessa for Ch of the East	
564	Columba and Celtic monks go to Iona, begin mission to east	
590	Gregory the Great is first monk to become a pope	
597	Augustine of Canterbury arrives to re-Xnize England	
622	Muhammad goes Mecca-to-Medina; Islamic calendar begins	MUSLIM
635	Nestorian Bp Alopen received in China, sets up Xn monasteries	
7th c	Arab armies conquer, from Persia to Spain	
711	Tariq ibn Ziyad takes Spain; it becomes Al-Andalus	
716	Boniface crosses Rhine in mission to Saxon Germans	

People Timeline

726	Byzantine Emp Leo III initiates iconoclastic controversy	
731	Venerable Bede completes *English Church History*	
732	Charles Martel checks Muslims at Tours in France	
756	Umayyads in Spain have "Land of Three Religions" (until 1031)	
780+	Church of East Katholikos Timothy I consecrates bp for Tibet	
787	Bps E and W hold last of the seven ecumenical councils	
793	Vikings pillage Lindisfarne monastery and, in 806, Iona	
Late 700s	Someone composes *Donation of Constantine*, a forgery	
800	Pope Leo III crowns Charlemagne k of the Franks	FRANKISH
804	Alcuin, who led Charlemagne's Carolingian Renaissance, dies	
843	Empress Theodora restores icons, for Triumph of Orthodoxy	
850±	Anskar, apostle of the North, works in Scandinavia	
869	Vikings siege Constantinople; Patr Photios tries to convert them	
862	Cyril and Methodius conduct mission to Moravia	
863	Khan Boris of Bulgaria accepts Orthodox not RC baptism	
878	K Alfred of Wessex defeats Danes/Vikings; Danes become Xn	
905+	"A-Vikings" raids continue on wn Eur to Italy	NORDIC
925	St Odo establishes the monastery at Cluny, first of 1000 charter houses	
955	Otto the Great defeats Magyars at Lechfeld	FEUDAL
960	K Harold Bluetooth of Denmark baptized	
962	Otto the Great crowns himself Holy Roman Emperor	
963	Athanasios starts great lavra/monastery on Mt Athos	
966	Prince Mieczyslaw of Poland baptized	
975	Duke Geza accepts RC—not Orthodox— baptism for Hungarians	
988	Prince Vladimir of Kiev, a Rus, baptized by Greek monks	SLAVIC
993	P John XV canonizes first saint: Ulrich of Augsburg	
1000–1300	Farmers and others prosper during "Little Optimum" global warming	

Brief Christian Histories

1054	E Orthodox patr and W Catholic p issue mutual anathemas
1059	Order of Augustinian monks starts (Martin Luther will be one)
1066	Wm Conqueror wins Battle of Hastings, gives 1/4 of England to ch
1076	P Gregory VII excommunicates K Henry IV, who repents
1086	Masters and students start U of Bologna, Oxford 1096, Paris 1150
1095	P Urban II at Cluny calls for Holy Crusade against Muslim "infidels"
1098	Theologian Anselm writes *Cur Deus Homo*

HIGH CHRISTENDOM YEARS (1100–1450 CE)

1118	Peter Abelard, theologian teaching at U of Paris, castrated	
1141	Mystic Hildegard of Bingen writes and sings	
1145	Bernard of Clairvaux, head of Cistercians, preaches 2nd Crusade	
1150s	Elizabeth of Schönau has visions of Mary's assumption into heaven	
1165	Prester John, a Xn k, *said* to rule in sub-Sahara	
1170	Thomas Beckett murdered in Canterbury Cathedral	
1187	Saladin at battle of Hattin retakes Jerusalem from crusaders	ARAB
1190±	Joachim of Fiore has apocalyptic "three ages" vision of history	
1204	Wn crusaders sack Constantinople for Venetians	
1215	K John forced to sign *Magna Carta* at Runnymede	
1215	P Innocent III calls 4th Lateran Council, which made rulings on transubstantiation, mandatory confession, celibacy for priests, marriage as sacrament, more	
1216	Dominic founds order of Preachers	

People Timeline

1219	Sava, first archbp of Church of Serbia, reforms Mt Athos monastery
1223	Francis of Assisi's Friars Minor approved; also Clare's Poor Clares
1260	Muslim Mamluks defeat almost-Xn Mongols at Ain Jalut
1265±	Townspeople build Chartres Cathedral; other cities build too
1270	Yikunno Amlak restores Solomonic Xn line in Ethiopia
1272	Thomas Aquinas pens *Summa Theologiae*
1290	K Edw expels Jews from England (as happens later in France and Spain)
1291	Last crusaders leave Acre
1302	Boniface VIII issues *Unam Sanctum* on papal supremacy
1305	Giotto paints *Adoration of the Magi* in Arena Chapel
1309	Popes are in Babylonian (Avignon) Captivity for 40 years
1321	Dante writes *Divine Comedy* ITALIAN RENAISSANCE
1341	Petrarch crowned poet laureate in Rome
1348	People start dying in Black Death, 1/3 of Eur population dies
1349	Sergius of Radoezh founds Holy Trinity lavra near Moscow
14th c	Unknown Monk writes *Cloud of Unknowing*
1380	Wyclif inspires translation of Latin Bible into English
1378	Popes Urban-Clement-Alexander are in great papal schism
1387	K Jogaila of Poland leads Lithuanians into RC baptism
1393	Julian of Norwich completes *Showings of Divine Love*
1400s	Medici family promotes Renaissance in Italy
1408	Theopanes paints *Transfiguration* for Mt Athos monastery

Brief Christian Histories

1415	John Hus of Bohemia burned at stake as heretic	
1418	Thomas à Kempis writes *Imitation of Christ*	
1431	Joan of Arc burned at the stake	
1435	Henry the Navigator searches W Africa for Prester John	NAUTICAL/MARITIME

REFORMATIONS/NEW WORLDS ERA (1450-1650 CE)

1453	Ottoman Turks take Constantinople, end Byzantine Empire	
1456	Gutenberg invents printing press	TECHNOLOGICAL
1476	Wm Caxton sets up printing press in Westminster, England	
1483	Dominican Torquemada appointed inquisitor general in Spain	
1492	Columbus reaches the New World for Spain	
1492	Ferdinand and Isabella expel all Jews and Muslims from Spain	
1494	P Alexander divides Atlantic, E for Portugal, W for Spain	
1498	Vasco da Gama rounds African Cape of Good Hope	
1512	Michelangelo completes Sistine Chapel mosaics	
1514	Bartolomé de Las Casas defends Native Americans	
1517	Luther posts 95 theses; Protestant Reformation begins	MAGISTERIAL
1519	Cortez defeats the Aztecs, Franciscans convert native people	
1520s	Monk Filofei at Pskov proclaims Moscow as "Third Rome"	
1525	Katherine von Bora Luther becomes first pastor's wife	
1525	C Grebel baptizes G. Blaurock by immersion, the start of Anabaptists	
1526	Alfonso, K of the Congo, plans evangelism for his country	
1531	Peasant Juan Diego has vision of Our Lady of Guadalupe	

People Timeline

1534	Henry VIII breaks with Rome, creates Ch of England
1536	Calvin writes *Institutes*, starts Reformed Protestantism
1540	Ignatius of Loyola gets Jesuits their Bull of Foundation
1543	Copernicus sets out solar universe theory
1545	P Paul III convenes Counter-Reformation Council of Trent
1549	Cranmer publishes *Book of Common Prayer*, includes evensong
1549	Jesuit Francis Xavier on world mission arrives in Japan
1559	John Knox returns to Scotland, sets up Presbyterianism
1563	Council of Trent concludes for Tridentine (Latin) Catholicism
1572	French K Henry IV's St. Bartholomew's Day massacre of Huguenots
1582	Jesuit Matteo Ricci dresses as Confucian scholar in China
1596	Jesuit Martinez becomes first bp in Japan
1596	Ruthenians by Treaty of Brest become Orthodox Uniate-Catholics
1609	John Smythe in England baptizes self/others by immersion
1611	K James I puts name on *King James Version* of Bible
1620	Pilgrims land on Plymouth Rock, New England
1625	Edw Herbert posits religion based on reason/deism ENLIGHTENMENT
1633	Galileo before an Inquisition recants Copernican theory
1639	Roger Williams establishes first US Baptist ch in Rhode Island
1648	George Fox heads Society of Friends/Quakers
1648	Parties agree to Peace of Westphalia, ending Thirty Years' War

Brief Christian Histories

1649   Puritan Cromwell executes K Charles of England

THE ECUMENICAL/GLOBAL AGE (1650 CE–PRESENT)

1650	Descartes of *Cogito ergo sum* dies	
1664	Monarchy restored in England	
1666	Isaac Newton posits theory of gravitation	SCIENTIFIC
1683	Turks defeated at Vienna on September 11	
1685	Louis XIV revokes tolerant (for Huguenots) Edict of Nantes	
1700	John Locke, following Descartes, advances reason	
1704	P settles rites controversy, ends Jesuit mission in China	
1721	Peter the Great takes control of Rus Orth Ch from patr	
1727	J S Bach composes *St. Matthew Passion*	
1738+	John and Charles Wesley preach/sing in Methodism	
1742	Handel composes oratorio *Messiah*	
1740	G Whitefield and J Edwards lead Great Awakening in colonies	
1773	P dismantles Society of Jesus (restored in 1814)	
1780	Richard Raikes starts Sunday school movement in England	
1788	R Johnson, Ch of Eng, arrives in Australia with prisoner settlers	
1789	Madison/Jefferson separate ch and state in US Constitution	
1790	French revolutionaries (Jacobins) tear down abbey at Cluny	NATION STATES
1794	Russian monks come into Alaska, establish mission	
1795	Wm Carey in India translates Bible into native tongues	COLONIALISM
1799	K Wilhelm III unites German Lutheran and Reformed churches	
1800s	Protestant missionaries go all over the world	
1801	American revivalists start 2nd Great Awakening in KY	

People Timeline

1801	Napoleon and p concordat brings Catholicism back in France
1806	K Francis II abdicates HRE title (running since 962)
1827	Joseph Smith has first revelations for *Book of Mormon*
1804	Feuerbach ("God made in image of man" philosopher) born
1835	Schleiermacher in *Christian Faith* stresses feeling in religion — ROMANTICISM
1848	Karl Marx issues *Communist Manifesto*
1848	Talmadge in China pioneers indigenous congregations
1853	Antoinette Brown ordained in ministry, the first woman
1854	RC Council declares Mary's immaculate conception
1859	Darwin publishes *On the Origin of Species*
1860	American Xns divided on slavery, fight Civil War
1864	P Pius issues *Syllabus of Errors* against socialism and tolerance
1867	Worldwide Anglican bps convene at Lambeth Palace
1868	Lavigerie made archbp in Algiers, supports White Fathers
1870	Vatican Council I declares papal infallibility
1871	Reporter says, "Dr Livingstone, I presume," in Africa
1890	Rauschenbusch leads in social gospel movement
1892	Mokone starts "Ethiopian" Ch in Transvaal, Africa
1906	Seymour's Azusa St revival starts Pentecostalism
1907	Korean Xns make a single national Presbyterian Ch
1910	Mott and Oldham lead at Edinburgh World Missionary Conference
1910+	Princeton theologians start publishing *The Fundamentals*
1915/6	A million+ Armenian Xns die in Ottoman Turk genocide
1917	Tikhon elected Rus patr; in 1920s Soviets start persecution
1918	Karl Barth pens *Commentary on Romans*

Brief Christian Histories

1922	Turks burn Smyrna, ending 3000-year Greek culture there	
1925	John Scopes is key witness in "monkey trial"	
1932	Reinhold Niebuhr publishes *Moral Man and Immoral Society*	
1934	Bonhoeffer and German Confessing Ch reject Nazism	SECULAR
1948	Ecumenicals organize World Council of Churches	
1950	Mother Teresa organizes Missionaries of Charity, Calcutta	GLOBAL
1962	P John XXIII convenes 2nd Vatican Council	
1963	M L King Jr. leads civil rights march on Washington	
1964	Patr Athenogoras and RC P Paul VI embrace in Jerusalem	
1968	RC bps at Medellin outline liberation theology	
1970	Christians participate in first Earth Day	
1974	Billy Graham supports Lausanne Conf on World Evangelization	
1980	Archbp Oscar Romero martyred in El Salvador	
1990	Aleksii II made patr in Russia as Communism crumbles	
1990s	Rosemary Radford Reuther, other Xn feminists, speak out	
1994	Archbp Tutu leads Truth and Reconciliation Commission in S Africa	
2001	Muslim extremists destroy Twin Towers in New York City	WIRED
2003	Xns around world in largest peace rally in history	
2013	Benedict XVI retires; cardinals choose Francis I of Argentina as p	

Chapter 2

Christians' Ethics
Historical Trajectory on Relating to God and Neighbor

And what does the Lord require of you but to do justice, and to love mercy, and walk humbly with your God?
—Micah 6:8

There is some one good thing which alone is an end beyond which there are no further ends, we may call that the good of which we all search. . . . Happiness more than anything else appears to be just such an end. . . . Happiness, then, the end of which all our conscious acts are directed, is found to be something final and self-sufficient.
—Aristotle, *Nicomachean Ethics*[1]

Huck Finn said, *They* [the slave bounty hunters] *went off and I got aboard the raft, feeling bad and low, because I knowed very well I had done wrong* [lying to the hunters to save his friend Jim], *and I see it warn't no use for me to try and*

---

1. Aristotle, *Nicomachean Ethics*, 36–37.

Brief Christian Histories

learn to do right; a body that don't get started right when he's little ain't got no show.... Then I ... says to myself s'pose you'd 'a' done right and give Jim up, would you felt better...? No, says I, I'd feel bad... [so, he decides, after this,] *always to do whichever come handiest at the time.*[2]

—Mark Twain, *The Adventures of Huckleberry Finn*

For Halloween one year, a church in Denver did a Hell House. They had rooms in which the sponsors tried to frighten young visitors into sin-free lives by revealing consequences of various identified sins and evils. So they had a teenage girl suffering in hell for having had an abortion, a young man tormented by demons because he'd smoked pot, and still another in the fire of hell for homosexuality. Such is one understanding of what constitutes *immorality* in the world.

That same weekend in Colorado Springs another group of Christians issued an *Active for Justice* newspaper. In the publication they too identified sins and evils of the world. Their list included homelessness, capital punishment, and "Star Wars" weaponry development.

Other Christians will identify yet other sinful things, such as saying "Goddam," polluting the environment, not genuflecting, human trafficking, and wearing lipstick. Through the millennia of our religion, there have been many different things, persons, practices, places, values, and beliefs identified as unclean, forbidden, punishable, or an abomination to God. Any list of wrongs has, of course, its opposite list of what is right/good/proper/moral for the faithful. Consideration of sin and of rightness—of what is evil and what is good—is ethics or morality, two words used interchangeably in these pages.

As a framework for thinking about ethics, a fourfold typology is employed. This typology is derived from the thought of Christian ethicists H. Richard Niebuhr and Robin Lovin.[3] They suggest that, in and for the moral life, there are four ethics:

- an ethic of command
- an ethic of ends
- an ethic of response

2. Twain, *Huckleberry Finn*, 89.
3. Niebuhr, *Responsible Self*, 47–68, and Lovin, *Christian Ethics*, 19–20.

- an ethic of virtue

Below is a brief description of each, and when I refer to these ethical-stance modalities in the chapter, I shall **bold** the concept.

Basic to an **ethic of command** is a "thus says the Lord," "do this, don't do that" understanding of life. Christians act in obedience to directives given in the Bible, contained in church law, or prescribed by one's community of faith. Niebuhr says the human image for the command ethic is that of "wo/man-the-citizen," one who makes laws and abides by them. To change the image a bit, we are actors playing out the script of God.

The **ethic of ends** is one that considers where the believer is headed, to what envisioned goal or *telos* he or she is directed. If people look forward, for example, to a just society, the Kingdom of God, or to heaven-as-home, they then shape their conduct toward that goal. Niebuhr says the human image is that of "wo/man-the-maker," one who constructs things, including himself or herself, according to an ideal. He or she acts for the sake of realizing that end.

Niebuhr's third way of doing ethics is by **ethic of response**. Here people are considered response-able beings who react to actions on their lives by God, other people, and the world. The human image is that of "wo/man-the-answerer." This is a present-tense, here-and-now ethic, as distinguished from wo/man-the-citizen, which is more past-oriented, and wo/man-the-maker, which is more future-oriented. The ethic of response asks about what is fitting more than about what is right (ethic of command) or what is good (ethic of ends).

The fourth category is the **ethic of virtue**, or living a life that is good. Robin Lovin here says that the ethical person is asking what kind of person he or she wants to become. The concern is character, inward integrity, virtue, or what the Greeks called *arete*. The look is neither behind with rules, or before toward goals, or beside in response, but within. The human image is that of "wo/man-the-upright."

Elements of all four ways of being and behaving (1) in the world, (2) with others, and (3) in relation to God are found in Christian history.

(Note: I considered calling this chapter "The *Evolution* of Christian Ethics" and thought to offer a *progressive* interpretation of moral history. But too much evidence weighs in against such an interpretation. Reinhold Niebuhr, brother to H. Richard Niebuhr, says, "Man's [sic] story is not a success story." What I know is that we continue to struggle with how to live rightly. *By God's grace* we sometimes get a few things right. Still, the

Christian situation is often three steps forward, two back—and sometimes four in reverse. Even so, we trust we've made a little progress, affirming with Martin Luther King Jr. that "the arc of a moral universe is long, but it bends toward justice."[4])

In this chapter, my hope is that the reader will get some better understanding of the Christian moral life in its many dimensions over historic time . . . so that he or she might gain some better insight on how to put life together faithfully/morally in our own time.

PRE-MONARCHIC MILLENNIUM (2000–1000 BCE)

The Older Testament of the Bible begins with theological and anthropological stories. They are ancient but altogether relevant. True observations are made about humanity "in the beginning." Genesis 1 says that humankind was created *imago Dei*, in the image of God, and that what God created was good. To start off, then, there is a positive affirmation of *homo sapiens*. Men and women, the Bible says, are likenesses of God in who we are and what we do.

But something else is also said about us.

We are fallen creatures. Genesis 3 tells the story of the first man and woman. Living in the garden of Eden, these two are **commanded** not to eat of the tree of the knowledge of good and evil, it being reserved for God alone. They eat anyway. Thus they disobey, and for their disobedience—their sin—God expels them from Paradise. They "fall" from grace. They discover guilt and shame. They suffer and ultimately die. This story, the Bible writers want to say, is not about a twosome in year 4004 BCE. It is about every contemporary man and woman. The truth is that we "miss the mark," the classic definition of sin. We posture as God. And we are punished. The story of Adam and Eve is, of course, mythological, yet profoundly true. The novelist Thomas Mann rightly says, "Myth never was but it always is."

This is the basic paradoxical understanding in the Christian religion about humans: though made *imago Dei*, we are flawed. We have "original blessings," *and* we are in a state of "original sin." We think both too highly *and* too lowly of ourselves, when we ought just to be thinking harder *about* God and neighbor.

---

4. King is quoted in Howell, *Exploring Christianity*, 34.

Christians' Ethics

The neighbor's importance in Christian ethics is revealed with the first murder. In Genesis 4, Cain, one of the two sons of Adam and Eve, in greed and jealousy slays his brother Abel. It is a primordial act of violence with intended cover-up. God then comes and asks Cain where Abel is. Cain lies, "How should I know? Am I my brother's keeper?" Cain has it that he is **not responsible**, but our ancestors in the faith have always known that the correct answer to God's question is, "Yes, I am my brother's keeper, for I am my brother's brother."

Christian ethics from the beginning, then, is triadic, involving (1) God, (2) the self, and (3) neighbor. The following figure reminds us of the dynamic:

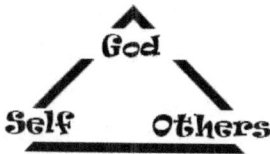

The moral agent is always the individual, and we, as moral agents, are always in relation to others. Given our *imago Dei* potential, given human sin, and given human **response-ability** to brothers and sisters, our faith ancestors were working early on to say how we might live rightly.

The next major section of the Genesis story also contributes to ethical understandings. Genesis 12–50 is the account of the patriarchs and matriarchs of ancient Israel. What might be noted is that an **ethic of ends** operates in the stories of our legendary ancestors. Abram and Sarai in faith left their homeland in Chaldea (southern Iraq) to go to a place God would show them. They put their life together with this goal in mind. They settled in Canaan/Palestine after a brief sojourn in Egypt.

As the book of Genesis ends, our ancestors are again in Egypt. There they remained for 450 years . . . until the time of Moses and the exodus from Egypt. For Moses' time and during the decades to come, three of the basic ethical ways in our faith history are shown. Consider first the **ethic of ends**. About the year 1250 BCE, the enslaved Israelites under Moses' leadership fled Egypt and began a trek that would lead them back to Canaan, to their "promised land." They were drawn there by Moses, whose very name, interestingly enough, means "drawn."

As a consequence of this exodus event and of forty years of wandering in the Sinai wilderness, the escapees came together as a coherent people: the People of Israel, people in **response-able** relationship with God and one another. There was give-and-take among Moses, God, and the people as they made their way along. Ultimately they came to realize what is needed to live and work together, and their main guide in this regard became the

Ten Commandments, sometimes called the Decalogue. Such was given them, they affirm, by God through Moses. Thus the **commandments** came to be owned by the People of Israel in a covenant made with God and each other.

Over the millennia, these Ten Commandments have had greater influence on ethical thinking and behavior than anything else in all Christian moral history. They are worth reviewing, here condensed:

1. I am Yahweh your God. Have no other god than me
2. Don't make any graven images or bow down to any such
3. You shall not take the name of Yahweh, the Lord, in vain
4. Remember the seventh day, keep it holy, on it do no work
5. Honor your father and mother
6. Do not kill
7. Do not commit adultery
8. Do not steal
9. Do not bear false witness/lie
10. Do not covet anything that is your neighbor's

The Ten Commandments are listed twice in the Older Testament, in Exodus 20 and Deuteronomy 5. Though they are called *commandments*, note that the first commandment, "I am the Lord your God," is a declarative sentence, not imperative. It recognizes that these people are **acting in response** to God's prior action toward them. All that follows in the other commandments, then, may be understood as answering God.

Still, the *sense* of **command** is there. The first five have to do with duties toward God, including parents, who stand with God, and the last five concern life with others in the community.[5] Traditionally they are understood to have come from "on high," given by God to Moses on Mt. Sinai and then etched in stone tablets. They were to be obeyed by all Israelites according to the Sinai covenant between Yahweh and the People of Israel. The stone tablets became so important to the People of Israel in the wilderness with Moses that they were housed in a special trunk called the Ark of

---

5. Some, like St. Augustine and the Latin Church, say only three commandments are about duty to God, while other traditions, notably that of Eastern Orthodoxy, has a four-six split of the Ten Commandments, weighting human duties more heavily than the five-five split.

the Covenant and carried by long poles. Each night during the wandering in the desert, the Ark was placed in an area called the tabernacle. The Ark-in-the-tabernacle, then, was watched over by a special coterie of priests, known as Levites. Physical artifacts and their handlings, notwithstanding, it is the tablets' instructions for the people that was of utmost importance. In community one was to observe them, put them into practice.

From this second millennium BCE, we may discern still another ethical dimension at work. The book of Exodus puts the reader on notice regarding social justice. Once slaves of the Egyptians, our Israelite faith-parents had experienced oppression. Evil had been imposed on them *from without*. It had an *externality* to it. They knew oppression entrenched in social, political, and economic structures. They experienced pharaohism, a system with ruling elites. In their bones they came to abhor such domination, wanting it not for themselves or for others. Our ancestors came to value freedom and justice, two high ethical passions that, when *internalized*, become dispositions reflecting an **ethic of virtue.**

While the Ten Commandments from the Sinai covenant are the main ethical features to be identified for this period, the commandments were actually predated by oral rules governing life in the desert. In the nomadic Middle East, a law of hospitality was widely observed. To welcome desert guests, for example, was expected behavior, as in Genesis 18, when Abraham set the table for three desert wanderers. Conversely, to be inhospitable—as were the inhabitants of Sodom to a desert guest—was considered wrong.

In addition to the law of hospitality, there is an ancient Holiness Code recorded in Leviticus 19. In it the faithful are called to be holy *because God is holy*. The code has instructions on sacrifice, harvesting, eating, not stealing, paying one's workers, witchcraft, the treatment of strangers, and more. Most importantly, there is a high-water ethical one-liner: "Love your neighbor as yourself" (Leviticus 19:18). To each command in the Holiness Code is added the *reason* to obey: because "I am the Lord your God." Such refrain makes the code's ethic of command also an **ethic of response.**

The law of hospitality and the Holiness Code are quite gracious, especially compared with some other vengeance practices mentioned in the Bible, most notably Genesis 4:23. There a man by the name of Lamech tells his wives, "I have slain a man for wounding me, and a young man for striking me." Lamech's action was unequal vengeance. An improvement on such conduct was reflected in the idea of balanced retribution: if someone knocks out your tooth, you may take one of his teeth but *no more* than that! Technically this is called *lex talionis* or "law of (proportional) retaliation." Leviticus 24:19–20, with its "eye for an eye" rule, was actually an ethical improvement over Lamech's way of acting.

Joshua, the People of Israel's leader after Moses, and the rise-to-the-occasion "judges" who followed Joshua (Othniel, Deborah-Barak, Gideon, Samson, etc.) seem not to have practiced *lex talionis* very well, if at all. Instead, they meted out unequal—even unprovoked—violence on others; for example, in taking the city of Jericho, Joshua's men "devoted to the sword all in the city, both men and women, young and old, oxen, sheep, and donkeys" (Joshua 6:21). Other examples of such mercilessness, usually "in the name of the Lord," can be found. Concerning such horrors found in the Bible, Older Testament scholar Walter Brueggemann reminds us that the Bible is a "book in travail." It is ethically unequal, but some better ways can be found in it.

TIME OF THE KINGS AND PROPHETS (1000–550 BCE)

In time, the Ark holding the commandments was brought into the city of Jerusalem, Jerusalem being the city King David captured and made capital for all the tribes of Israel. This was about the year 1000 BCE. David's son, Solomon, in turn, built a great temple in Jerusalem, and in that temple's center-most room, called the Holy of Holies, he placed the Ark. Believers then came to the temple to fulfill their ethical duties to God and to be reminded of their duties to others in the covenant. In the faith of our ancestors, the **ethic of command** continued at the center.

Liveliness was added to the "in stone" Law by prophets who delivered "the word of the Lord." The prophets became the living-law spokespersons for Yahweh. They were not, please note, priests with vested interest in worship and cultic activity, but independent voices who emphasized evolving theological and, especially, ethical interpretations of God's will. The prophet Samuel, for example, spoke for Yahweh and acted for Yahweh. He anointed Saul to be the first king in Israel. When Saul failed to be obedient, Samuel replaced him with David, "a man after God's own heart" (1 Samuel 13:14).

David was certainly God's anointed, but at one point he acted as if he were above the law. Instead of going to war as kings are *supposed* to do in the spring of the year, he sent others and stayed home. "Late one afternoon," so 2 Samuel 11 tells it, from the roof of his house, David saw a woman bathing, "and the woman was very beautiful." He enticed the woman, Bathsheba, into an adulterous relationship and then orchestrated the death of her husband, Uriah, one of the leaders of his army. For this, Nathan the prophet came with "the word of the Lord." The writer of the book of Samuel is clear that David's sins were unacceptable to God and a violation of covenant community. David would suffer: the child whom Bathsheba bore died.

In the case of David, he was not punished with a personal death sentence for his adultery and murder. In fact, he was forgiven. Something about mercy—God's mercy—was fitted into early moral equations of our religion. Jews, Christians, and certainly Muslims speak always of "God the Merciful." God's mercy exceeds God's wrath. David lived and had a successful forty-year kingship. Whatever else we may say of David, it should be noted that he was a *godly* man, able to confess his sins to the God in whom he believed.

Even so, the biblical notion that "the sins of the fathers shall be visited on the children to the fourth and fifth generations" came true in David's house. One of his daughters was raped by one of his sons, while another beloved son rebelled against him and in the insurrection, much to David's sorrow, was killed. Toward the end of the tenth century BCE, the unified kingdom, which David put together and Solomon maintained, broke apart. It split north and south. The ten-tribe northern kingdom of Ephraim had Samaria as its capital, while the two-tribe southern kingdom of Judah stayed centered in Jerusalem.

The main chronicler of the reigns of the kings of the kingdoms of Israel and Judah is the D writer, known as the Deuteronomist, or Second Law Giver. In the year 621 BCE a priest in the temple of Jerusalem discovered a manuscript that specified right worship practices and right behaviors for kings and people. Specifications for obedience were applied to histories of the kings. The northern kings, the D writer said, did what was wrong in the sight of the Lord. The main thing those kings got wrong was that they allowed the worship of Yahweh to take place in their own northern cities rather than exclusively in Jerusalem. *Place* of worship, though, was not the Deuteronomist's only criterion for making judgments. Kings were also judged on the basis of whether they fulfilled their justice responsibilities for the people. Only a few kings got passing grades.

Brief Christian Histories

A value of the Deuteronomist's history is that he joined theological considerations with ethical judgment. How he joined them, of course, was in a cause-effect relation:

Sin = Punishment

Righteousness = Reward

This joining of God and morality during the first millennium continues to the present. Judaism, Christianity, and Islam are all *ethical* religions, in which talk is first about God, then about the community's relationship to God and people's relations one with another and with neighbors. The prophets especially drew attention to the three-way covenantal relations. The Deuteronomist's ethical understanding holds through all "his" books: Joshua-Judges-Samuel-Kings. His formula was adopted by all the prophets too. Only the writer of the book of Job, a few centuries before Christ, would raise the question of *theodicy*—why do the righteous suffer, why do bad things happen to good people?—to a level that questioned the Deuteronomist's basic cause-effect formula.

In the eighth century BCE, three prophets—Amos, Isaiah, and Hosea (who have books bearing their names)—were Yahweh's spokespersons within the covenant. These prophets focused hardly at all on cultic purity but, rather, on how people treated one another. The three shared perspective—on the holiness of God, for example—and all were passionate about justice.

Consider Amos. He was unrelenting on the idea of the righteousness of God and the need that justice be done in the covenanted community. He pounded on themes of economic inequality, writing, "Let justice roll down like waters, and righteousness like an ever-flowing stream" (Amos 5:24). Three millennia later, Martin Luther King Jr. quoted Amos's words in Washington, D.C., in a speech about civil rights for black Americans.

Amos also railed against "the noise of solemn assemblies," meaning temple worship, where leaders attentive to ritual did not care adequately for "the widow, orphan, and stranger at the gate." In truth, every major prophet made treatment of the least and lost a touchstone for faithfulness to Yahweh.

Consider Isaiah, usually referred to as First Isaiah. This prophet is best remembered for his *mysterium tremendum* experience with Yahweh in the temple, recorded in Isaiah 6. He came away from that encounter knowing that God was holy and that God wanted holiness among his people. Isaiah was the first radical monotheist. He understood that even a hated enemy could be doing God's will. So Assyria might be understood as "the rod of God's anger," chosen to visit God's judgment upon the nation of Israel. The reason for Yahweh's anger, Isaiah said, was because of those who "turn aside the needy from justice and rob the poor of my people of their right" (Isaiah 10:2). This eighth-century prophet has been inspiration for much social justice preaching. Even so, he also talked about mercy and forgiveness, which the southern—but not the northern—kingdom experienced.

Thirdly, consider Hosea, the prophet who best articulated mercy. He held that, though Israel had played the harlot, God, for whatever inexplicable reasons, still loved Israel and would not let her go. Even if Israel were a slave on an auction block, rightly to be sold, Yahweh wanted to buy her back! Hosea's perspective is quite wonderful. It absolutely undoes the sometimes-spoken view that "the God of the Older Testament is a God of wrath." Not so, says Hosea 10. Yahweh of old is a loving, forgiving God.

The prophets, of course, were **ethicists of command**, couching their judgments with the phrase "Thus says the Lord." Certainly the prophet Micah operated in this way when he asked in that high-water-mark passage of Micah 6:8, "What does the Lord *require* of you?" and answered with the words, "to do justice and to love kindness and walk humbly with your God."

Some of the prophets, though, expressed more of an **ethic of virtue**. Jeremiah, for example, spoke of a "new covenant" that God would write. The new covenant would not be like the old covenant, which the Israelites broke. No. It would be *written on people's hearts*, so no one would have to say to a neighbor, "'Know the Lord,' for they will all know me, from the least of them to the greatest, says the Lord; for I will forgive their iniquity" (Jeremiah 31:34). Jeremiah's vision, while it drew people toward the new covenant and promised good life from the inside, would come only as a gift of Yahweh.

Yahweh, though, first had to bring judgment.

So it was. In 586 BCE the city of Jerusalem was captured and destroyed by the Babylonians. The leading citizens of the city then were taken off to live "by the waters of Babylon." In that foreign land they operated with an "interim ethic," most like an **ethic of response**, trying to figure out what to do in their changed situation. The answer was to build houses, plant vineyards, and "seek the welfare of the city where I have sent you into exile" (Jeremiah 29:7), which city belonged to their captors.

In exile, though, the prophet Ezekiel had visions of a reversal of fortune when the dry, dead bones of Israel would be re-fleshed. He held out hope, which relates to the **ethic of ends**.

SECOND TEMPLE PERIOD (550–20 BCE)

In time, the Babylonians were defeated by Cyrus the Persian, and in 538 BCE Cyrus allowed the captive Judeans, forty thousand in number by tradition, to return home to Jerusalem. So their hope came to a reality, at least in part. Once home they built a new temple, raised a wall around the city, and began to live according to their sacred texts, which at this time were being assembled.

They came home from Babylon, though, with a few different ideas. During their years in exile, the former Judeans were exposed to the cosmology and stories of the Babylonians. The result of such exposure shows up in the biblical material being assembled. The authors-compilers-editors borrowed a Babylonian account of a great flood, for example, and retold it to talk about God's judgment and mercy. Also, they borrowed thought from their new rulers, the Persians. The Persians were Zoroastrians, operating with a dualistic worldview. Dualistic thinking sets up polarities for ethical decision making:

God vs. Satan

Good vs. Evil

Heaven vs. Hell

Angels vs. Demons

So, in the book of Job, written during the Persian period, 538–333 BCE, we meet the fallen angel Satan, a being who had *not* been around in stricter monotheistic years. Satan sought to do Job in.

Once presented, the opposing-poles worldview, we know, never goes away. In the Newer Testament, Jesus deals with demons. There is certainly a Hades in Dante's *Inferno*, written during the Middle Ages. In late-seventeenth-century-CE New England witch trials happened. A twentieth-century American president spoke of an international adversary as an "evil empire." Credit such thinking, adopted by our faith-parents, to the ancestors of people now living in Iran.

So there was an *external*—in this case, Persian—influence on our faith-parents' ethics, and there was *internal* shaping, coming from their own history and reflection, especially as related to the assembly of the Bible. During this Second Temple Period, the first five books of the Bible took final form. The Torah or Law, greatly revered, became "The word of the

Lord," instructional for religious observance *and* ethical behavior. Some 613 laws can be identified in the Torah—the supposed number of seeds in a pomegranate—and these laws, the faithful held, were to be followed as scrupulously as possible. There were/are rules on holiday observance, for the keeping of Sabbath, sexual relations, diet (what foods not to eat, e.g., catfish), and much, much more. Modern folk might think this emphasis on detailed rules is obsessive, even oppressive, but the Hebrew people did not find them so. They liked this **ethic of command**, as revealed in Psalm 119, verses 97, 103, and 105, where the writer speaks rapturously of Torah:

Oh, how I love your law! It is my meditation all day long . . .

How sweet are your words to my taste, sweeter than honey to my mouth . . .

Your word is a lamp to my feet and a light to my path.

If one wants to know what to do—the ethical question—the answer is, "Check out Torah." Millions of people, ancient and contemporary, do. The creation of Torah, then, was in this period *the* great achievement for ethical direction.

As we moved toward the Common Era, Torah was supplemented with scrolls for the Prophets and for the Other Writings (such as Psalms and Proverbs). By the year 90 CE the canon of the Hebrew Bible was fixed. The whole corpus became sacred scripture, guide to faith *and morals*, ultimately valued by Jews, Christians, and Muslims.

One of the things detailed in the emerging Bible is a symbolic way to handle sin and to excise it. Leviticus 16 describes a ritual in which, once a year, citizens selected a goat on whom individual and corporate sins might be cast. So casting their sins, they then drove the animal from their village, never to allow it reentry. If this ritual scapegoating worked spiritually, ethically, and psychologically, it set people in the community right with God and with one another. Later Judaism would have a High Holy Day called Yom Kippur, in which sins, individual and corporate, were confessed and atonement—that is, at-one-making—with God and neighbor was effected.

The Older Testament or Hebrew Bible or Tanakh (Torah+Prophets +Other Writings) was valued both by Jews who lived in and near Jerusalem *and* by the faithful dispersed throughout the Mediterranean Middle Eastern world. After 333 BCE, when Alexander the Great of Macedonia wrested power from the Persians, the world of our ancestors became increasingly

Greek. The faithful, in **ethic of response**, had to discern how to relate to this quite different culture.

As our faith-parents attempted to adapt, a major division in the house of faith began to grow. On the one hand, there was a group, both in Jerusalem and in the *Diaspora* (Jews scattered in places outside of Palestine), who emphasized law-abidingness. They wanted scrupulous obedience to the Law, with purification of the faith, bordering on "ethnic cleansing." The priest Ezra, for example, forbade marriage of Jews with non-Jews, and his writings told husbands to give up their foreign/Gentile wives.

On the other hand, some believers felt that religious and ethnic separateness was not right. *Second* Isaiah, author of Isaiah chapters 40–55, writing in mid-sixth century BCE at the time of the return from Babylon, envisioned something more than just restoration for old Jerusalem. He saw a "New Jerusalem" in which religion and righteousness would be realized, with Zion becoming a magnet city for the nations. He envisioned Gentiles—all people, really—being drawn in peace to Jerusalem and to Yahweh. His was an *inclusive* ethic. In the same vein, the writers of Ruth and of Jonah pleaded against withdrawal from the wider world. They said the right thing to do was to reach out and include Gentiles in the historic faith. God's message is universally valid, they contended, and faithful people have an ethical opportunity to share it broadly. The sharing is so that God is made known in all the world and that persons everywhere realize they are received in God's great inclusiveness.

Hundreds of years after Second Isaiah, Ruth, and Jonah, a Nazarene prophet by the name of Jesus picked up on this larger vision and talked about an inbreaking Reign of God for all people.

Living in the wider Greek world, some Jews, notably Philo of Alexandria, attempted a synthesis of Hebrew religion with Greek notions of Wisdom or *Sophia*, an idea by which men and women were guided. Walking in the Way of Wisdom is extolled, for example, in the book of Proverbs. "Lay aside immaturity, and live," Proverbs 9:6 says, "and walk in the way of insight." Much practical advice on how one should live morally is suggested in this book, as well as in other Wisdom literature, such as Ecclesiastes and Wisdom of Solomon. Wisdom, personified, is portrayed as having been with God "from the beginning." Now, walking in Wisdom's way while eschewing folly was the correct course for righteous living. Adherence to Wisdom would enable one to become habituated into Sophia's holy ways. This is an **ethic of virtue**. What faithful people would hope for themselves is that they might embody Wisdom well enough to realize what "good life" would be vis-à-vis God and one another.

NEWER TESTAMENT TIMES (20 BCE-110 CE)

Jesus of Nazareth was an itinerant rabbi and healer from Galilee in northern Palestine. He came on the scene with a basic message of love, God's love for all people. Gathering a small coterie of men and women, he taught them in terms of a revolutionary vision of a now-breaking-in Basileia/Reign/Kingdom of God. His was primarily a great **ethic of ends,** in which he invited people to become *makers*—H. Richard Niebuhr's image—or *builders* of the Kingdom of heaven.

Jesus, however, was not singular in his ethics. Besides an ethic of ends, those who tell his story also say Jesus employed an **ethic of command**. In this regard, the twentieth-century preacher Harry Emerson Fosdick said, "As with the prophets, so with [Jesus]. The major motivation in all his thinking about God was not cosmic curiosity but moral seriousness."[6] Jesus' moral seriousness is compressed in his famous Sermon on the Mount. In that Sermon we hear him say time after time,

"You have heard it said of old . . .

regarding killing, adultery, divorce, revenge, swearing falsely, and so on

but I say to you . . .

don't be angry, look lustfully, divorce one's spouse, swear, and so on"

All this is in Matthew, chapter 5. Matthew 7:29 contends that Jesus "taught them as one having authority." That authority, his disciples affirmed, was the authority of God . . . so that his words came to be understood as the Word/the Command of God. Jesus' prescriptions were also radical, involving turning the other cheek to an oppressor, loving your enemies, having purity of heart, attaining righteousness (exceeding that of the most righteous), practicing nonviolence, being nonanxious, trusting God totally, and much more. Living in just such a way also would be to have inner integrity, to live by an **ethic of virtue.**

---

6. Fosdick, *Understanding the Bible*, 40.

Besides being ends-, command-, and virtue-driven in his ethics, Jesus was also one who lived an **ethic of response**. Note, for example, how he regularly asked and responded to questions and people. From the time of his being with elders in the temple when he was twelve years old to his last hour on the cross, with two thieves beside him, he was dialoguing. He was ever searching for the loving-forgiving-"fitting" thing to do.

However construed, Jesus' words about how to live and be in this world, vis-à-vis God and neighbor, brought him into conflict with two establishments of his day. The first was that of the Pharisees. These teachers kept themselves *pure* by strict adherence to rules. They did not approve of Jesus' associating with "unclean sinners," such as lepers and tax collectors, nor could they accept his acts of healing on the Sabbath. Secondly, there were the Sadducees, who followed the oldest interpretations of the Law, asserting, for example, there is no hereafter. The Sadducees rigorously protected the temple and were angered when Jesus tried to "cleanse" it, driving money changers out. Eventually these two religious establishments conspired with the Roman political authorities to arrest, try, convict, and crucify the man from Nazareth. On a cross, he died.

Three days after Jesus' death his followers came to proclaim that, by God's power, their Lord was raised from the tomb. So Jesus became the Risen Christ. How that resurrection happened is shrouded in mystery, open primarily to the eye of faith. Some people, however, offer an "ethical explanation" of the resurrection, saying it happened because Jesus' teachings about God and his ethic of love took hold of his followers as "still true"/"right on," even though he was gone. When that realization transpired, it was as though he was still among them, alive. However we explain Christ's resurrection, it ensured that his radical ethic would be remembered.

In all this, the fact that he died on a cross would be a strong suggestion that his followers might suffer similarly. We will come to consideration of this possibility shortly.

Jesus' life and teaching are presented in the Gospels of Matthew, Mark, Luke, and John. The first contributor to Newer Testament scripture, however, was Paul of Tarsus. Traveler that he was, Paul wrote letters to the churches he founded and to individuals. The letters were with regard to all manner of belief, belonging, and behavior. His central teaching was/is that humans are saved by faith and not by works. He distrusted all works righteousness. Not that Christians do not act justly, give generously, or live mercifully, Paul would say. They can and do. It is just that our actions should not be based on the Law's *demands*, or on hope of heaven's *reward*, or emerge from a place of inner *virtue*, but, rather, should come primarily out of response to God's love and mercy toward us in Christ Jesus.

Paul's doctrine of "justification by faith alone," we shall see, regularly surfaces in subsequent Christian history. What it meant in terms of ethics at this era is most interesting. Christians are free to relate to God and one another in nontraditional ways. Working as he was among the Gentiles (that is, among Greeks), Paul realized that certain traditional Jewish practices were not necessarily required—notably circumcision (the usually-infant right of male initiation into the People of Israel) and keeping a kosher kitchen (a complex collection of rules about menu and food preparation). In the freedom of Christ, he said, such things can be let go.

Most dramatically, these early Gentile Christians abandoned the Sabbath-day commandment. They began to worship at sunrise on the *first* day of the week! They practiced something called Holy Communion or Eucharist (from the Greek word for "thanksgiving"). They observed open table fellowship, letting slaves and women be there. They shared their resources across borders. And much more, all in the spirit of love. Greek Christians were responding in fresh ways to the Good News of God's love addressed to them in Jesus. The writer of the letters of John captured the **ethic of response** best when he wrote, "We love because God first loved us" (1 John 4:19).

As open, even progressive, as Paul and other early Christians were, they were also limited by the mores, culture, and self-understandings of their time. Some of Paul's instructions now seem narrow, even wrongheaded. *If* he wrote all the letters attributed to him, he would be understood as one who condoned slavery, required women to keep silent in church, and eschewed same-sex relations. Paul thought singleness is better than being married, and he counseled strict obedience to governmental authorities, saying, "Be patient in suffering" (Romans 12:12)—which is just to say that he was a first-century-CE person.

Some of the reason for Paul's thinking about behavior was because he and the earliest Christians looked for the imminent return of Jesus. Even late in the first century CE, the writer of the book of Revelation was holding out for the second coming of Jesus. Other Christians, notably Gospel writers Luke and John, suggested that the Lord had *already* returned, in the presence of the Holy Spirit. The Spirit of God the Father and Christ the Son, they believed, was with them and would lead them into *all truth*, including new truth and new responsible ways of being in the world. They struggled, though, to define how to be *in* but not *of* this world, the issue in chapter 4 of this book.

Always Christians sought to live out an ethic of love. Sometimes they succeeded. One of the highest compliments ever paid the early Christians was the tribute of the pagan philosopher Celsus, who commented, "Behold how they love one another!" Indeed, love (*agape, caritas*, self-giving, unconditional love) became the ethical ideal of Christians. Paul wrote. "And now faith, hope, and love abide, these three; and the greatest of these is love" (1 Corinthians 13:13). *Agape* (a-GAH-pay) love became the Christian aspiration. It was/is a love that is beyond familial love (Greek *storge*) or friendship (Greek *philia*) or romantic love (Greek *eros*). *Agape* love, the early church believed, is what God has toward humanity. Such love is "of-the-will-pertaining," more than a natural affection. Christians are ever called to *agape* love, which has **command-ends-response-virtue** dimensions in it.

The love that the earliest Christians affirmed and practiced, according to the book of Acts, was taken out into the world broadly. After the Feast of Weeks or Pentecost experience, involving "speaking in tongues"—probably foreign languages, more than holy babble—Jesus' followers became "witnesses in Jerusalem, and in all Judea and Samaria, and to the ends of the world" (Acts 1:8). Thomas by tradition went to India, Mark to Alexandria, John to Ephesus, Peter to Rome, Mary Magdalene to France, and James to Spain.

STRUGGLING CENTURIES OF THE CHURCH (110–500 CE)

Christians, in trying to live out Jesus' love ethic in the first several centuries, did some unique things. For love of God and God's people (all humanity), they refused to serve in the army. That until about 170 CE. They refused to attend gladiatorial circuses. Magicians, jugglers, and mountebanks who became Christian had to give up or modify their professions. People of the Way (an early name for the Christian church) would not expose unwanted babies, a widespread pagan custom. Sometimes Jesus' early followers practiced a form of communism, sharing their wealth with those who had need. When they worshiped and broke bread in an Agape Meal, they even allowed women to preside at the table.

As a consequence of such ethical practices and *because of* Christian beliefs, a number of Gentiles were drawn to this new movement. Greeks who had been initially attracted to Judaism, who were known as God-fearers, came in, as did women, slaves (representing up to 80 percent of the population), and the poor. There were also people of prominence, education, and means in the movement. For them all, Christianity presented "a more excellent way" (1 Corinthians 12:31).

Philip Wogaman in his history of ethics says, "The early church was deeply engaged in moral teaching! Moral instruction was not a side interest; it was at the heart of the presentation of the gospel to believers and nonbelievers alike."[7] Some of the moral instruction is in *The Didache* or *Teaching of the Apostles*. It is an **ethic of command** book. In the book, caring for the needy is prescribed. Such practice turned out to be another plus for the faith's attractiveness. People liked Christianity's (1) incarnate God, (2) its sacred scripture, (3) its organization, the church, and (4) its caring ethic and practice.

Not everyone in the empire, however, appreciated this emerging new branch of old Judaism, partly because it was *new*. The Romans tolerated old religions, and Judaism was considered old. So it was put up with. But this Christianity was an *upstart* faith, perceived as dangerous. Its adherents, for example, did not give due deference to the historic Roman gods. Thus the early Christians were considered "atheists," nonbelievers in the Roman gods. As far as near-kin Jews were concerned, the followers of Jesus were "di-theists," believers in two gods, a father and a son.

Beginning in the first century CE, and continuing irregularly over the next two hundred years, emperors and provincial governors would require citizens to show their loyalty to Rome by putting a pinch of incense on coals burning in front of a Roman statuary god—or the bust of a Caesar who had declared himself divine. Many Christians decided that the incense offering was tantamount to denying their faith in Jesus, who, they affirmed, was their *only* Caesar/Lord. They made the ethical decision not to do the pinch. Persecution of Christians was the government's sometimes response.

Persecution ended in 313 CE when a new emperor, Constantine, issued an Edict of Toleration. His conversion or generosity toward Christianity may be attributed to one of three influences. The first is because he had a vision of Christ just before an important battle, a battle that he won (see the icon at the start of this section; Chi and Rho are the first two letters in

---

7. Wogaman, *Christian Ethics*, 25.

the Greek word for "Christ"). Or Constantine's acceptance of Christianity may be attributed to the positive urgings of his Christian-believing mother, Helena. Or, for a third thing, Constantine may have seen something persuasive in Christian ethics, something that might help him be a successful ruler. Certainly he observed how the church cared for the general welfare of people through its orphanages, hospices (early hospitals), and feeding efforts. He needed such social services for effective governance, so he gave the church money, that such caring might continue, even be expanded.

In time, tolerance went to outright favor. In 381 CE Christianity was made the official religion of the Roman Empire. Such favor, however, created a problem recognized early on by Christians in Egypt. There, as persecution slowed down, believers began to ask, "How do we *suffer for Christ*, as prescribed in scripture, and suffer like Jesus, if we're accepted by the world?" Many men and women answered that question via *self*-imposed sacrifice, fasting, and various asceticisms. Some went alone to the desert to test themselves. Others joined in close community to live lives of poverty, chastity, and obedience. By the late two hundreds CE the monastic movement was underway. By the five hundreds it was the superior way in the Christian life. So identification and union with the crucified Christ became the *goal* of such believers. This was the practice of an **ethic of ends**.[8]

In these early centuries of the church, the essential guide for Christian belief and practice was the Bible. First of all, there was the Older Testament with its Law codes, prophetic utterances, and Wisdom literature. It had been translated from Hebrew into Greek centuries earlier. Then there was the Newer Testament with its ethical teachings by Jesus and the apostles. It was available in the Greek-speaking world from the start, as it was written in the *lingua franca* of the day, Koine (pronounced koy-NAY), that is, everyday Greek. For *Latin*-speaking and -reading Christians, however, translation from Hebrew and Greek into Latin was needed. St. Jerome provided that in the late fourth century. Thus the Ten Commandments, the justice-and-mercy prescriptions of the prophets, and Jesus' moral teachings became available broadly. Given the reach of the Roman Empire and the spread of Christianity within it, we may speculate, then, that Jesus' Sermon on the Syrian Mount, originally rendered in Aramaic, made its way to be preached on the green hills of England in Latin!

---

8. We'll come to a fuller consideration of monasticism in the next section of this chapter.

The greatest theologian and ethicist of the Western or Latin Church was Augustine, bishop of Hippo in North Africa, writing in the early four hundreds. Several things applicable to ethics stand out in his thought. One was his **ethic of response** in the famous dictum: "Love God and do what you please," an idea that gives real freedom and real responsibility. Equally well known is his thinking on original sin, a doctrine implied in biblical thought, now made explicit by Augustine. In his autobiographical *Confessions*, he examined his own deeply flawed character, his lust, and his sinful pride/concupiscence. Augustine thought that such is the condition of all people, and that separation from God and neighbor was there "in the beginning":

> In Adam's sin,
> we fall,
> one and all.

The doctrine of original sin became part of subsequent Christian thought, taken seriously yet today. It is subscribed to in the great American novel *Moby Dick* and spoken of by the English writer G. K. Chesterton as "the only Christian doctrine that can be empirically verified." Though the doctrine paints a grim picture of "human nature," it is most useful in calling attention to the need for (1) God's grace and (2) **responsive** human faith.

A less pessimistic view of the nature of humanity, distinct from Augustine, is that of Clement and Origen of Alexandria. They suggest that humanity can make moral progress, can do something about salvation. So began "moral theology," which a thinker like Thomas Aquinas and most of the mystics hold to be the case. We are not helpless, in total depravity, the Alexandrians said.

If men and women choose the good, as Clement and Origen say, they/we walk in the Christian theological **virtues** of faith, hope, and love. These virtues practiced can create a "good life" leading toward heaven, avoiding "purgatory"—a concept of the afterlife also originating with Origen. Ethicist Mark Douglas says that from this time on an **ethic of virtue** is what drives the church's moral life.[9]

---

9. Mark Douglas, professor of Christian ethics, Columbia Theological Seminary, Decatur, Georgia, shared this thought in a personal conversation, December 18, 2001.

THE AGE OF MONASTICISM (500–1100 CE)

Augustine died in 430 CE. After him there is less significant theological and ethical writing for hundreds of years. There was, though, great Christian moral earnestness and practice. Basically it continued through the monasteries and convents of the Eastern and Western churches, which topic was briefly touched on above. St. Basil's guidance for Eastern or Greek Orthodox Church monastic life was put into a *Rule*. St. Benedict in Italy did the same for Western or Roman Catholic monasticism. He started writing his *Rule* in 529 CE. In it he laid out *ora et labora* (prayer and work) practices for the religious to follow. It specified times for prayer, responsibilities to one's superiors, the obligations of the prioress and abbot for their members, foods for the seasons, and much more, such as emphasis on hospitality toward persons who come to the gates of the house. Maintaining community in obedience and humility is central in *The Rule of Benedict*, as it also is in Basil's. Both reflect an **ethic of command**.

Monasteries and convents in this early medieval period were especially important in preserving both Christian faith and Christian practice, for in the fifth century CE western Europe was being overrun by invading Germanic peoples. Periodically these barbarians—meaning, literally, "bearded ones"—wearing pants, not togas, swept into the empire from northern and eastern Europe. They came looking for warmer climes, fertile lands, and the wealth that the West had. The tribespeople were not much interested in Roman culture, literature, or art, much less Catholic/Nicene Christianity. If they were anything but pagans, they were Arian (anti-Nicene) believers. An Arian barbarian general by the name of Odoacer deposed the last Western emperor, Romulus Augustus, in 476 CE, providing a date for the fall of the Roman Empire. Certainly much of Western Christianity was in some danger of being snuffed out. In England, established Christianity disappeared almost entirely when Roman troops withdrew after 476.

One bastion of significant Christianity *not* overrun by the barbarians was Ireland. Though the Irish had adopted Christianity only a century earlier, a Celtic monk by the name of Columba was ready in 564 CE to take the faith east to Scotland, the land of the Celtic Picts. On the island of Iona he established a monastery. From there he won the Picts/Scots over to Christianity. Columba's fellow monks kept traveling, south into Wales and east to the Continent. Wherever they went, they founded monasteries and rekindled love of Christ and the love of letters, for the Celtic monks were great manuscript copyists. They created fresh islands of *ora et labora* throughout Europe, right alongside the rough world of the Germanic tribes. The monastic communities practiced peace in a world of violence, offered sanctuary to those who fled to their door, and reached out in ways of social service, creating homes for unwed mothers, orphanages, and hospices.

The big turnaround in sociopolitical circumstance for Western Christianity happened in France through the rising royal house of the Carolingian monarchs, most notably Charles the Great, Charlemagne (742–814). He first defeated the barbarian Saxons in Germany—pushed them back across the Rhine River—and then, on Vatican request, subdued the pagan Lombards in northern Italy. In the year 800 CE, Pope Leo III gave Charles the crown and title of king for his empire, whereby he became "the protector of the popes and their domains, the patron of reformers and missionaries, and the guardian of orthodoxy."[10] Charlemagne advanced learning during his Carolingian Renaissance and encouraged the work of Christian monks and nuns, notably sending Christian Saxon monks from England to the pagan Saxons of Germany. After 900 CE the giant French monastery at Cluny took the lead in planting monasteries across Europe and winning people—especially Norse/Vikings—to Christian faith and practice. The monks modeled Christianity, practicing the poverty-chastity-and-obedience (**command**) ethical values along with *ora et labora*.

By the end of this first millennium, Christianity was well reestablished in most of Europe, including the Scandinavian countries where missionary monks had gone. The Vikings, who had raided up and down the Atlantic coast—and into the Mediterranean—in time settled into England, Normandy, and Sicily. Once settled, the monks and kings (like Alfred the Great of Wessex, England) brought the Vikings into the faith. Deep in Europe, when the Magyars (aka Huns/Hungarians) were defeated by Otto the Great in 955, they finally turned to align themselves with Western Catholic Christianity, rather than Eastern Orthodox Christianity, though the latter had initially been considered. It was Duke Geza who led the Hungarians into ties with Rome.

Orthodox monasticism, closely allied with the Byzantine emperors in Constantinople, was a strong and ongoing presence in the Eastern empire. We remember Egyptian desert fathers like Anthony, Syriac monks like Simeon Stylites, cave-centered Cappadocians (in central Turkey), and Greek island communities. All suggest the pervasiveness of monastic

---

10. *Westminster Dictionary*, 179.

Christianity in these regions. When Islamic horsemen came out of the Arabian Desert conquering during the seventh century, Eastern monasticism and Christianity (of several forms) began to decline under Arab domination. Islamic law, for one thing, required Christians to pay some special taxes. Even so, many Christian believers in Egypt, Syria, and Babylon hung on *and* have continued to hang on, even to the present day. In Baghdad today there are a half million Chaldean or Nestorian Christians, but they are only a shade of their former prominence. Back in the eighth century CE, the Nestorians were vital enough to send missionaries as far as China and India. They were operating under Jesus' **command ethic** to "Go and make disciples of all nations . . . teaching them to observe all that I have commanded you" (Matthew 28:19). The heterodox Christianities of Coptic Egypt, Ethiopia, and Armenia of the early Middle Ages also have managed to continue to continue, however diminished.

As Greek Orthodoxy's numbers in the eastern Mediterranean shrank, new growth happened further north. In the year 988 the czar in Kiev adopted Christianity for the Rus. From Kiev it spread north into Muscovy and Lithuania. Today Russian Orthodoxy is the third or fourth largest expression of Christianity in the world, behind Catholicism and Protestantism—and perhaps Pentecostalism, as we shall discover.

Generally speaking, wherever Greek, Russian, Coptic, or Chaldean Christianity has lived, it has been quite conservative or traditional, keeping to inherited worship practices. In the East, Orthodox really means "right liturgy" more than "right belief." Only in a few exceptions, as when priests and monks challenged imperial authority during an icon controversy in the eighth and ninth centuries, have Orthodox religious challenged secular power. Perhaps it has had to be so, for these Christians ever lived under the domination of Byzantine, Persian, Arab, and Ottoman rulers. In Russia the church was controlled by the czars and then, during the twentieth century, by the Communists, who sought to destroy it. Through all circumstances, in Russia, in Greece, and in other places where Orthodoxy maintained, there were holy persons called *hesychasts,* who sought God in pilgrim wanderings and in the practice of stillness. Hesychasts lived, we must say, by an **ethic of virtue**, desiring inner rightness with God and gentle association with humble people. One Russian hesychast walked a thousand miles, continually repeating the Jesus Prayer: "*Lord Jesus Christ, Son of God, have mercy on me, a sinner.*"

*

Christians' Ethics

East or West, the church tried to provide a moral compass for people, including kings and emperors. Such compass included guidance on war, using Augustine's just-war theory,[11] for example. In addition, bishops might censure princes who lived licentiously or merchants who charged interest on money, aka usury. In the case of usury, this prohibition came from scripture (Exodus 22:25). In the eastern part of the empire, law-abidingness was especially regulated by the law code of Emperor Justinian (529–565 CE), built from ancient Roman law. One aspect of Justinian's law code, still honored if not always observed, is that persons are considered innocent until proven guilty.

In Western Europe, law was more nearly set by Germanic tribal law codes with the general prescriptive formula, "If a man does *x* wrong ... then *y* should be his penalty." One horrific aspect in the justice system of the early Middle Ages, which originated with the Franks, was the trial by "ordeal": if a magistrate could not decide judicial cases by eyewitness testimony or forensic proof, litigants could prove claim of innocence by retrieving a small rock from a cauldron of boiling water. Then the hand was bandaged; if, after three days of coverage, an examining priest found no damage to the hand—which would be a miracle—that person was considered to have told the truth. Otherwise, no.[12]

One of the things to consider is how the moral life looked in terms of ordinary Christians. This was an age of piety. "Do-right" things might include almsgiving, going on a pilgrimage to a holy shrine, venerating icons or relics, praying the stations of the cross, fasting, or walking a labyrinth. (We shall look at these and other practices and pieties more fully in chapter 3). All that was done as duty to God (**ethic of command**) and to attain heaven (**ethic of ends**).

Regulating conduct happened especially through the church's penitential system, an inheritance from Celtic Christianity, where it began via "tariff books." We would probably call them legal guidelines. Over time the tariff books set up a system that took into account (1) the sin, (2) personal confession to a priest, (3) the priest's assessment of appropriate penance, followed by (4) doing the penance, which generated both (5) satisfaction

---

11. Just-war theory includes ideas such as last resort, legitimate authority, self-defense, chance of success, goal of peace, proportionality, and protection of noncombatants.

12. There also was a "trial of iron" (carrying superheated metal in your hand three paces), a "trial by water" (if in drowning one floated, he/she was judged guilty, but sinking confirmed innocence), and a "trial by the cross" between litigants (an endurance contest to see who could keep their arms extended the longest).

and (6) absolution (forgiveness of the sinner). The penitent might be required to fast, abstain from sex, be flogged, go to prison, pay a fine, or do a repeated recitation of the Psalter in position of discomfort. The penance was supposed "to fit the crime." In the Middle Ages for the sacrament of penance there a double-compartment confessional booth with a grid or lattice separating the penitent from the priest-confessor was used. Always the ethic involved was one of **ends**, trying to help the person be cleansed for heaven. Doing proper penance was believed to shorten one's stay in purgatory. Purgatory, a nonbiblical notion, was a major Christian category from the fourth century on, fully put to use now.

In the Eastern Church there was not a penitential system per se or any talk of purgatory or limbo. The differences in "crime and punishment" style, if you will, between East and West were one dimension to creating the great schism by which, in 1054, Orthodoxy officially separated from Catholicism. Pope in Rome and patriarch in Constantinople each thought, of course, that he was doing right in issuing an anathema/curse on the other.

HIGH CHRISTENDOM YEARS (1100–1450 CE)

In the year 1095, though Orthodoxy and Catholicism were officially separated, Emperor Leo III in Constantinople asked Pope Urban II in Rome to help him repel Islamic Turks who were taking over Byzantine lands. Pope Urban then called for Western European armies to fight against "the infidels." What, though, did such a call mean? If Christians practiced nonviolent pacifism in the first centuries of the Common Era, and if, from fifth century on, they were guided by Augustine's just-war theory, now a radically different face was shown: that of the holy war. Kings and princes, monks and priests, simple peasants of western Europe responded to Urban by marching and sailing to the Levant for the next two hundred years. St. Louis of France and Richard Lionheart of England were among those who made Crusades. The crusaders' goal (**ethic of ends**) was to wrest the Holy Land—especially the Holy City of Jerusalem—from Muslims (Seljuk Turks, and, later, Arab Egyptians). The slaughter wrought by the crusader knights was indiscriminate. A *Christian* Arab was just as likely the target of a crusader's lance as a follower of Muhammad.

Though Christian pacifism and just-war theory were forgotten in the Crusades, a "more excellent way" (1 Corinthians 12:31) was remembered within a new religious order, the Order of Friars Minor. St. Francis of Assisi and his Franciscans took on the traditional vows of poverty, chastity, and obedience, but instead of retreating *into* cloistered life they went *out* preaching, serving the people, and receiving sustenance from what was offered. The mendicant brothers came as close to living out Jesus' Sermon on the Mount ethic as anyone since the first centuries of the church. Among other things, Francis, risking martyrdom, went out to Cairo to be a witness for peace to the sultan of Egypt. Though he could not bring hostilities to an end, appreciation of Islam and of oriental Christianity increased. Francis acted with an **ethic of response**.

Interestingly, Francis's thought included love of the natural order—the sun and moon, birds and animals—which love made him patron saint for ecojustice in modern times.

In the early twelve hundreds, besides the Franciscans, another mendicant order, the Dominicans, was birthed. The Dominicans engaged in public preaching, much of it to win back heretics to the faith; and they went into teaching in newly founded universities. There, especially at the University of Paris, they worked up moral theology. Foremost among the Dominican scholastic thinkers was Thomas Aquinas. Aquinas received conceptual tools from Islamic scholars in Spain, who shared the lost thought of Aristotle. In particular, Aquinas was drawn to Aristotle's ideas on "natural law." Natural-law philosophy suggested there was right and wrong in the natural order, which reason could decipher and use as basis for human decision making. Aquinas believed natural law coincided with revealed/divine law. Abortion and contraception, for example, were considered against the law of nature and, therefore, against the will of God. Aquinas's conclusions were controversial in their time, but in the sixteenth century his great philosophical/theological/ethical system became Western Catholicism's primary guide.

Thomas's thinking was hierarchical, as was all thought in the Middle Ages. So in moral valuing it was held that all beings *aspire* toward God, the uppermost, the highest. Moral action was based on doing that which moves the actor toward the Ultimate Good, toward God. This is a clear **ethic of ends** with **ethic of virtue** closely tied. If identification and union with God was the goal, one moved toward God by "habit of virtue." So there developed the...

Seven Cardinal Virtues and   Seven Deadly Sins

Prudence	Pride
Justice	Covetousness
Temperance	Lust
Fortitude	Envy
Faith	Gluttony
Hope	Anger
Love	Sloth

Of the cardinal virtues, the first four were derived from the Roman ancients and last three from 1 Corinthians 13. Of the seven deadly sins, one of my teachers said to remember them by using the acronym PIGLAWE, standing for pride, idleness/sloth, gluttony, lechery/lust, avarice/greed, wrath/anger, and envy.

Even as the thinking of Thomas and other medievalists was hierarchical, that is, *upward* to heaven, it also went *downward* to hell. Speculation about punishment in the life hereafter went apace, to include notions of (1) limbo, a landing place for Older Testament (pre-Christian) patriarchs and unbaptized infants; (2) purgatory, a realm for punishment for all until one is redeemed; and (3) hell itself, with various levels of torment for the damned. Dante (1265–1321) described much of this in his great moral critique *The Divine Comedy*. Fear of hell operated quite fully as a negative **end**/*telos* motivation. Eventually, medieval moral tradition took prescriptive shape. A **command ethic** came to be, governed by the confessional booth: "Do this, not that, for the sake of your eternal soul." This was *not* Augustine's "Love God, and do what you please" ethic of responsive freedom, but it is why Thomism came to be charged with a "salvation by works" stance.

In *Distant Mirror*, a book about fourteenth-century Europe, Barbara Tuchman says that three things made the century "calamitous." One factor was the marauding knights returned from the Crusades, who took law into their own hands. Secondly, it was calamitous because bubonic plague swept Europe at regular intervals, killing up to half the population. And thirdly, Tuchman says, was the corruption of the church. In spite of Franciscan and Dominican witness and in spite of the rise of universities and the building of the great Gothic churches, Catholic practice showed much was not right. The papacy itself came into general ill repute; for instance, at one time there were three popes: an Italian pope, a French pope, and a German pope! Church offices were sold to wealthy families, who might place a pubescent son in a bishop's chair. Once the papacy was bought for an eleven-year-old boy. Some clerics became personally wealthy, kept mistresses, had children, and bequeathed estates. Many were simply worldly, hardly saintly. Monk John Scotus Erigena, one of the better theologians of the Middle Ages, once said at the death of the too-political archbishop of Rheims:

> Here lies Hincmar, crook.
> But [leaving] savage greed aside,
> He did one truly noble thing: he died.

The church also began to grant indulgences ("Get Out of Purgatory Free" chits), first to pilgrims and soldiers who went on a Crusade and later to whoever would pay the price. So, if a person feared that he or she—or someone dear—had not been moral enough in this life to get into heaven, their way could be paved/paid. Much potential for abuse can be seen in such practice. Much protest might also be made. It came.

REFORMATIONS/NEW WORLDS ERA (1450–1650 CE)

Protests against church abuses and efforts toward reform happened in the late Middle Ages. Some reformers, such as the Cistercian monks and the Franciscan friars, stayed within the folds of the Catholic Church. Some, such as the Waldenses in northern Italy during the thirteenth century, broke with Rome. So did the Hussites of Bohemia in the early fifteenth century. Whether staying or leaving, these movements for change were preliminary to a full-blown revolution that occurred in the early fifteen hundreds: the Protestant Reformation. This protest—against Rome and for biblical faith—brought with it significant changes in the way that northern European Christians believed, belonged, and *behaved*.

The foremost reformer was Martin Luther of Wittenberg, Germany. First off, he said that selling indulgences was clearly wrong. Soon he questioned other practices, such as the veneration of relics or saints' bones and the efficacy of pilgrimages. Most of all, in matters of authority, Luther urged a return to the Bible. *Sola scriptura* ("scripture alone"), he said, was the way to decide what is right, not papal bulls or encyclicals by church councils. He opposed works righteousness generally and the penitential system in particular. Instead, he advocated return to earlier Augustinian and Pauline understandings, that the Christian is justified not by works but *sola fide*, "by faith alone." Faith, as Luther understood it, was a *response* to God's gracious action, and morality a further spontaneous response. Ordered by Emperor Charles V and the leading prelate from the pope at the Diet of Worms in 1525 to recant his views, Luther responded, "Unless I am convinced by reason and the Bible, I will not recant. Here I stand. God help me. Amen."

He did not recant.

Great contribution was made to Christian ethics by John Calvin, a French lawyer become Protestant theologian. He tried to institute a rule of God or theocracy in Geneva, Switzerland, and so began a long Protestant tradition of concern for the social, economic, and political order. Calvinists took seriously the idea of building God's kingdom "on earth, as it is in heaven," an **ethic of ends**.

Geneva's civic and moral model received a second major embodiment in the New World a century later, specifically in North America. It happened this way: Englishmen who had studied with John Calvin came back from Geneva wanting to purify the Church of England. Though King Henry VIII broke the English church off from Rome in 1534, these "Puritans" thought there was not yet separation enough from "popery." They wanted no truck with "bell, book, and candle," that is, ornamentation, written prayers, and high liturgy. Having little success with their reform ideas in England, many Puritans went to *New* England to begin a rule-by-God commonwealth. In this reconstituted society, Puritans dressed plainly and lived simply, enacting rigid rules for themselves and other colonists. For one thing, Sunday/Sabbath closing laws came about and stayed on the books well into the twentieth century. In their theocratic New England, these Puritan reformers opposed

- crosses on the roofs of their meeting houses (they substituted rooster weather vanes)
- organs (they threw an organ belonging to the Church of England into Boston harbor)
- marrying and burying by clergy (the Bible warranted only baptism and communion)
- Christmas (which they clearly saw as a "mass")

Shedding things wrong, they hoped to remake the church and themselves into a cleaner image of God. They were "wo/man-the-maker," operating primarily by an **ethic of ends** to build New Jerusalem in the New World. W. C. Fields said, not too unfairly, "Puritans were a people who were afraid that someone somewhere might be having a good time!"

Even more radical than the Puritans were the Anabaptists. Also following the *sola scriptura* way, the Anabaptists reaffirmed Jesus's practice of nonviolence. Like first- and second-century Christians, they refused to take up arms. The Anabaptists came to emphasize the equality of all believers before God; in doing so, they basically attacked medieval hierarchy. Moreover, by favoring biblical adult believers' baptism and not infant baptism, they were negating the registration function of the state, saying no to secular governing authority. At core they were for *individual* conscience; so they were soon subject to persecution and martyrdom themselves—even by other Protestants. Modern democratic thinking, however, owes much to the Anabaptist reformers.

*

Against the various Protestant stirrings, the Catholic Church launched a Counter-Reformation. The Council of Trent met from 1545 to 1563 to clarify and correct church doctrine and practices. At this time the church officially adopted Thomistic moral theology as normative for the faith. It included classification of sins as *mortal* (ultimately damning) and *venial* (serious but forgivable). Moral theology continued to be a rigorous discipline, with moral rectitude—**virtue** by habituation, the way to go/to be. Reemphasis was given to the sacrament of confession for dealing with sin and guilt.

None of these adjustments in the Catholic Church worked to bring Protestants dissidents back into the Vatican's fold. So in southern European countries, notably Spain, the Inquisition was reinstituted. Trials, torture, and burning at the stake were used to hold rebels in check.

Catholics of gentler mind and ways were also in the world. One was Thomas More, who opposed the breaking off of the English church from Rome. Sir Thomas, maintaining his resolve, integrity, and sense of **virtue** in the face of King Henry VIII's demands, was beheaded. Another virtue-guided Catholic was Erasmus of Rotterdam, who considered becoming a Protestant but finally concluded, "I will put up with this Church until I see a better one; and it will have to put up with me, until I become better." Both More and Erasmus, friends as they were, were irenic spirits.

Divisions within European Christianity deepened, however, as the sixteenth century unfolded. Bitter and bloody conflict engulfed the principle religious parties, Catholic, Lutheran, and Reformed. There seemed to be "war of all against all," culminating in the Thirty Years' War. Finally, in 1648 at Westphalia, a peace treaty was made among the major parties. By then, sensitive folk had had enough killing in Christ's name—or almost of *anything* in Christ's name. Increasingly, thoughtful people turned away from religious solutions.

New solutions were sought in several ways. One, hinted at above, was through nautical escape. New Worlds came onto the horizon. Travel to, exploration of, and discovery in Africa, the Orient, the Americas, and the South Seas began.

The first sending nations, notably Portugal and Spain, went to find trade routes to the Orient. In discovering America they also found gold *and* new peoples, misnamed Indians. The conquistadors often saw indigenous Americans as less than human. Some of the priests and religious order brothers, however, recognized a shared humanity. The Dominican friar Bartolomé de Las Casas opposed the enslavement of Native Americans, saying that they too were made *imago Dei*. He helped ameliorate some of the suffering. Sadly, though, Las Casas's work on behalf of Native Americans only opened the door to new enslavement and forced transport of Africans to America. African slaves were in the West Indies and Virginia before the Pilgrims' *Mayflower* set sail for North America. **Response** ethical issues about slavery and human rights were being set for the next five hundred years.

As some people went around the world to explore, convert, and exploit, others went more to settle, plant crops, raise families, and enjoy religious liberty for themselves. Witness the Puritans discussed above. They and other incoming groups operated especially in terms of an **ends ethic**, seeking to make something good in the places they landed. The very landscape influenced their sense of what to do and be. As women and men stood on the edge of new frontiers, their position had to create a huge "sense of freedom under God"—an important moral category. With freedom comes a sense of responsibility.

Certainly Jesus' instruction "Go . . . and make disciples of all nations" (Matthew 28:19) received new impetus from the sixteenth century on. The Jesuit Francis Xavier went to India and finally made his way to Japan. Even Russian Orthodox monks went out, in their case to Siberia and east, ultimately into the Americas, evangelizing among Eskimo and Inuit Indian people. In the nineteenth century Protestants became missionary minded, journeying into Africa, Asia, and the South Pacific. All may have gone out under biblical mandate, the **ethic of command**, but of necessity they had to function by **ethic of response** in new surroundings and among unique people. A white, European-influenced Christianity did not always fit in easily with distinctly different languages, customs, worldviews, and social structures. Prudish Protestants had to learn, for example, that Polynesian women need not cover their breasts to belong to Christ. Sometimes good adaptations were made, as when the Jesuit Matteo Ricci in China fitted Roman Catholic rites to indigenous cultural mores. He found a Chinese word for "God" and used it; he saw the Chinese gown for scholars and wore it. (His adaptations, though, were later disallowed by Rome as too much accommodation.)

THE ECUMENICAL/GLOBAL AGE (1650 CE– PRESENT)

Besides looking to the Bible or councils or to lands abroad for moral compass, some people looked within. René Descartes (1596–1650), thoroughly disgusted by religious wars and ways, put himself in a box and thought until he could say, *Cogito ergo sum*, "I think, therefore, I am." His own mind became the ultimate source of authority. The Age of Reason or Enlightenment was born. It invited people to question traditional authority and standards. Many joined the rationalists, rejecting church by whatever name. They stopped baptizing, praying, or taking communion. "Too much hocus-pocus, superstition, and nonsense," their actions said. One early Enlightenment thinker was Baruch Spinoza, a Jew, who wrote *Ethics* in 1677. In it he said that God was not concerned about good or bad, but God was simply God. In such understanding Jewish or Christian ethics were *not* necessarily a product of God's will. That was a different take indeed!

Simultaneous with the Enlightenment was the rise of science. It began in earnest in the mid-sixteen hundreds, continuing full force right down to the present day with life-altering discoveries. Consider such figures as Galileo in astronomy, Newton in physics, Hutton in geology, Hegel in history, Darwin in biology, Marx in economics, Curie in chemistry, Pasteur in medicine, Freud in psychology, Crick in genetics, and so on. Such people operated with the belief that scientific investigation would unravel the secrets of the universe.

The Enlightenment and rise of science placed great emphasis on *humans* as discoverers and makers of their own destiny through the use of reason. These modern men and women, who did not subscribe to traditional religious sources for moral conduct, devised new ways in ethics:

- John Locke advocated for a "social contract" understanding of human interaction, a **response ethic**, hoping thereby that ideals of justice and equality would be kindled.
- Immanuel Kant wrote about a "categorical imperative," **command ethic**, which directed persons to act in terms of the highest universal good.
- Karl Marx had vision of a "classless society," **ends ethic**, in which the proletariat would be able to throw off their chains and all people be equal.

These ways of being and acting taken together emphasize objectivity and reason. What is real is the physical, not the metaphysical. "Man," with his mind and will, is in control. There is no original sin, just errors. Regarding heaven, there seemed not to be such, once scientists threw out the three-storied universe.

The God present in Enlightenment thinking was deistic, a creator of a mechanistic universe and subsequently uninvolved with humans. There was morality, though. Most of the rationalists believed that human moral compass was bestowed by Nature or Nature's God. People could and would do the good *naturally*, if not hindered by despots or divines. Kings were rejected, even as church authority was forgotten. *Individual liberty* became the greatly valued thing in the Age of Enlightenment. A sense of individual autonomy came to characterize the modern age. Free individuals, it was believed, then would join together in a social contract to ensure "life, liberty, and the pursuit of happiness"—a new trinitarian formula. It went into the American *Declaration of Independence*. How Enlightenment thinking played out more broadly was that people (1) believed there was a Creator to whom they were ultimately accountable; so they (2) acted accountably/morally in relation to other citizens . . . constituting a **response ethic.**

In the Bill of Rights of the new American *Constitution* a separation of church and state was instituted. Thus a fifteen-hundred-year way of church-state intertwining, dating back to Constantine in the fourth century CE, was broken. Caesaropapism (a cozy relationship between government and church, often with political leaders making church decisions) would not exist in America. This separation put churches more on their own, having to raise their own money, build their own buildings, and become intentionally evangelical.

Revivalism, which had started in the eighteenth century with the Great Awakening, became a major ongoing institution. Revivalism worked via an almost-forgotten theological interpretation of humans, the Arminian. Arminianism regarded humans as free agents, not predestined creatures. So faith and church membership were not what you were born into, and did not need to wait on God's timing alone. Rather, these were matters of personal decision, owning the faith for oneself and willing your own eternal destiny.

This reconsideration of humans as beings with free will was supported by a new pietism or "religion of the heart." We recognize pietism earliest among the Moravians, whose singing, praying, and gentle interacting had great and wide effect. They powerfully influenced an English Anglican priest by the name of John Wesley . . . got him to looking for a new way of being faithful. One ordinary evening at a Moravian prayer service in London, Wesley's *heart* was "strangely warmed." Inspired, he generated the Methodist movement. This eighteenth-century reformer introduced new appreciation for enthusiastic religion. He espoused a "method" of study, prayer, and community by which persons might know "sanctification" before God. Wesley thought that the truly devout could "move on to perfection," an **ends ethic** idea. The Methodist *Book of Discipline* with "Rules for Methodist Societies" specified what the ways were: daily reading of the Bible, prayer, feeding the hungry, and visiting the sick and those in prison. The *Discipline* also specified what was unacceptable: alcohol, tobacco, rings, jewelry, loaning money at interest, frivolous talk, profaning God's name, coiffured hair and hats. Great gospel songs enhanced moral fervor in Methodism, especially songs that Charles Wesley composed, six thousand all told.

Twenty-first-century Christians might smile about some of the Methodist disciplines, but those rules gave answer to the question of what one ought to do to attain a sanctified life. Such a life is what the Methodists were after, and the rules provided guidelines for getting there. So, an **ethic of command** is behind the rules, and yet there is the **ethic of virtue** operating here too, for the sanctified life would be attained by habituation in doing what was right.

Piety in Methodism, interestingly enough, went beyond individualism and *personal* ethics. In England, Methodists spoke for the rights of miners and pressed for changes in child-labor practices. They also addressed the issue of slavery. Wesley opposed the American Revolution because he thought the colonists were not inclined to abolish slavery soon enough, as he thought the English were.

Slavery, yes or no, certainly was *the* burning ethical issue in the nineteenth century. The religious body most outspoken against slavery was the Society of Friends, otherwise known as the Quakers. Guided in the moral life by "Inner Light" (**virtue**), they concluded that slavery, though allowed in the Bible, was no longer God's will. A leading spokesperson for the abolition of slavery was New Jersey–born John Woolman, who sparked the movement in England that eventuated in abolishing the slave trade.

In the increasingly Less-united States, there were Protestant clergy and church people on both sides of the slavery issue. Chief among the antislavery folk was Congregationalist Henry Ward Beecher, who addressed the subject from his pulpit. His sister, Harriet Beecher Stowe, wrote against slavery in her influential novel, *Uncle Tom's Cabin*. Former black slaves Harriet Tubman and Sojourner Truth also spoke for abolition, worked the Underground Railroad for runaway slaves, and practiced civil disobedience. Eventually an uncivil war, the Civil War, was fought to settle the question of slavery's rightness or wrongness. For Northerners, the ethical issue was one of **ends**: "What kind of society do we want to build?" Southerners were following the Bible under an **ethic of command**.

Slavery was a large *social justice* issue, one of several ultimately addressed in the social gospel movement. Social gospelers, living during the Progressive Era of the late nineteenth and early twentieth centuries, saw the evils brought on by industrialization, classism, and inequitable distribution of capital. Some Christians were active suffragettes, working to win the vote for women. Another issue addressed was that of "demon rum." In 1920 Prohibition was made the law of the land, but in 1933 it was rescinded. During the 1930s social gospel focus went toward helping labor organize. Theologian-pastor Reinhold Niebuhr was so engaged and so wrote one of the most important books on ethics of the twentieth century, *Moral Man and Immoral Society*. In it he recognized that good people get caught in social and economic systems, collectivities that are evil-doing and need to be changed.

In Germany during the 1930s, confessing Christians had a role to play against National Socialism, aka Nazism. Neo-orthodox theologian Karl Barth and others said in their Barmen Declaration that "Jesus is *Führer*," meaning *not* Hitler. One Lutheran pastor, Dietrich Bonhoeffer, was executed because he took part in a plot to assassinate *der Führer*. He wrote a book on ethics titled *The Cost of Discipleship*. He knew both sides of discipleship. Bonhoeffer was an **ethics of response** theologian.

In the last half-century, Christians have been active in a number of social justice causes. Consider:

- In the 1960s, clergy and laity, black and white, gave leadership in the American civil rights struggle.

- Some Christians also raised voice about the "military-industrial complex," warning with theologian Walter Wink that "violence is the ethos of our times. It is the spirituality of the modern world. It has been accorded the status of religion, demanding from its adherents absolute obedience to death."[13]

- Most recently the socially aware arm of the church has thought in "whole earth" terms, turning attention to ecology and the environment. One conference of the World Council of Churches focused on *Justice, Peace, and the Integrity of Creation*.

- Christian social ethicists have drawn attention to other issues—medical ethics, gender issues, and globalization, to name three.

Much of this social justice engagement was inspired by neo-orthodox theology, which took biblical **command ethics** seriously, such as the command to care for the least and lost and to work for the peace of the city.

Meanwhile the focus on individual ethics has never let up. Christians desired to live personally upright lives, all related to the **ethic of virtue**. Much individual focus has been on avoiding "sins of the flesh." Things like premarital sex, adultery, abortion, homosexuality, pornography, and even dancing were strong no-no's for many Christians. Some too with alcohol, gambling, and drugs. In recent years, conservative Protestants have joined with Catholics to try to limit or outlaw abortion. Throughout the modern centuries Catholics have, through papal encyclicals, spoken ethically, doing so in terms of Thomistic natural law. So sex, for example, has been understood as only for procreation: why then use contraception?

Hope or liberation theology began to show up in the late sixties within Catholic ranks. It percolated through the church and manifested itself in a 1991 encyclical affirming God's "preferential option for the poor." Even

---

13. Wink, *Engaging the Powers*, 13.

before this encyclical, and certainly after it, liberation theology and ethics operated in Third-World countries, especially in South and Central America. Similar liberation movements among Protestants took place in the United States, led by and for blacks, Hispanics, Asians, women, and, quite recently, gay and lesbian Christians. All ask the society to consider again the ancient foundational question of Cain: "Am I my brother's keeper?" (Genesis 4:9), *and* the question that a lawyer put to Jesus, "Who is my neighbor?" (Luke 10:29). Jesus' answer in Luke 10:30–37 still shines through:

> "A man was going down from Jerusalem to Jericho, and fell into the hands of robbers, who stripped him, beat him, and went away, leaving him half dead. Now by chance a priest was going down that road; and when he saw him, he passed by on the other side. So likewise a Levite, when he came to the place and saw him, passed by on the other side. But a Samaritan while traveling came near him; and when he saw him, he was moved with pity. He went to him and bandaged his wounds, having poured oil and wine on them. Then he put him on his own animal, brought him to an inn, and took care of him. . . ."
>
> "Which of these three," Jesus asked, "do you think, was neighbor to the man who fell into the hands of the robbers?"
>
> The lawyer replied, "The one who showed him mercy."
>
> Jesus said to him, "Go and do likewise."

*

Of the four basic ethical stances reviewed in this chapter, **command, ends, response,** and **virtue,** currently the **ethic of ends** may be the more ascendant, at least among Catholics and mainline Protestants. Christians doing process theology speak about men and women acting *toward* Christ, who beckons—even lures—them toward the future. God is understood to have had "a primordial nature" with an initial aim for the world and a "consequent nature," made known by what happens/processes over time. That consequential nature will be realized as men and women work alongside one another toward the Holy One, even the Cosmic Christ ever before the faithful. The French Jesuit theologian and paleontologist Teilhard de Chardin wrote that we are moving to an Omega Point in evolutionary consciousness, in which there will be unity in mind and spirit. For Teilhard and others, love continues to be the main virtue needed in moving toward the fulfillment of the world, God, and humanity.

This writer says, "Let it abound!"

*

Questions for Reflection and Discussion

1. In the Bible are both the Ten Commandments and Jesus' Sermon on the Mount. They are related, but does one weigh more heavily in practice than the other? Why and why not?

2. Is there such a thing as "natural law"? Thomas Aquinas thought so, as did the eighteenth-century rationalists. Is their thinking the same?

3. The categories of **command, ends, response**, and **virtue** have been used to speak of Christian ethics. Does one of these four characterize your usual moral orientation? Which? Does it blend with another?

4. How are the four modalities in ethics being lived out today among different groups? Catholics? Evangelicals? Pentecostals? Which modality is most prevalent in Christian observance? Should it be?

5. What do you think are the most pressing social ethical issues today?

Chapter 3

Practices and Pieties of The Pilgrimage
With Matching Quizzes for Historical Periods

To thee I lift up my eyes,
O thou who art enthroned in the heavens!
Behold, as the eyes of servants
look to the hand of their master
... so our eyes look to the Lord our God,
till he have mercy upon us.

—PSALM 123:1–2 (RSV)

1. Am I consciously or unconsciously a hypocrite? ... 4. Am I a slave to dress, friends, work or habits? ... 7. Do I give the Bible time to speak to me every day? ... 8. Am I enjoying prayer? ... 9. When did I last speak to someone else of my faith? ... 11. Do I get to bed on time and get up on time? ... 13. Do I insist upon doing something about which my conscience is uneasy? ... 15. Am I jealous, impure, critical, irritable, touchy or distrustful? ... 16. How do I spend my spare time? ... 20. Do I grumble or complain constantly? ... 21. Is Christ real to me?

—JOHN WESLEY, HOLY CLUB SELF-EXAMINATION QUESTIONS (1729)

Practices and Pieties of The Pilgrimage

Here's an Amish man's testimony: "Christ said, 'Follow me,' not 'Study me.'"
—Recorded by Carrie Taintor Wiser, PBS Documentary, 2012

A YOUNG AMERICAN WOMAN took a job after college with a newspaper in Guatemala. During her second summer in that country she met a man who taught karate. They fell in love and were practically inseparable until "one day in February." It was on a Wednesday. He announced that for the next forty days he would be tied up each evening.

"Doing what?"

"Carrying a bier for the Virgin."

"A what?"

"A bier, a portable platform. It bears the statue of the Virgin Mary. I and about thirty other guys take her in procession through the streets each evening. It's how I observe Lent."

The young woman, a nominal Protestant, had heard of "giving up chocolate for Lent," but this was different. Indeed.

*

Through the centuries, people of Christian faith have had different ways of being holy, practicing their religion, demonstrating piety, keeping promises, denying themselves, and behaving as good believers. In this chapter we do two things: (1) look again at our four-thousand-year religious history, this time lifting up the ways the believers "showed forth their faith" and (2) consider what contemporary Christians still might do—or not do—with those practices of old.

As we move through these pages, when I mention a particular practice or identify something used in holy observance, I will bold whatever it is, such as **venerating icons**.

At the end of each section covering a historical period is a matching quiz exercise that the reader may complete. The challenge is to connect current practices and pieties with historic events/people/developments. *Contemporary practices* are shown in the left-hand column, while *faith history happenings* are listed on the right. Below each exercise I show my answers.

Brief Christian Histories

PRE-MONARCHIC MILLENNIUM (2000–1000 BCE)

There may be no practice more common among religious people than **lighting candles**. Certainly many Christian services of worship today begin this way. Likewise, for centuries Jewish families have begun *Shabbat* with the mother offering a prayer while circling her hands over a flame. Contemporary ceremonies that celebrate birthdays invariably use candles. There is something special about fire, something that speaks to people of the holy presence. It may be a primordial collective unconscious thing, from tens of thousands of years of our ancestors gathering around campfires. There they told stories and recounted episodes from the lives of their forebears.

One such story in our tradition is of an Abram/Abraham, possibly living 3,800 years ago. As the story goes, he was called by God to go on a journey "to the land I will show you" (Genesis 12:1). From Ur in Babylon, he went north and west, then traveled south and west along the Fertile Crescent of the Middle East, around to Canaan/Palestine, to what we now call the Holy Land. In the story of the journeying of Abram/Abraham and his wife Sarai/Sarah we have precedent laid for millions of subsequent **faith journeys**, often called **pilgrimages**. Twenty-first-century Christians do the same, as across Spain to Santiago de Compostela. My wife and I did this in 2005—on foot, five hundred miles.

In the Bible's Abraham-Sarah story we also learn that bones are important. During a time of famine, this couple went down to Egypt. There they died. Five hundred years later, according to tradition, their bones were brought back to Israel for final burial. Such honoring of the remains of deceased holy persons is a **veneration of relics**. Such practice, of course, was a deep piety of the Middle Ages CE.

Campfire stories with regard to the patriarch Jacob are told in our Bible too, and today his story is recounted when young people gather 'round a campfire to **sing a spiritual**, often enough "We Are Climbing Jacob's Ladder." It remembers that patriarch's Genesis 28 vision of angels ascending and descending a ladder connecting heaven and earth. After the end of Jacob's mystical experience, the scripture tells us, he **makes a covenant** with God. It is not too much of a stretch, I think, to consider **shaking hands in church** as a kind of covenant making, a pact of mutual faithfulness. In remembrance of the covenant, Jacob put up a stone pillar, which he said was "God's House." That pillar became a shrine to which later generations returned. Even today, **shrine visiting** is a well-known activity of Christians.

Practices and Pieties of The Pilgrimage

Foremost among the tribes of Israel's campfire stories were those of their greatest leader, Moses. Many Jewish and Christian rituals observed today stem from Moses and what the Older Testament says he did about the year 1250 BCE, especially his leading the enslaved People of Israel out of Egypt. That leading-out became so important to subsequent generations that a most **holy meal** is done to remember what God through Moses did "for us." The Passover or Seder meal observed by Jews involves many foods, not the least of which are bread and wine. It is, of course, out of observance of this meal that the Christian sacrament of **Holy Communion** came. So today, when Christian people come down an aisle and receive a flat disk of unleavened bread, there are whispers of the time of Moses. If it's *unleavened* bread, it's because, in the flight from Egypt, there was no time to let bread rise.

Other religious practices can be traced to Moses, he being the one who shepherded the Israelites through forty years of desert wandering. The **number forty** thus became important, counted many times and many ways throughout our faith history. Elijah, for example, lived in the desert for forty days, fed by a raven. When the writer of the Bible's Noah and the flood story put that account on papyrus, he floated Noah on the billowy sea for forty days. According to the Gospel accounts, Jesus was tempted by Satan in the wilderness for forty days. In the Middle Ages a calendar of the church year began to emerge, and it included forty days for Lent, leading up to Easter. When today people in a forty-day observance of Lent do any of the following

> **give up something**, like chocolate (which the American girl knew about)
>
> **march in procession** (which the Guatemalan karate instructor did)
>
> **read a devotional booklet daily** (which many Christians do, e.g., *The Upper Room*)

they do so, in part, because of events related to Moses 3,250 years ago.

A story of Moses *before* the exodus explains yet another contemporary practice. On a journey back to Egypt from the Sinai Desert, Moses was struck down by God. At the point of death, Moses' wife, Zipporah, circumcised their son, and so saved the son's and her husband's lives. **Circumcision** is still widely practiced among Jews *and* Muslims *and* Christians, though contemporary Christians may think they do this for hygienic, medical reasons.

Brief Christian Histories

Three other Moses stories bear on present practice. The first two have to do with God's name. In a revelatory experience of a burning bush not consumed by fire, Moses encountered God. In that awe-full meeting, Moses asked for the name of the Holy One. The name given was Yahweh, which means something like "I am who I am/I will be who I will be." That's one name story.

The second is this: after the exodus event and in desert wandering, Moses ascended Mount Sinai. There he received the Ten Commandments. These commandments, of course, have been foundational for people of our faith ever since. One of the commandments says, "Thou shalt not take the *name* of Yahweh your God in vain." Whatever it meant then, it now means to pious folk **no swearing**, that is, saying the name of "God" with a "damn" in anger or dismay. That certainly is a piety. Also with the name "Jesus Christ." (Humorously, because of these aversions, there now arise expletives like "Got All Muddy" and "Cheese and Crackers"!)

The third story has to do with the staff or rod of Moses (the icon of this section). Moses' staff, when thrown down, became a snake that consumed the staff-snakes of Pharaoh's priests. It's a major symbol of authority present through the ages with princes and pilgrims, seen today when an Anglican bishop, for example, carries **a staff** in a church procession.

In subsequent centuries, when the Hebrew people got around to giving explanations of origin, they told about Adam and Eve, Cain and Abel, Noah, and others of the ancien régime. In Noah's case, after the flood, a rainbow covenant was made. God promised never to destroy the earth again, at least by water. Now every "O God" spoken in extremity of circumstance (when frustrated) is **invocation for God**, and every "O God" in response to beauty in sunset is an **ejaculation of praise**.

So . . . here are some of the seminal events in this earliest period of our faith story, from which a considerable number of today's pieties and practices can be traced.

For this period match

contemporary practices	*faith history happenings*
a. lighting candles at Christmas	1. Ten Commandments
b. shaking hands at church	2. Jacob's rock pile
c. visiting shrines	3. covenant making
d. having a male child circumcised	4. the exodus event

e. saying "fiddlesticks" instead   5. tribal campfire gatherings
f. taking the communion wafer   6. Moses saved by Zipporah
g. giving up something for Lent   7. forty years in the wilderness

(My answers to the above are a-5, b-3, c-2, d-6, e-1, f-4, g-7.)

TIME OF THE KINGS AND PROPHETS (1000–550 BCE)

After forty years in the wilderness, the People of Israel entered the Holy Land of Canaan/Palestine. They entered under the leadership of Joshua, the one who a song says "fit the battle of Jericho." After Joshua, leadership arose mostly from within various tribes in response to threats of invasion. Deborah and Gideon were two such leaders, called judges. The most famous judge is Samson, remembered as drawing strength from his long hair. It was uncut because he was a *Nazarite*, one who swore never to be shorn, never to touch a dead body, *and* never to drink strong drink. Samson's **abstinence from alcohol**, through the years, has been a piety that many observed. Witness John the Baptist, John Wesley, and, after a time, a recent American president, George W. Bush.

The last of the judges seems to have been Samuel, also a priest. As priest, Samuel crowned first a man named Saul and later a shepherd lad, David, to be king. In and by such an anointing, the king was vested with divine authority. Israel, however, never did what the Egyptians did—and what the Greeks and Romans tried to do later—namely, deify their pharaoh or king. Nevertheless, they came to believe that the welfare of the nation, in part, rested with the health of the king. People then and ever since join in **shouting "God save"** and **"God bless"** for the ongoing health of their sovereign. This happened at medieval coronations and happens still. In the United States at every presidential inauguration a cleric will at least **ask God's blessing** on the new leader. In turn **the leader says, "God bless America"**—a pious mantra seemingly required. In other countries in earlier centuries, people would bow before the ruler, thought to rule by divine appointment. In the United States vestigial bowing happens when people hear and respond to "All rise!" as a judge enters the courtroom. In church, one may observe the **genuflecting,** bending the knees/tipping the head, toward the cross at the front of a church.

With David, more can be said. When he brought the Ark of the Covenant housing the stone tablets inscribed with the Ten Commandments into his new capital city, Jerusalem, he "danced before the Lord with all his might" (2 Samuel 6:14). David's wife Michal, however, was embarrassed by that dancing—and came to despise him. Ever since, there has been considerable **dance aversion**, it being "too frivolous for serious Christians"; but, even more, there has been **dancing** through the centuries. One cannot imagine Christianity in Africa or on a Navajo reservation without dancing.

David's son Solomon poured his energies into building the first temple of Jerusalem. This temple—and two later reconstructions of it—became the center for worship for a thousand years. Temple worshipers brought there "first fruits" offerings, that is, the first cuttings of barley grain, the first extracts from the olive-oil press, and the first portion of dates. Our custom of **tithing**, giving 10 percent of one's income to the church, may be traced to this firstfruits practice. Tithing is also mentioned in Genesis 14:20, an early action of Abraham; and it is commended in Malachi, the last book of the Older Testament. Besides crops and monetary gifts, people brought animals to the temple for sacrifice on an altar. Today's church altar or communion table, on which bread for Christ's body and wine for Christ's blood are placed, is not unrelated to ancient temple ritual. Christians **eat and drink in remembrance**.

Deep in the interior of Solomon's temple was a room called the Holy of Holies. The Ark of the Covenant was kept there. It was believed that God hovered over the Ark. The care and respect accorded the Ark and the tablets therein, as *objects of the Divine*, certainly has had its historical counterparts. Consider, for example, the way believers in the Middle Ages practiced **veneration of relics**, including, in addition to bones of the saints, wood from the "true cross" of Jesus and milk from Mary's breast. The Shroud of Turin, supposedly bearing the imprint of the face of Jesus, has been an object of veneration for centuries. There also are

- icons/paintings, which Orthodox believers kiss
- crucifixes, which Roman Catholics, especially, wear
- Bibles, which Protestants handle with care

This third piety, regarding the Bible, I remember well from fourth grade in a public elementary school. The rule in the classroom was that nothing should ever be placed on top of the scriptures. Once a girl tattled, "Teacher, teacher! Jimmy left his lunch sack on the Bible."

Practices and Pieties of The Pilgrimage

*

As it turned out, the years of a united kingdom for the tribes of Israel were few, fewer than seventy-five. By the end of the tenth century BCE, only two tribes of the original twelve were still attached to Jerusalem and the temple. The other ten functioned around different sacred centers in the north: Shechem, Bethel, and Dan. In all cases, temples were built on an elevated ground, up there, "nearer to God," even as native Canaanite people had "high places" of worship. So began and has continued the practice of **pointing up to God** with church towers and steeples, and **looking up to heaven** in prayer.

This several-centuries-long period, with north and south monarchs and capitals, witnessed two other developments of tremendous historical importance.

One is the appearance of prophets. These were holy men of the marketplace and palace (sometimes of the temple) who called the nation back to faith in Yahweh. They wanted to maintain the covenant, especially in ethical dimension. Elijah, for example, was a prophet of the ninth century BCE who critically engaged his society and its elites. He chastised King Ahab and Queen Jezebel for allowing foreign gods to be worshiped in Israel, and he challenged their priests of Ba'al to a contest on Mount Carmel. With Yahweh's "fire power," Elijah won that contest. **Speaking for God and challenging the way things are,** then and now, is also a kind of holy practice. Jesus, John Chrysostom, Menno Simons, and Martin Luther King Jr. exemplify that ancient prophetic tradition.

Elijah also may be honored for another contribution to the way Christians yet live out their faith. After he defeated the prophets of Ba'al, Elijah was forced to flee from the wrath of King Ahab and Queen Jezebel. His flight led to a mountainous cave where he hid. He was summoned out of that cave, however, to experience "earthquake, wind, and fire." But God was not in these natural phenomena. No. God spoke to him only in a "still, small voice" or "sheer silence" (1 Kings 19:11–13). His experience of the way God speaks to people has carried forward, especially in the great mystical traditions of Christianity and in **ordinary silent prayer and meditation.** "In quietness there is holiness," Elijah let us know. Many faithful souls—from Anthony of the Desert (third century CE) to the unknown monk of the fourteenth century CE who wrote *The Cloud of Unknowing* to last weekend's **contemplatives praying** in retreat houses—are following in Elijah's holy way.

There are, of course, other prophets... but let the prophet Isaiah stand in for them all. His call to be a prophet is recorded in the sixth chapter of the book that bears his name. In the temple he had a vision of God and learned that *holiness* is God's main attribute. The seraphim (bronze, six-winged angelic creatures) came alive for him inside the Holy of Holies. They called out, "Holy, holy, holy is the Lord of hosts." Our **singing the Sanctus** ("Holy, holy, holy") in church today comes from this ancient encounter. For Isaiah, though, true holiness was shown in right ethical behavior, especially care of "the widow, the orphan, and the stranger in your midst." So it has been that Judaism, Christianity, and Islam are *ethical* religions. When Christians today **engage in social action and service**, such as demonstrating for housing policy reform, taking part in a peace march, or serving in a soup kitchen, they are keeping faith with the prophets.

In his Holy of Holies *mysterium tremendum* encounter with God, Isaiah established an order of worship that is followed widely:

1. adoring/praising God
2. confessing one's sins
3. receiving absolution

The volunteer church secretary faithfully **typing the Sunday bulletin,** which contains the threefold liturgical action, reproduces Isaiah's order of interaction with God.

The other major event to underscore for this period is the destruction of both the northern and southern kingdoms. Israel in the north fell to the Assyrians in 721. Judah in the south succumbed to the Babylonians in 586. The year 586 BCE is a "year that lives in infamy." It's when the temple and city were destroyed and the leading citizens of Judah carried off into exile. They were marched six hundred miles away, to live by the waters of Babylon, where "we sat down and wept" (Psalm 137). They longed for Jerusalem, which was no more. **Remembrance and honoring of Jerusalem... or sacred places... or loved ones long gone** continues. When we piously say, immediately after mentioning the name of a beloved place or person, "Let its memory live forever," or "May she rest in peace," Christians speak with the psalmist. If one is **weeping**, that too is a well-known faith-related occurrence, tears considered by many as "sign of the nearness of God."

Practices and Pieties of The Pilgrimage

Now, for this period, match

contemporary practices	faith history happenings
a. kissing an icon	1. fall of Jerusalem
b. tithing	2. David crowned king
c. genuflecting in church	3. Ark with tablets
d. being a teetotaler	4. firstfruits on the altar
e. meditating, praying	5. Elijah before the cave
f. saying, "Rest in peace"	6. prophets' ethical call
g. visiting in a nursing home	7. Samson the Nazirite

(My answers to the above are a-3, b-4, c-2, d-7, e-5, f-1, and g-6.)

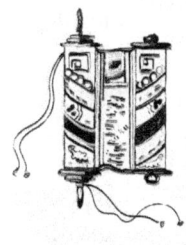

SECOND TEMPLE PERIOD (550–20 BCE)

The remnant people of Jerusalem living in Babylon were allowed to leave that land of exile in 538 BCE, allowed because Cyrus the Persian defeated the Babylonians and granted the exiles reprieve. Many returned to Jerusalem. In the course of the century to follow, the returnees (1) rebuilt their temple, albeit less grandly, (2) made Jerusalem a walled city again, and (3) reinstituted government according to Jewish Law. This third accomplishment is detailed below.

First, though, let it be noted that many "Jews," people who originated from Jerusalem of *Judah*, were scattered throughout the new Persian Empire and around the Mediterranean. At the time of return from exile, most expats probably did *not* return. Our ancestors in faith stayed where they had been planted. Yet they kept the faith. Unavoidably, though, they were influenced in thought and practice by the cultures of which they were a part, as will be discussed more fully in chapter 4, "Christ and Culture Interacting." Those influences in distant locales shaped religion and life and, over time, even shaped the life of coreligionists back in Palestine.

When considering the two hundred years of Persian influence, remember that the Persians were a people whose religion was Zoroastrianism, which sees the world dualistically and divides it between God and Satan, heaven and hell, angels and demons. Our monotheistic faith-parents of the Diaspora were exposed during these years to the Persian dualistic way of thinking. It should be no surprise, then, that the literature began to

113

talk of angels and archangels. "Angel piety," if you will, began then and has never gone away. Angelolatry resurged in strength during the Middle Ages, as Renaissance paintings attest. It came again in the last century as angel boutiques, angel home décor, and angel jewelry bear witness. Not a few women will be seen **wearing "an angel on my shoulder,"** it being gold, the wearing *not* merely a fashion statement.

Some of the practices we exercise today around death and burial may also be attributed to Persian influence. Traditional Judaism believed that the deceased went down to Sheol, a "land of deep shadows," and that was the end of it. The Zoroastrians, on the other hand, held to a doctrine of a bodily resurrection to heaven. Some Jews, notably the Pharisees—and, later, both rabbinic and Christian Jews—came to believe in a heavenly place of ascendance. Such belief shows itself today in burial practices and funeral rites: **embalming, selecting a casket, and tucking goodbye notes in the casket,** saying, "Mum, we'll meet again in heaven."

One book of the Bible, Daniel, is about the problem our ancestors had keeping the faith while in a foreign land. An incident in this book reminds us of a practice that went on at that time—about 200 BCE—and that may *always* have gone on, and has certainly continued. The practice? **Praying and giving thanks.** In the book of Daniel, chapter 6, verse 10, we read that Daniel "went to his house where he had windows in his upper chamber open toward Jerusalem; and he **got down upon his knees** three times a day and prayed and gave thanks before his God, as he had done previously (NRSV)/as was his custom (KJV)." This customary behavior of Daniel's is surely one of the longest standing—we should say "kneeling"—traditions of the faith. By prayer, more than anything else, Christians show forth relation to and trust in God.

From Daniel also comes a **fasting** tradition, one modern version of it is actually called "the Daniel fast," which is a diet for Lent, having only food from seeds—vegetables, fruits, unleavened grains—and drinking only water. Most often the diet is done along with **daily devotions.**

Besides practices and pieties developing while under Persian suzerainty, there was Greek influence. In 333 BCE Alexander the Great of Macedonia conquered the Persians. He established a Hellenic *political* presence in the Middle East that lasted two hundred years and a fifteen-hundred-year *cultural* influence. The worldview and practices of Greek culture shaped our religion tremendously. With regard to understanding "what happens after death," for example, the notion of each person having a *spirit* that returns to the realm of Pure Spirit/Perfect Forms/God is a Greek belief. On the occasion of a funeral, for example, we now **say, "Auntie's spirit is with God in heaven."**

Not everything about Greek culture, of course, was adopted by our faith-parents. There were resistances. The Greeks exalted in the beauty of the human body, for example, and easily accepted nakedness in art and in gymnasium sports. Hebrew and Semitic people, on the other hand, were scandalized by such nudity. Their aversion is noted in the book of Genesis, where Adam and Eve, having gained knowledge of good and evil, knew thereby that they were naked and so were ashamed. Their shame, according to the story, was covered by God, who clothed them. Today, in solidarity with the fig-leaf-covered first couple, many faithful people **wear modest attire.** About sexuality, most Christians are careful, **observing monogamy in marriage**—or, at least valuing it—as a way of "doing what God intended for us to do." In the same vein, **forgoing premarital sexual intercourse,** while *not* forbidden in the Bible, is a way some Christians show forth the faith.

Some of our practices and pieties arise in the several centuries BCE. The major religious accomplishment for these years was the putting together of the Bible, what Christians call the Older Testament. First came the Torah, aka the Law or the Pentateuch, the first five books of the Bible. By ancient rabbinic count, the Torah has 613 laws. To follow those laws was "to walk in the way of the Lord." To this day, Orthodox Jews strive to live by these laws in what they wear, how they eat, when they worship, and ever so much more. **Obeying the Law** became the mark of the faithful then, right down to the present. Many of the things now considered "right and wrong" reach back, at least, to these four hundred years before Christ—for example, **not shaving the beard,** as is the custom of Old Believer Russian Orthodox men and Amish Protestant Christians.

The Bible, of course, has other laws, for instance, with regard to usury (changing interest on money loaned). In the Middle Ages churchmen would not engage in usury. It was seen by church authorities as a major no-no. Today, not charging interest is a practice conspicuous by its absence! In trying to obey the law about keeping the Sabbath holy, some pious folk do so by **not cooking any hot food on Sunday.** That was a piety my fraternal grandparents observed.

After the Torah, the next two major blocks of the Older Testament are the Prophets and the Other Writings. These sections took their final form in this period. Among the books in the Other Writings is the book of Job, a literary account of a one man's suffering struggle to understand the justice of God. Essentially Job raises the question that is the title of a popular book, *When Bad Things Happen to Good People*. As Job argues about God's justice with three "comforter" friends, he does so "**repenting in sackcloth and ashes.**" Many a monk **wearing a hair shirt** in the early Middle Ages imitated Job. Many an Anglican lass **accepting ashes on her forehead** at the beginning of Lent is doing something *in kind* with Job.

Let me note too that the Bible generated in this period prescribed certain festivals for observance. In rabbinic Judaism these festivals came to be called High Holy Days. Yom Kippur and Passover are two. Hanukkah (which commemorates the important mid-second-century-BCE throwing off of Greek rule) and Purim (an imaginative remembrance of how a woman named Esther saved her people in Persia) are lesser holidays. Christians in time **observed festival holidays** too, sometimes recasting older holy days. Most notably, Jewish Passover segued into Maundy Thursday Communion. Fifty days after Passover/Easter is another holy occasion, when Shavuot or Weeks for Jews became Pentecost for Christians.

The Law, Prophets, and Other Writings became sacred text for both rabbinic Jews and Christians.[1] **Reading/studying/meditating upon/following/arguing about/honoring the Bible** is, without question, a key characteristic of many peoples' faith behavior. Jews, Christians, and Muslims all understand themselves to be people of the book.

In this period another great value of the Bible was discovered: it is *portable*. Survival of faith, our foreparents found, was not tied to Jerusalem or temple worship. The Tanakh

Ta = *Torah* ("the Law")

Na = *Nevi'im* ("prophets")

Kh = *Ketuvim* ("writings")

was sufficient for religious cohesion. Whether the Bible was in papyrus scroll, vellum binding, or paperback, it moved! Indeed, scripture has traveled with God's people throughout the world.

In the synagogues of the Diaspora, reading the Bible became the main focus of Shabbat services *and* for everyday study. It is not too much

---

1. Jews set the books of the Tanakh in canon by 90 CE. Christians honored those rabbi-chosen books along with a few *extra*canonical books, like Esdras, Tobit, Judith, and Maccabees. In the sixteenth century Martin Luther said that the Jews' more limited early choice was good enough for him and, so in time, that is what is in most Protestant Bibles.

to suggest that **attending Sunday school**, which Protestant children and adults from the eighteenth into the twenty-first centuries do, is very much the legacy of the Bible having been assembled in the Second Temple Period. The book is a "movable feast." For twenty-five hundred years people have been reading

"In the beginning God..."

"Hear, O Israel, the Lord your God is..."

"What are human beings that you are mindful...?"

"...do mercy, love kindness, walk humbly..."

Reading, hearing, knowing, speaking Bible is central to faith in the centuries prior to the advent of Jesus and has remained so to the present moment.

For this period match

contemporary practices	*faith history happenings*
a. not cooking on Sundays	1. Persian/Zoroastrian culture
b. studying the Bible	2. Tanakh assembled
c. attending Sunday school	3. temple festival days
d. wearing an angel pin	4. Adam and Eve stories
e. observing Christmas and Easter	5. the trials of Job
f. dressing modestly	6. codification of 613 laws
g. praying daily	7. Daniel's daily ritual
h. receiving forehead ashes	8. synagogues of the Diaspora

(My answers to the above are a-6, b-2, c-8, d-1, e-3, f-4, g-7, and h-5.)

NEWER TESTAMENT TIMES (20 BCE–110 CE)

If there is any single, widespread, overt Christian practice and piety in America, it is **going to church on Sunday morning**. This custom, of worshiping on the first day of the week rather than on the seventh (as prescribed in the Bible), was begun by the earliest Christians. They often stayed up all Saturday night to greet the sun, doing so because dawn is the time and Sunday the day their leader/teacher/master/prophet/healer/Lord, Jesus of Nazareth, came back to them from death. At that time and on Sunday he appeared to some of his followers. Today people may study Jesus' teachings, marvel at his acts of healing, wonder at stories concerning his birth, affirm his loving message, be inspired by his social passion, and admire his integrity; but had there been no resurrection, all those other aspects to the life of the rabbi from Nazareth would be forgotten.

So the resurrection is starting place in the history of Christian faith as *Christ*ian.

On one particular day each year, Easter Sunday, upon hearing the proclamation, "Christ is risen!" **worshipers respond, saying, "He is risen indeed!"** Such a call-and-response has been a Christian practice for almost two thousand years. From the resurrection, the rest of the story follows. The meaning of Jesus' death was a problem needing to be explained. One of Jesus' followers, Saul of Tarsus, who became our Saint Paul, addressed the issue, saying Jesus' death was the means of reconciling estranged humanity to God. He said that humanity was alienated from God by sin, but the willing, sacrificial death of one who was sinless—namely, Jesus—canceled the debt owed God. Paul's doctrine of substitutionary atonement, to be sure, is not the only way of interpreting Christ's death, but it suffices to suggest that something significant happened for us because of that death. So, almost two thousand years later, Jesus' followers will be heard **saying, "He died for me."** Such assertion means much. It signifies an *at-one-ment* with God, one's reconciliation with all that is Holy, in spite of all alienation.

From the resurrection and crucifixion, let us continue "reading backward."

The night before Jesus was crucified, he celebrated a Passover meal with his closest disciples. During the course of the dinner, he took bread and broke it, took a vessel of wine and poured it. Jesus told them, "This is my body. . . . This is my blood." He further instructed them to eat the bread and drink the wine that he might be re-membered to them, be re-presented to them. So Holy Communion, the central worship ritual of Christian people, began. It has been called, variously, the Mass, the Lord's Supper, the Eucharist, and the Feast of Our Lord. **Taking Communion—eating the bread, drinking the cup**—thus became Christians' most significant ritual observance.

Continuing *back* in investigation, our faith-parents wanted to know the things Jesus did. So they learned about his wonder workings (miracles), his faith healings, his travels, and his interactions with all kinds of people

Practices and Pieties of The Pilgrimage

. . . many dimensions of his life that in turn suggested to followers ways to "go and do likewise" in their own lives, such as showing forth the faith in **ministries of healing** and **feeding the hungry**.

As for *getting back* to his words, the early disciples remembered stories, such as the Good Samaritan parable with its double lesson about **helping the beaten down** and **not stereotyping others**. As Jesus' teachings were collected, some of them went into a Sermon on the Mount, which included commands about **turning the other cheek, practicing nonviolence**, and **loving one's enemies**—actions that, ever since, some Christians, such as Francis of Assisi and Leo Tolstoy of Russia, have tried to embody.

Other religious practices developed in connection with early Christian worship, some of which are recorded in the Newer Testament. Paul in a letter speaks of **praying with hands raised**. The palms up and lifted tradition of praying exercised in the early church gave way in time to an **on-your-knees/head-down/hands-together praying** posture, especially during the early Middle Ages. During that era the story was born that the apostle James had been so constant in prayer that his knees became like those of a camel! Persons, ancient or contemporary, who practice Christian meditation seem to follow an **on-your-lap-palms-up praying** position. All three ways are part of the practice of prayer.

In the book of the Acts we learn the origin of other still-current customs. Acts reports that at Pentecost, the Holy Spirit/Wind of God came upon those assembled. The Spirit came as tongues of fire. With that, Jesus' followers got enthused! They began **speaking in tongues**, meaning either that they spoke in the *foreign* languages of Pentecost bystanders or that they spoke in a *spiritual* language called *glossolalia*. Perhaps both. Today's Pentecostal movement, which is having wide resurgence throughout the world, connects with the glossolalia tradition.

From the Pentecost event something else started: **proclaiming the Good News** of God's love made known in Christ Jesus. Jesus' followers became "witnesses in Jerusalem and in all Judea and Samaria and to the ends of the earth" (Acts 1:8). Expansion of Christianity was under way. By tradition Jesus' disciple Thomas went to India, Mary Magdalene to southern France, Mark to Egypt, Peter to Rome, and so on. The early missionary imperative, of course, still moves Christians. So, even with people who never become a missionary or ever evangelize overtly, there is reach-out behavior over the back fence, a **witnessing for Christ**, which Christians do, some just by the way they live. St. Francis in the thirteenth century CE said it best: "Proclaim the gospel; use words, if necessary."

This 130-year section of Christian history—with Jesus the Messiah at the heart of it—is the most faith-shaping time for Christians in all our four thousand years. It stays alive to us through the Newer Testament, a collection of twenty-seven books, most written during the eighty years after the resurrection of Christ. Consider: Jesus died about the year 31 CE. In the forties and fifties Paul wrote letters to the churches he'd started and/or visited. The four Gospels, which give detail of Jesus' life and teachings, were assembled in the sixties (Mark), the seventies or eighties (Matthew and Luke–Acts), and the nineties (John). Other writings, including the book of Revelation, came about at the turn of the first century. Most were finished by 110 CE. **Reading and sharing the Newer Testament** is definitely an act of ongoing Christian faith.

For this period match

contemporary practices	faith history happenings
a. taking communion	1. Paul's instructions
b. attending Sunday worship	2. Jesus' Last Supper
c. praying with hands/palms up	3. Acts of the Apostles
d. speaking in tongues	4. Christ's crucifixion
e. attending Good Friday services	5. Pentecost experience
f. witnessing to Christ	6. Christ's resurrection

(My answers to the above are a-2, b-6, c-1, d-5, e-4, and f-3.)

STRUGGLING CENTURIES OF THE CHURCH (110–500 CE)

In Judea in the years 70 and 135 CE, there were rebellions against Roman authority. The rebellions were put down violently. After the first uprising, the temple of Jerusalem was razed. After the second, all native residents, including Jews and Jewish Christians, were expelled from the city. The name of the city was changed to Aelia Capitolina. Thus the Romans made our faith ancestors, Jewish and Christian, a people without a temple, without a city, and without a Holy Land. We were scattered, spread out in a new Diaspora.

Practices and Pieties of The Pilgrimage

Judaism now was no longer temple-centered and priest-directed but synagogue-located, Torah-centered, and rabbi-led. It became *rabbinic* Judaism. The other major form of historic Judaism I give the name *Christian Judaism*. These two branches of the historic faith were very close to each other, though at odds. As things progressed, the latter branch, Christian Judaism, proved to be quite attractive to Gentiles. So Christian Judaism increasingly took on Greek and Roman character.

It should be noted that rabbinic Jews, identified as closer to historic Judaism, were in a favorable position within the Roman Empire. They were exempt from doing obeisance to the Roman gods. Christian Jews (increasingly Gentile), however, were not exempt. They were considered a "new religious body" or cult and so were required to do homage, to put a pinch of incense on the coals burning before the bust of Caesar. Many of our ancestors, however, said they would not comply. Many were willing to be imprisoned, tortured, suffer, and die before bending the knee to anyone but Christ/the Lord.

The first several hundred years of Christianity per se, then, were centuries of persecution, though intermittent, here and there. Such persecution made for a tradition of **suffering for and with Jesus**. Those who were killed for him became martyrs, meaning "witnesses," to the faith.

In addition, early Christians also practiced behaviors such as **not serving in the military, refusing to take oaths, not attending coliseum circuses,** and **never exposing babies to the elements for death**. In time, the latter two Christian practices were adopted by society, but *all* the early practices show up now and again in our history. So there are Christians today who are **practicing pacifism, not paying taxes, not watching football,** and **not condoning abortions**. The early Christians also practiced **caring for widows and orphans**. These various behaviors set them apart from much of society.

It is a wonder that anyone would join the ranks of such a different and persecuted folk, but many did. Converts were attracted to Christianity's monotheistic God, who, they understood, revealed himself in a Savior, and whose devotees **lived an admirable set of ethics**. Slaves (estimated to be 75–80 percent of the population), freed slaves, women, emigrants, thoughtful Greeks, and occasionally Roman officials were among those attracted. Coming into the faith from the Gentile world, new Christians needed instruction in discipleship. A second-century document called *The Didache* or *Teaching* indicates that people could join the church only after several years of instruction, culminating with their **taking part in an all-night Easter vigil, being baptized,** and **receiving first communion**. Every single one of these customs lives today, though not necessarily all done at the same time.

In popular memory, the early Christians were persons who met secretly, underground, in the catacombs of the dead. That seems to be true especially for city-of-Rome Christians. They **worshiped, had communion,** and **honored the deceased in graveyards**. Such honoring of the dead, it should be noted, was a long-standing Roman custom. What Christians did was **mark tombs with symbols of the resurrection**. There was the symbol of Jonah in a whale, suggesting that, as Jonah was in the fish's belly for three days and then thrown back into *new life*, so it was with Jesus, and so it shall be for one's departed. Sometimes a beardless youth, a shepherd with a lamb about his shoulders, is on a tombstone. The shepherd is Jesus bearing new life.

Though persecuted erratically for 250 years, a reversal of fortune for Christians occurred in the year 313 CE. In that year a Christianity-inclined Roman general, Constantine, defeated an imperial military rival and, with a coemperor, issued an Edict of Toleration for Christians. The edict gave our ancestors the right to practice their faith openly. Insofar as Christians today **practice tolerance**, they can do so remembering gratefully what Constantine did for them in the early fourth century CE.

When Constantine finally was sole ruler of the Roman Empire, he sought ways to unite and govern all the lands and people around the "Roman Lake"/Mediterranean Sea. One of the ways he saw coherence happening was by bringing together the loosely organized—but *organized*—Christian church bishops for consensus building in regard to doctrine and practice. The First Ecumenical Council then met in northwest Asia Minor/Turkey at Nicaea in 325 CE. Under Constantine's eye, the church fathers worked out an affirmation of faith for the church, the Nicene Creed. **Reciting a faith creed**, the Nicene or other, such as the 150-CE Apostles' Creed or the 451-CE Chalcedonian Creed, is a practice of the faithful worldwide today.

During the fourth and fifth centuries CE, further clarification of church doctrine was needed, especially to cope with heretical ideas and to overcome internal schism. The church fathers (Athanasius, the Cappadocians, Ambrose of Milan, for example) and at least one church mother, Macrina, struggled to put Christianity's theological house in order. They began to carve out a practice in the faith of **doing theological thought and**

Practices and Pieties of The Pilgrimage

writing. The greatest reflector and author of this period was Augustine, the bishop of Hippo in North Africa. He integrated traditional Hebrew thought with Greek Neoplatonism and wrote his works in Latin. Especially he picked up on the thought of St. Paul that "we are justified by faith." He went on to pen the dictum "Love God, and do what you will"—a generous guide in the Christian life. Augustine is also remembered for having written the first personal autobiography in the world. His *Confessions* provided a model for **acknowledging with particularity one's sins** before God. Any modern 12-step program, which includes **asking forgiveness** of those one has offended, is a version of Augustine's pioneering example.

Chalcedon of 451 CE, mentioned above, proved to be a "breaking-apart event." Christians in the East took different stances on "the nature of Christ." Some, such as Coptic, Syriac/Jacobite, and Armenian Christians, called Miaphysites or Monophysites, emphasized essential oneness of Godhead and humanity in Christ. Others, such as the Church of the East or Nestorian Christians, called Dyophysites, wanted to keep Christ's human and divine natures distinguishable. Miaphysites suggested "oneness," as when wine and water blend in one cup; Dyophysites imaged the joining of oil and water in one cup, where the two do not mix. Majority-opinion Eastern/Greek and Western/Latin Christians held to the language of the Chalcedon formula: "one person of two natures." The differing interpretations of the creed are subtle but significant. Disagreement led to irreconcilable fracturing of Christian bodies. The Church of the East/Nestorian branch of Christianity was also less inclined to call the Virgin Mary *Theotokos*, "God-Bearer," whereas Orthodox/Catholic Christians strongly accepted such a title for her. That acceptance led to nonstop **honoring of/devotion to the Virgin**, Moscow to Madrid, Mexico City to Manila, Maine to Manchuria, still today.

Some unique practices developed during these early centuries. Christians in Armenia (a nation *outside* the Roman Empire and the first country to officially adopt Christianity) **slaughter a lamb** at the end of their worship services. The sacrifice likely was a pagan/pre-Christian practice, but it could be related to Christ, the sacrificial Lamb of God.

In 410 CE Rome fell to barbarian Visigoths.[2] That fall had major implications in the shape and practices of Christian faith, as we shall see when moving into the next half of the first millennium CE. Before that, though . . .

---

2. Though barbarians, their religion was Christian, albeit *Arian* Christian.

Brief Christian Histories

For this period, match

contemporary practices	*faith history happenings*
a. reciting a faith creed	1. the Roman catacombs
b. honoring the dead	2. the *Didache* or *Teaching*
c. taking instruction for baptism	3. Augustine's *Confessions*
d. not going to movies	4. martyrdom of the saints
e. acknowledging one's sin	5. Constantine's 313 Edict
f. suffering/dying for Jesus	6. ecumenical councils
g. tolerating differences	7. no circus attendance

(My answers to the above are a-6, b-1, c-2, d-7, e-3, f-4, g-5.)

THE AGE OF MONASTICISM (500-1100 CE)

Moving into this next six-hundred-year period, we back up briefly to underscore the beginnings of monasticism. This religious crystallization showed fully in the early Middle Ages, aka late antiquity.

As soon as Christianity was officially tolerated in 313 CE, persecution stopped and involuntary suffering ended. There were those, however, who started a practice of **voluntary suffering**. Some Christians, known as the desert fathers, retreated to the remote areas of Egypt and the Middle East. There they could deny themselves and take up rigorous ascetic disciplines. These men were the first Christian monks (from Greek *monos,* meaning "alone"), also known as solitaries, anchorites, or eremites (from Greek word for "desert" and from which we get the word "hermit"). The solitary monks were followed shortly by monks who lived in community, known as cenobites. Whether solitary or communal, the vow of the monk was to **live a life of poverty, chastity, and obedience**—not easy practices in any age.

Besides rigors of the body, such as **fasting**[3] and **denying themselves sleep**, some practiced other unique disciplines, such as **eating grass** (the grazer movement) and **living out their lives on top of tall pillars** (the stylites). Some monks known as "holy fools" **would feign madness and**

---

3. Fasting is by no means unique to Christianity. It predates these first millennial monks and is a worldwide religious discipline, considered "good for the soul."

Practices and Pieties of The Pilgrimage

break social rules, like running naked in public, which brought ridicule and beatings on themselves. They believed St. Paul commended such in 1 Corinthians 3:18: "become fools so that you may be wise." Monks, nuns, and laypeople who committed themselves to celibacy *and* virginity were called "athletes of God."

Communal life was ordered in Eastern Mediterranean Christianity by St. Basil and in Western Europe by St. Benedict. Each wrote a *Rule* for monastery governance and practice. Benedict started writing his around 529 CE, setting forth the hours for prayer, times of silence, when to work, how to treat guests, and so forth. The primary observance east and west was **doing *ora et labora*—**prayer and work. Guidelines prescribed then are guidelines in many monasteries yet today. For contemporary clergy in the world and laypeople, a version of traditional monastic life is seen by **going on a spiritual-life retreat** or **working with a spiritual director.**

Within the monasteries, music played an essential part. Monastic worship was especially enhanced during the eight hundreds CE by Charlemagne, who encouraged Gregorian chants. He wanted worship to be enjoyable. **Chanting**—and, later, **hymn singing**—thus became a major feature in Christian worship. Such music, we know, often continues to resonate in weekday life. In the sixth and seventh century, **ringing a steeple bell** was introduced by Celtic monks. The practice spread widely and is of long observance. In the eighth century **playing the organ** became possible; so **listening to music meditatively** began. Such ringing and playing continues today as people **join a handbell choir** or, for a Sunday school class, **plink out a hymn tune on the piano.** Jumping ahead, music in Christian worship developed even more fully in the High Middle Ages; then we encounter four-part chorales, requiem masses, and orchestras in worship services. Today **strumming a guitar** at a summer camp vesper service or **listening to Christian radio** are behaviors related to the music of the monks of the early Middle Ages. So **singing, composing,** and **playing music** such as *Te Deum laudamus* ("We praise you, O God") were and are ways in holiness.

The monasteries and convents of this period were magnets for men and women who wanted to practice a holy life and, in some cases, become educated. The cloistered life facilitated both. Some men—and it was *men*—went into the secular priesthood to live out their baptism. Their ordination ceremony might have had them **lying face down before the altar of Christ,** then a bishop consecrating the candidate by the **laying on of hands.** As discussed previously, the laying on of hands dates back at least to Samuel's anointing of Saul and David in the eleventh century BCE.

Considerable Christian practice has foundation in the Bible, such as **going on a pilgrimage**, heralded in Psalms of Ascent, such a practice becoming tremendously important early in the Common Era. It never went away. Even before Constantine granted tolerance to Christians, there were those who traveled to the Holy Land to walk the streets where Jesus walked. In 327 CE, Constantine's Christian mother, Helena, was a pilgrim. She ordered churches built on the traditional site of Jesus' birthplace in Bethlehem and his traditional burial site/sepulchre in Jerusalem. Millions upon millions of pilgrims through the ages—this writer included—traced Helena's/Jesus' footsteps on the *Via Dolorosa*. Once pilgrims returned to their homes in Europe, they established "stations of the cross" along the walls of their churches. **Walking and praying the stations of the cross** are still done.

An additional wrinkle on pilgrimages is reported out of the Russian Orthodox tradition. One faithful holy man went on a thousand-mile trek to a holy shrine. He prayed without ceasing, "O Lord Jesus Christ, Son of God, have mercy on me, a sinner," aka the Jesus Prayer. **Reciting the Jesus Prayer** happens millions of times a day throughout the world. We should note too that **reciting the Lord's Prayer** happens tens of millions of times daily.

Pilgrims began going toward destinations other than Jerusalem. Some went to Rome, others to Santiago de Compostela in Spain, or Canterbury in England, as remembered in Chaucer's *Canterbury Tales*. When people arrived at a holy locale having a cathedral on it, they sometimes found that inside they could **walk a labyrinth**. What drew them most to a site, however, were relics, the bones of the saints, or some other holy artifact. According to tradition, on her visit to the Holy Land, Helena found the true cross of Jesus—a piece of which, Russians believed, could be seen in the pectoral cross worn by their czar. Jesus' cross seems to have been made of *ever-growing* wood, for it is said that there was enough true-cross lumber in Europe to build a battleship!

Cynicism aside, the **relics of the saints were venerated**, held in awe, and considered to have miraculous healing power. Hear what St. John of Damascus said to his emperor about Saints Barlaam and Joasaph's relics: "We carry about these clean and holy bones, O king, because we attest in due form our love of those marvelous men to whom they belong: and

Practices and Pieties of The Pilgrimage

because we would bring ourselves to remember their wrestlings and lovely conversation, to rouse up ourselves to the like zeal."[4]

Prior to the fifth century CE, whether in churches or homes, there was not much **displaying of a crucifix**, that is, a cross with Christ's body depicted on it. *That* cross was much too raw and shameful for Christians to "glory in." Over time, however, this ignominious death symbol lost some of its shame. That cross began to show up more prominently in the early Middle Ages. This was truer for Christians in the West than for those of the East. Eastern Christians tended to emphasize the triumphant/risen/coming-again/judging Lord, not the human/suffering/dying One. Regardless of *how* Christ or the apostles or saints and martyrs were depicted, the point is that they *were* remembered, often in art. Thus an artist and his patron could **show devotion to Christ graphically**. Those who viewed such art were drawn into it for understanding and inspiration. Then—perhaps far earlier—people would cross themselves (head-to-stomach-right breast-to-heart (if Orthodox) or heart-to-right breast (if Catholic). Coming into and out of church, or before taking a shot in a basketball game, pious folk still **cross themselves**.

Artistic depiction, though, had its naysayers. In the eighth and ninth centuries CE, the Eastern empire had a huge "iconoclastic controversy." As Islamic armies came out of the Arabia, successfully taking land and peoples from the Byzantines, Emperor Leo came to the conviction that his losses were because Muslims obeyed the commandment to make no graven image, whereas Christians did not. In **venerating icons** (especially statues), Leo feared that his subjects were in fact worshiping idols. He hoped he might win back God's favor if icons were destroyed. So he set out to rid the church of them. The pope in Rome, monks, and common people everywhere, however, wanted to hold on to the depictions. To them icons were holy. Thus the controversy. In the end, the Eastern Orthodox finally settled for two-dimensional art, with Orthodox believers then and now showing their devotion to Christ, to Mary, to the saints by **kissing icons**. Meanwhile the Western Catholic Christians kept three-dimensional art. So **carving, sculpting, bas-relief-ing**, as well as **drawing, painting, frescoing, tile/mosaic placing** were—and are—holy practices.

---

4. John of Damascus, *The Precious Pearl*, 248.

Brief Christian Histories

Praying to and/or **through the saints** is also a practice continued—west, east, south, and north—in Christendom (though usually not among Protestants).

The six-hundred-year period here under consideration is described by historian Will Durant as the Age of Faith.[5] We've seen some of the signs of it above in deepening Jesus' people in asceticism and aesthetics. Christianity also inspired believers **to move, to spread the faith**. Nestorian believers belonging to the Church of the East sent missionaries east—and east still more—all the way to India, China, and Tibet. Coptic Christians in Egypt spread their witness south into the Sudan, where, interestingly, priests called—and call—the desert faithful to worship by **ringing resonant stone slabs** suspended in the air. Catholic monks in the West journeyed to transport Christianity to still-pagan parts of Europe or areas taken over by Germanic invaders. Quite early, Christianization—or re-Christianization—of western and central Europe was undertaken by Celtic/Irish monks. St. Columba, for example went from Ireland to Scotland, and in time his follower, St. Aidan, went to England's isle of Lindisfarne. Legend has it that on the west side of Ireland, St. Brandan and others **floated out into the ocean in animal-skin boats to let the Spirit blow them where it would**—to Iceland, Greenland, even Newfoundland! The Celtic wild goose icon shown above captures this Spirit movement well. Here's a poem about this dangerously unique, free-floating practice:

> I am the coracle upon the fearsome wave.
> I am the dragon rising from the deep.
> I am the petrel wheeling.
> I am your tiny knife.
> Your one drop left of sweet water
> Against a terrible thirst.
> I am your sextant
> As I am your star
> > Pilgrim, when you return to tell your story,
> > All your tales shall be of me.[6]

As noted previously, wherever they went, these Celtic monks emphasized **personal confession of sin**. They made **doing penance** have

---

5. Durant, *The Story of Civilization*, vol. 4, is named *The Age of Faith*.

6. Poem by RoMa Johnson, Colorado Springs, Celtic pilgrim, visiting Ireland in the 2000s.

Practices and Pieties of The Pilgrimage

meaning. Personal penance, including **mortification of the flesh,** is not much practiced in the Bible, but it certainly became a common practice in the Middle Ages.

As Irish monks went in motion during the sixth century, so there were Anglo-Saxon monks moving in the eighth century. Carolingian/French rulers intentionally sent Anglo-Saxon monks from England to convert their pagan Anglo-Saxon kin in Germany. Wynfrith, aka Boniface, was the apostle to the Germans. In the last centuries of the millennium, Cluniac monks of the Franks went to lands occupied by the Vikings, both in Scandinavia and in Normandy and Sicily.

Besides sending monks out, the Carolingians via Charlemagne established "parishes" for believers. So **attending one's parish/local church on a Sunday morning** became something Christians did then and do now. Prior to this time, cathedral or monastery or guild or nobility churches were the rule.

Another gift to the present from the Franks is the "language of worship" set up for centuries. Charlemagne in the ninth century CE insisted that ancient Latin be reinstated in worship services. "Why?" one may ask. Answer: because *Charlemagne believed God understood only Latin.* So, he thought, if a priest's baptismal prayer was not rendered in the proper tongue, God could not hear it to wash away original sin. The Latin reconstituted by Charlemagne is used today in traditional Catholic rites, in Vatican documents, and in 2013 in the Sistine Chapel, where cardinals debated who would be the next pope.

Meanwhile in eastern Europe, Cyril and Methodius, monks of the Greek Orthodox Church, left Constantinople for points north, establishing beachheads for Christianity among the Bohemians (in today's Czech Republic) and in 988 BCE among Slavic-Viking people in Kiev, beginning with the baptism of Prince Vladimir. The latter effort ultimately resulted in the Christianization of Russia, where, by the fifteenth century, czars and patriarchs were calling Moscow the third Rome.

To **engage in mission effort** was then a Christian practice, as it had been in previous centuries. It is still in operation. Among the most prominent of missionaries today are Korean Christians, who are going out broadly, even to South America.

Brief Christian Histories

For this period, match

contemporary practices	faith history happenings
a. taking spiritual direction	1. the rise of Islam
b. praying stations of the cross	2. Gregorian chants
c. fasting and self-denial	3. the desert fathers
d. trusting God in adversity	4. Cyril and Methodius
e. listening to Christian radio	5. coracle ocean-going
f. worshiping no graven images	6. *Rule of St. Benedict*
g. going on a mission trip	7. holy site pilgrimages

(My answers to the above are a-6, b-7, c-3, d-5, e-2, f-1, and g-4.)

HIGH CHRISTENDOM YEARS (1100–1450 CE)

In the second millennia CE, we have the centuries of the High Middle Ages leading to the early modern period. Midway through these centuries, a general revival of culture transpired in western Europe. Especially there was the Italian Renaissance, with advancement in literature and art. Along with this Italian resurgence, the Roman Catholic Church was reinvigorated. The Vatican in general and popes in particular began to wield greater sway in politics, culture, *and* everyday life. It was even more Durant's Age of Faith, with the church in the center of many things. Something like "Christendom" came to be. We note these high Christian years in several ways.

When Frankish armies—encouraged by the pope—advanced into Islamic Spain and captured Toledo, they found a library of depth there. Among the treasures in that library were the works of the fifth-century-BCE philosopher Aristotle. What happened next was that the religious order of the Dominicans, established by the pope in 1216, took interest. In particular, Dominican scholar Thomas Aquinas mined the ancient Greek philosopher's thought for new understandings in Christian theology. The Dominicans encouraged scholarship; so, during these years, the great universities of Europe opened. **To study, teach, and write as a scholar** was one way then—and now—for a Christian to show forth his or her commitment to God.

The arts started to flourish at this time. Maritime powers Genoa and Venice went out east and brought back art treasures—often by stealing.

Practices and Pieties of The Pilgrimage

What they showed awakened Western artists. Now they began to paint in oil, sculpt with stone, and work with stained glass as never before. Much of this fresh art went into the great new Gothic cathedrals that architects designed, using Arabic math and knowledge. Even today, to enter these cathedrals is to be transported into a heavenly realm through beauty. That people today **express their faith through the visual arts** was decidedly encouraged by the example of Christian artists in this period.

The infamous Crusades of the twelfth and thirteenth centuries were initiated and sanctified by the church as holy wars to wrest ancient Christian lands from Islamic Turks and, later, Islamic Arabs. Pope Urban II called for the First Crusade, and the great Cistercian abbot Bernard of Clairvaux preached one. Hundreds of thousands of western Europeans, especially Franks/Frenchmen responded. Kings and nobility, knights, monks and priests, ordinary laypeople as pilgrims—even children—went out. However misguided, they crusaded for reasons of faith, more than for financial gain, glory, or adventure. **"Killing for Christ"** was what such Christians did then—and many think they are permitted to do today. "Noble cause" motivation *best* shows itself today when Christians **nonviolently go out on a mission of human service**, for example, to teach in Africa . . . or organize in an urban barrio . . . or sling a hammer with Habitat for Humanity. *That* kind of going out is better Christian practice and piety, more in keeping with Christ's directives and motivated by a desire to do something significant for God by helping others. The Crusades of the Middle Ages turned out to be *not* noble cause.

Even so, Urban II's call for a crusade—and, the fact that he got one—strongly suggests that the pope in Rome wielded immense political power. As a matter of historical record, popes sometimes confirmed kings, and in this period they more and more began to regulate the lives of ordinary Christians. Part of the power of control was exercised through the sacramental system, set in place by the Fourth Lateran Council of 1215. The system designated seven basic rites, called sacraments, as essential to salvation. If, therefore, one wanted to do the will of God, that he/she might go in heaven, that person would (1) **be baptized** and (2) **confirmed** in the church, (3) **make confession**/do penance regularly and (4) **receive communion** at least yearly, (5) **have his/her marriage** or (6) **ordination consecrated in/by the church**, and finally (7) **receive last rites**/extreme unction from a priest. By these system rites, many people today demonstrate their faith. "By **attending mass daily**," a person might say and believe, "I know that I am a Christian, that I am saved." Many of the sacraments are received with **head bowed, knees on the floor, and hands pressed together**. All this keeps with the feudal hierarchical system where one bowed and curtsied to royalty and, in like manner, to the highest royalty, God.

The Middle Ages were hierarchical through and through. So when the great doctor of the church Thomas Aquinas wrote, he conceived of the world in terms of a hierarchy of beings,

at the top	God
then	angels and archangels
followed by	saints and martyrs
	clergy
	royalty
	artisans
	peasants

in that order. (Other folk thinking hierarchically put the nobility at the top, followed by the clergy, then serfs, these being the "three estates.") The point is that one knew one's place, and the idea was to **live one's station well, honor those above you**, and **care for those below**.

There were, however, those who thought faithful living out should be done closer to the model that Jesus himself provided. Dominican and Franciscan brothers appeared in the early-thirteenth-century scene to **wander, beg, teach, preach, do good works,** and **live simply**. Their example provided a high-water mark for Christian piety of yore and of now. The Franciscans kept very close to the people and encouraged "Marian practices," such as **saying the rosary**, a necklace with forty-forty-forty "Hail Mary, full of grace" beads spaced between larger beads, the larger reminding believers to recite the *Pater Noster* (Latin for "Our Father," the Lord's Prayer) when fingered to them. In these years, the Virgin Mary certainly became the prime subject of artistic imagination and popular devotion. Over the years she has only increased in stature in both Catholic and Orthodox traditions. **Marian devotion**, then, is a great passion for Christian millions worldwide. In the 2012 Olympics, one successful female sprinter upon winning pulled from her running bra a picture of the Madonna and Child to show the camera!

Devotion to Mary notwithstanding, **love of Jesus** was on equal, if not superior, footing. During these years in the Eastern Orthodox Church, the transcendent Christ became the triumphant *Pantocrator*, supreme ruler, in

Practices and Pieties of The Pilgrimage

mosaic form high on church interior dome ceilings. Beneath the Pantocrator, worshipers always stood before the iconostasis/stand, on which icons of holy figures were placed. Believers then **kissed the icons.** Outside the onion-domed churches, wandering through the country were Orthodox hesychasts, holy men who sought union with God in **stillness, rest, quiet, and silence.** They were descendants of a long eremitic/hermit, sometimes called holy fools. The hesychasts engaged in **continuous repeating of the Jesus Prayer**: "Lord Jesus Christ, Son of God, have mercy on me, a sinner."

In the Western Church, more and more, Christ was seen as Savior on the cross, dying. The crucified Christ came to dominate front and center altar space in churches. Worshipers identified with this Jesus and often sought to join him in his passion. In the fifteen hundreds Thomas à Kempis wrote *The Imitation of Christ*, in which he encouraged **voluntary suffering.** When this medieval piety of suffering like Christ made its way across the ocean into Native American culture, it sometimes lead to **self-flagellation—even self-crucifixions,** as in northern New Mexico's Penitente practice. Self-flagellation was also practiced in Europe during the time of the plagues/Black Death (1348 on), flagellants hoping thereby to suffer enough for their sins and thereby avoid death, if not for themselves, then for others.

If the high-water mark for Catholic Christendom was in the thirteenth century, by the fifteenth, low-water conditions were present. It happened in several ways, but especially around money. The selling of church offices, called simony, became a lucrative church business. Bishoprics were bought and sold. Pope Alexander VI, for example, sold offices—or gave them to relatives, including his own children by his several mistresses. To raise additional money, indulgences (dispensations from eternal punishment) were offered for sale. **Believers bought indulgences** for themselves and for deceased others. These fund-raising measures remind us, though, that the institutional church does need money to do ministry. It could receive support, one would hope, by honorable appeal and generous response. **Giving money to the church** then and now is certainly one of the ways that people express their faith. Then and now some people **offer a tithe,** 10 percent of their income, to God through the church.

The general abuses of the medieval church created internal rifts. One rift was in leadership. For a while, there was a pope in Rome, another in Avignon (France), and a third in Ravenna (northern Italy). Each pope was beholden to a different European king. Church councils were called to help

Brief Christian Histories

settle things, but were only marginally effective. Division was the order of the fifteenth century.

Division also came from within the rank and file of the church. Many faithful folk—Waldensians in France and northern Italy, Lollards in England, and Hussites in Bohemia—wanted church reform. Each movement tried to institute change in church policy and practice. Among practices advocated were to give laypeople authority to preach, have the Bible translated into the vernacular, and let laypeople receive communion "in both kinds"—that is, bread *and* wine. Such reform-minded people, **offering criticism and working for church renewal**, stand in the company with the prophets of the Older Testament and with contemporary activists, such as Hans Küng (a Catholic), John Spong (an Episcopalian/Anglican), and Jim Wallis (an evangelical), who want a church more faithful to God and responsive to all people.

Up to the year 1500 CE those reformist efforts mostly failed because they were put down. Some leaders were even tried for heresy in inquisitions and burned at the stake. **Dying—and executing(!)—for Christ** happened. After 1517, however, renewed reform efforts succeeded, and some things were different. With those differences would come new expressions of fidelity.

For this period, match

contemporary practices	*faith history happenings*
a. receiving communion	1. Franciscan way
b. fighting for Christ	2. the Crusades
c. tithing one's income	3. transubstantiation
d. marrying in holy bonds	4. Gothic cathedrals
e. kneeling to pray	5. sacramental system
f. bearing pain bravely	6. feudal hierarchicalism
g. worshiping through art	7. Thomas à Kempis's *Imitatio*
h. living simply	8. simony, indulgences

(My answers to the above are a-3, b-2, c-8, d-5, e-6, f-7, g-4, and h-1.)

REFORMATIONS/NEW WORLDS ERA (1450–1650 CE)

What Martin Luther began in Germany in 1517, Huldrych Zwingli, Conrad Grebel, and John Calvin picked up in Switzerland just a few years later. Calvin, in his Swiss years (1536–49), made Geneva a training center for European reformers, such as John Knox from Scotland. In England, King Henry VIII and Archbishop Cranmer changed that nation's church more cautiously, but change it, they did—eventually to be called Anglican. A collection of other leaders like Thomas Münzer, Jacob Hutter, and Menno Simons pushed for even more radical changes in church and personal life.

The Protestant Reformation was on.

The Reformation had major doctrinal dimensions. It put emphasis on the sovereignty of God and justification by faith alone. It made major church polity/governance shifts through the idea of "the priesthood of all believers." And it had political implications for nations when worship services went from Latin to vernaculars.

What the Protestant Reformation brought on, through theological, ecclesiastical, and political change, also changed the ways people practiced their religion. If one tried to **live by faith alone,** then surely there could be no purchasing of admission-to-heaven tickets, that is, indulgences. Nor, they came to believe, would meritorious deeds—like saying prayers or going on a pilgrimage—amount to anything in themselves. Protestants thus developed more interiority or subjectivity; so they had greater outward reserve. In time, the nineteenth-century Lutheran Søren Kierkegaard would even describe the true "knight of faith" walking through Deer Park in Copenhagen with no one ever guessing by appearance that he was a Christian. Inwardly, though, with every step, his knight of faith was **affirming/believing "in virtue of the absurd" that God had visited humankind in the person of Jesus Christ, the God-man.**

Kierkegaard notwithstanding, there were several *outward* signs for Protestant piety. All the Reformers stressed **studying the Bible and basing one's faith on the Bible.** Rejecting the rule of popes and councils, Protestants found authority in the Bible alone, *sola scriptura* (Latin for "scripture alone") being their watchword. Five hundred years after Luther and company spoke, Lutheran-Reformed-Baptist heirs continue to build worship services more around the Word read and proclaimed than around the mystery of the Eucharist. Luther made preaching a virtual sacrament. The faithful especially began **listening for "the Word of God."**

What made the sixteenth-century Reformation possible, of course, was the printing press, invented a half century earlier by Johann Gutenberg. This invention began to put the Good Book on the table in homes, not just under lock of cathedral library. Thus, **having family devotions based on the Bible** was a new practice of faithful literate people. The printing press enabled still other forms of piety. Anglicans printed a *Book of Common Prayer*, and that did much to shape and influence communal and **individual praying**, as well as everyday language. The *Book of Common Prayer* is quoted (e.g., "for better or for worse") more often than Shakespeare. The Puritans who came to America in the 1620s carried with them their *Geneva Bible* and the *Bay Psalm Book*, the latter for congregational singing. What folk heard and sang of a Sunday morning, of course, went with them through their week, shaping thought and action. **Hymn singing** became one of the distinguishing characteristics of Protestants—Martin Luther, Charles Wesley, Isaac Watts, and others composing new lyrics and tunes to inspire and direct Protestant sensibilities.

As essential as hymn singing, Bible reading, and preaching were to Protestants, none of these practices rose to the status of an official, announced sacrament. Why? Because "the Bible doesn't tell us" they are "so." The only sacraments for which Luther and the Reformers found biblical warrant were baptism and communion. Thus five of the seven sacraments of the Catholic Church—confirmation, penance, marriage, ordination, and last rites—were renamed ordinances. Even so, these **ordinances were observed** in Protestant life. Interestingly enough, some were *not* observed by Puritan divines of New England; they refused to do marriages or burials, since neither was the proper business of a *Bible*-believing parson!

The two sacraments that were kept were transformed. Communion for Protestants became **taking in** both **kinds**, bread *and* wine, even as John Hus in Bohemia had argued in the early fourteen hundreds. Baptism was in for change too, especially among Anabaptists. They found no scriptural warrant for the baptism of children. So they began to practice **adult believers' baptism, by total immersion**.

Other, more radical changes in behaviors came through the Anabaptists. Not only did they practice believers' baptism, they found other almost-forgotten prescriptions in scripture. They read Jesus' Sermon on the Mount and started **practicing nonviolence**, turning the other cheek; they

Practices and Pieties of The Pilgrimage

became resisters to war, refusing to serve in the military. They **forswore swearing**, refused to take oaths in court. **Plain-speaking**, they also refused to tip the hat to authorities, calling no one "Lord." They simply were persons **living simply**—as had Jesus, Anthony, and Francis of Assisi—"taking no thought for what ye shall put on" (Matthew 6:25 KJV).

Lutherans, Reformed, and Anglican divines, however, thought the Anabaptists and their kind (Mennonites, Quakers, Moravians, Baptists) went too far. So the major Protestant bodies were less than tolerant of "the radicals," even promulgating their persecution. **Becoming a martyr** became a possibility for some—thousands, actually.

Church reformation in whatever form was *not* welcomed by Rome. The pope launched a Counter-Reformation that ultimately ensured the loyalty of the southern European peoples. The Roman Catholic Church also made some internal changes. The Vatican stopped selling indulgences and church offices. Rome's Counter-Reformation was spearheaded by the 1540-founded Society of Jesus. The Jesuits **did significant intellectual work**, such as ensconcing Thomas Aquinas's theology as mainline in classrooms and schools they started. Best of all, they **engaged in promulgation of the faith through mission work**. Jesuit missionaries went south to Africa, then far east to Japan and west to Brazil and what is now Canada. The Franciscan and Dominican orders took prime responsibility for missions to Central and South America (west of Brazil). In the seventeenth century, England used the sea to plant colonists with Church of England faith in North America. English Puritans and Pilgrims came over too. In the nineteenth century the English planted colonists in Australia using jail prisoners. Conceivably English officials were **practicing forgiveness**, but, truth be told, they were probably trying to reduce the costs of confining debtors. The nineteenth century, called the great century for missions by church historian Kenneth Scott Latourette, saw Protestants in America, England, and other northern European countries sending missionaries abroad. These **faith-bringing** women and men went out under the banner of various missionary societies, such as the London Missionary Society.

Wherever Christianity went, it regularly adopted and adapted indigenous practices unto itself, as calling people to worship with a wooden gong and accompanying services with gamelan music in Bali—as my wife and I experienced. Other practices include **worshiping in dance, with flags, using local musical instruments; accepting body painting; tolerating polygamy, nose rubbing, and breast nudity; and exorcizing demons.**

One protest that Protestants made was against Catholicism's attachment to Mary. From a simple reading of scripture, Marian devotion seemed unwarranted. Even so, the Blessed Virgin continued to be important. Apparitions of Mary took place. She appeared to a simple Indian peasant in Mexico, to some girls in France, and to other believers in sundry other locations, such as Medjugorje in Bosnia-Herzegovina. From these apparitions came shrines for pilgrimage, as at Lourdes and Guadalupe. **People visit shrines.** Widely, Catholic **people worship** through **Mary** with figurines of the Queen of Heaven prominent in home altars and on votive candle glasses and velvet wall hangings. Mary's place is one of the differences that developed in practices and piety between Catholics and Protestants. Here are three others:

Catholics kneel with rosary beads to offer prayers.

Protestants stand, sounding out songs of praise.

Catholics wear crucifixes about their necks.

Protestants wear crosses without the body of Christ.

Catholics worship in stained-glass beauty.

Protestants let the light of God in, only through clear glass.

These are a few of the distinctions that came to be, which, when all is said and done, may not be much more than variations on a theme: **loving God.** When the Counter-Reformation Council of Trent (aka the Tridentine) ended in 1563, priests **used only Latin** in the liturgy; Protestants **spoke to God in vernacular tongues.**

The differences between Catholics and Protestants of Lutheran and Calvinist stripe eventually broke out in war, including the Thirty Years' War of 1618–1648. It is doubtful if any positive religious practices or behaviors grew from these conflicts, but **dying for one's faith** and **killing (supposedly) for Christ** certainly happened.

*

By the time of Catholic-Protestant separating, the Greek Orthodox Church and Middle East church variations (Armenian, Nestorian, Syriac, and Coptic Christianity) were under the hegemony of the Muslim Ottoman Turks, who controlled a vast Euro-Asian empire. Only on-the-fringe Abyssinian Christianity in Ethiopia escaped domination. Constantinople fell to the Turks in 1453 and was renamed Istanbul. So Greek Orthodox

Practices and Pieties of The Pilgrimage

Christianity was less secure than in the days of its alliance with Byzantine rulers. Now more than ever, the focus of Orthodox Christianity was on staying alive, doing so by keeping to itself, especially by maintaining ancient liturgies. Characteristically, Orthodox services were conducted with **worshipers standing**—for long hours—in services that were candle-lit, icon-rich, and incense-filled. In their homes Orthodox faithful often **had a "bright" or "red" or "beautiful" corner where icons were placed and candles burned**. When my wife and I visited an Orthodox cemetery in Athens, we noticed that **mourning widows wore black dresses**. Such dark costume, of course, is not unique to Orthodoxy: my Methodist great-grandmother wore black for thirty years after her husband, "Mr. Wilden," died. Such attire reminds us that there is special appropriate dress for church by Christians, such as **wearing a white dress for First Communion** or **putting on a tie for church**—a custom that seems to be fading in America. Much, much more could be said about attire for Christians, from a priest's heavy, jeweled, gold-stitched chasuble to a Mennonite woman's simple hair bun.

Orthodoxy survived uniquely on the Athos peninsula in Greece. There, amazingly enough, it has been left pretty much alone, able to let continue monasteries of sundry national affiliations. Monasteries (aka lavras) related to Greek, Ukrainian, Bulgarian, Serbian, Russian, and so on Orthodoxies were built on the peninsula, existing to the present day. Hesychasm with its **silencing into God** was practiced at Athos and promoted from there. One regulation on Athos is that **women are not allowed on the peninsula**. A variation of gender separation in other denominations in other countries is **"Women sit on the pews to the right, men to the left."**

The one place where Orthodoxy did not come under Islamic domination was Russia. After Constantinople fell to the Turks in 1453, Orthodox believers in Moscow came to call their capital "the Third Rome," and today Russia is still the numerical stronghold of Orthodoxy. Differences in practice within Russian Orthodoxy exist: Old Believers **cross themselves with three fingers** (for the Trinity), while Greek-influenced Russian believers use **two fingers** (for the two natures of Christ). Wherever I've run across Orthodoxy—and that is in some widespread places (Jordan, Switzerland, Manitoba, and Russia)—I found the practices of **kissing the icons, crossing oneself repeatedly**, and **burning much incense**.

Brief Christian Histories

For this period, match

contemporary practices	faith history happenings
a. reading the Bible at home	1. *The Bay Psalm Book*
b. listening to sermons	2. communion "in both kinds"
c. singing hymns	3. *sola scriptura* way affirmed
d. "bright corner" devotions	4. Gutenberg's printing press
e. receiving the cup	5. Guadalupe apparition
f. nonswearing, nonviolence	6. Orthodoxy in Russia
g. following the *Book of Common Prayer*	7. Anglican Reformation
h. Marian devotion	8. Luther on "the Word"

(My answers for the above are a-4, b-8, c-1, d-6, e-2, f-3, g-7, and h-5)

 THE ECUMENICAL/GLOBAL AGE (1650 CE–PRESENT)

The year 1650 is chosen intentionally as the beginning for the ninth period for the Christian histories in this book. In 1650 René Descartes died; for many, Descartes is the symbol person who marks the start of the Enlightenment or Age of Reason/Rationalism. He was followed by such thinkers as Locke, Diderot, Rousseau, Voltaire, Spinoza, and Hume. The rise of science traces back to the mid-seventeenth century too. Its symbol person, Isaac Newton, was born in 1643, followed by such notables as Lavoisier, Hutton, Faraday, Darwin, Pasteur, and Einstein.

Reason and science greatly influenced what happened in Christianity, as illustrated in the case of the United States, a nation that came into being during the late seventeen hundreds, a nation whose leaders were guided by Enlightenment ideas. The *Constitution* for the new nation was drawn up with a Bill of Rights, its First Amendment creating a separation of church and state. Church-state separation also came about in France and Germany in 1806 when Napoleon ended the Holy Roman Empire. Even stronger changes came in most European countries over time—especially after World War I, but separation came first in America.

What the separation did in the United States was put religious institutions churches on their own for the first time in fifteen hundred years. No more public largesse was available to heat buildings or pay clergy salaries.

Practices and Pieties of The Pilgrimage

For Christian churches to survive, the "case for relevancy" of the faith to individuals had to me made. So all religious bodies in America—Protestant, Catholic, Jewish—had to be "customer oriented." Protestantism became quite evangelical. In great campground meetings and, later, tent revivals, there were "awakenings." The First Great Awakening was in the early eighteenth century, one leader being Jonathan Edwards. The Second Great Awakening occurred in the early nineteenth century, especially associated with Charles Finney.

The truth is that almost all Protestant preachers in America began **preaching for individual decisions in faith.** That was quite different from earlier patterns, where sovereigns chose their people's religion or one was simply "born a something." The majority of the population pulled away from dry rationalism and went toward heartfelt faith. Hereafter in America people could tell you when they were *moved* to **go down the sawdust aisle to "take Jesus as my personal Savior."** The words of a great spiritual spoke for many:

> If you cannot preach like Peter
> If you cannot pray like Paul
> **Go out and tell your neighbor**
> That "He died to save us all."

So they did—and do. In the last half of the twentieth century evangelical-pentecostal Protestants became the largest religious group in America with about 30 percent so affiliated. Catholics have 24 percent. "Nones" account for 17 percent, mainline Protestants 14 percent, black Protestants 8 percent, other faiths 3 percent, and Jews and Mormons each 2 percent.[7] **Belonging to a church**—or at least **professing a denominational preference**—is true for about 80 percent of the American population. It is a sort of piety. American Christianity, perhaps more than in other countries, puts emphasis on belonging to and **living in a worshiping community.**

Another way in which the religions of America responded to church-state separation was in education. With due diligence, local churches engaged in religious education. **Going to Sunday school** became a way of faithful life for many, many children *and* adults. In this context, **teaching a Sunday school class** became an important way for someone to "do religion." Also, to be noted: **singing in the choir, ushering, preparing a potluck supper dish,** and—a huge one—**serving on a church committee!** The point

---

7. Survey finding in Putnam/Campbell, *American Grace*, 17.

is that in the United States, the church found ways to get people involved and to show their faith. The effort helped American churches be strong and grow. In addition to Sunday schools, many parochial schools were set up. Christians founded colleges and universities; for example, Congregationalists did so from Harvard to Hawai'i Pacific. In Christian colleges or in state universities, Christian students may **take a religion class** or **be in an off-campus Bible study**. All educational efforts sought to ensure an educated and believing laity and clergy.

While the above is an account of what was happening with the Christianity in America, there was in the world seismic change around "knowing" itself. Pietism arose in Europe and spread broadly; it was a response to dry and intellectual theology, as well as to objectivity and materialism in science and reason. Pietism was a spiritual movement "of the heart," of emotion, of interiority. It influenced almost all Christian churches, best signaled in Moravianism and Methodism.[8] Pietism called for a **deepening of prayer life**, **regular study of scripture**, and **personal holiness**. If pietism had a most-articulate spokesperson, it would be Blaise Pascal, a Catholic, who wrote, "The heart has its reasons, of which reason knows nothing." Theologians and ordinary believers came to the conviction that the inner life is the primary realm of the Holy. So people **spoke more about their "feeling" for God**. God's existence was not to be proven by logic or pointing to historical events, much less made known by decisions of church councils or even sacred scripture. The oncoming modern religious world lodged itself increasingly in private "spirituality." Meaningful personal experiences/feelings, through nature, music, or story, came to connect believers to the Holy. One form that pietism took was to encourage **saying grace/giving thanks at meals**, a relatively new form of religiosity.

While pietism was happening for some, a secular way of life developed for many others, as many, especially in Europe, lost interest in religion. Some even came to hate it, most pointedly the Jacobins in late-eighteenth-century France and the Bolshevik Communists, who took over in Russia during the twentieth century. Each tried to stamp out the church—the Catholic Church in France, the Orthodox Church in Russia. Ultimately, neither stamping out succeeded. Napoleon worked out a concordat with Rome, and Gorbachev much the same with Russian Orthodox priests and believers in 1991.

---

8. See an opening quotation of this chapter to sample what pietism meant for John Wesley.

Practices and Pieties of The Pilgrimage

Two hundred years after the advent of pietism, two related forms of Christianity ignited. One formation was Pentecostalism, characterized by **speaking in tongues** or *glossolalia*, but also other Spirit manifestations, such as **casting out demons, divine interventions,** and **faith healings.** Sometimes in ecstatic worship what social scientists call "involuntary motor behaviors" occurred: **weeping, being in-tranced, exuberant singing, and dancing.**[9] The charismatic movement, as Pentecostalism is also called, began at the turn of the last century. The Azusa Street Revival of 1905 in Los Angeles is one of its starting points. In the course of the century, Pentecostalism swept through Latin America, Africa, Southeast Asia, and, really, one-can't-say-where-all. It was an ecumenicity of ecstasy, not of ecclesial structures. One group of Pentecostals began to **baptize in the name of Jesus only**, not the Trinity.

Spreading around the world, Pentecostal and other, older Christianities picked up features important in the indigenous cultures they entered. Masai Africans, by custom, ever bearing wooden staffs, affixed a horizontal bar to their staffs, so they now are found **bearing stave crosses**. In another tradition, Christian Maori in New Zealand continued to **tattoo themselves**, now with some Jesus symbols. Almost everywhere in southern Christianity there has been a renewal of miraculous healings, often performed by "prophets" (a functional office spoken of in the Bible but not much present in northern Christianity). People **come to the prophet for a-healin.'**

Conjoint with Pentecostalism was another religious movement of the last century, fundamentalism, a reaction to modernity and "liberal" Christian theology. This new conservatism's ideology took form from Princeton Seminary, beginning in 1910, theologians there issuing *The Fundamentalist Papers*. In the course of the century, fundamentalist Christians began to call themselves evangelicals. Though it was seemingly antiscience and antimodernity, ironically, fundamentalism-evangelicalism adopted the scientific worldview, making biblical faith *objective* and *literal*, not necessarily allegorical or mystical. Such a stance fit in well with the general cultural milieu in America. So it became the most popular expression of Christian faith in America. Emphasis always was on *individual* salvation and the responsibility to **testify to your neighbor**. During the course of the last one hundred years, many of the aversive pieties of early fundamentalism disappeared,

---

9. Screaming, howling, barking, numbness, weightlessness, shivering, profuse sweating, rolling on the floor, and frothing at the mouth also have been observed among some sects.

namely, **not dancing, not wearing lipstick or shorts, not shopping or cooking on Sunday, not going to movies,** and, often, **not drinking.** Evangelicals now do almost all of these. At the present they are mostly **against gay marriage and abortion.**

The numerical growth of Christianity, much of it via Pentecostal evangelicalism, has been phenomenal. In Africa the number of Christians in 1914 was about 4 million. By 2025 it is predicted that the number will be 633 million! In Africa today there are thousands of indigenous Christian denominations, sects, and movements and thousands of imported evangelical-pentecostal groups. They exist alongside longer-established Catholic, Anglican, Lutheran, and mainline Protestant churches. Of whatever brand name, hardly a one is not still **praying, in their own languages, "Our Father who art . . ."**

*

The social gospel movement, arising in the United States in the mid-nineteenth century within traditional Protestant circles and through the YMCA, was different from Pentecostalism and evangelicalism in that it was focused not so much on individual salvation but on social transformation. To show forth their faith, these Christians turned toward activism, **working to ameliorate unjust societal conditions**, especially conditions brought on by industrialization. Social gospelers were sympathetic to labor unions, encouraged women's rights, worked for Prohibition, spoke against war, and advocated for economic justice. Between the World Wars of the last century, the social gospel movement slowed down, but it took on new life and form in the last half of the twentieth century. Most notably, social arena effort was given to the civil rights struggle of black Americans.

Christians began **marching for integration**. A few years later they were **marching for women's liberation,** and regularly some **took to the streets for peace.** In the 1960s and 70s there was strong protest by mainline Protestants and Vatican II Catholic Christians against the war in Vietnam. On February 15, 2003, Christians of this type took part in the largest anti-war rally in the history of the world, against America's invasion of Iraq. In Rome alone three million people gathered in the streets to protest. It was, most unfortunately, to no avail. The powers that be "had their way."

In Latin and South American countries, especially among Catholic Christians, social concern took the name liberation theology. Liberation theology meant to **do the work of conscientization** in base communities, *awakening* the faithful in small groups with Bible study *and* social analysis, both emphases aimed at freeing and empowering the marginalized.

As to other issues shaping behavior, the environment itself came front and center for Christian response. In truth, environmental awareness was enlivened by men and women who study the earth, namely, *scientists*. They awakened Christians to work at healing her. A new modern piety, then, has come forward: **being ecological**. Widely now, Sunday school **children make Whole Earth posters, families separate their trash**, and in the spring each year **folks observe Earth Day**. All these acts are, for these Christians, acts of faithfulness.

Earth piety, however, should not be read to suggest that older, traditional Christian ways of being religious have disappeared. People still **attend Sunday worship, read their Bibles**, and **whisper "Now I lay me down"**—or an equivalent—at bedtime. Sometimes they/we **act toward the next door neighbor as toward Christ**.

In this 450-plus-year modern period under consideration, the world has grown smaller because of ships, trains, planes, television, cell phones, and the Internet. We know we are connected. Christians have always *said* so, and in this period attempts to connect and reconnect historic Christian groups have been made. The effort is ecumenism. The spirit of Christian unity was well symbolized when Pope John XXIII called together a council of bishops in the 1960s. Vatican II opened up Catholicism to the world in ways previously closed. It commenced conversations among separated Christian communions. So some people have "done their religious thing" by **taking part in ecumenical dialogues** and/or **observing World Communion Sunday**. Catholics, Baptists, and Orthodox have joined in **walking a labyrinth together**, perhaps in France's Chartres Cathedral, perhaps in the courtyard of a Kansas country church.

One encouraging aspect in present-day America is **growth of tolerance**,[10] as reported by Putnam and Campbell in their book *American Grace*. By large majority opinions, Mormons, Catholics, mainline Protestants, black Protestants, and evangelical Protestants believe that "people not of my faith, including non-Christians, can go to heaven."[11] If one asks how such a high degree of tolerance came about, the answer is Aunt Susan.

---

10. This may also be read as a victory of liberal or progressive Christianity in the culture war of the twentieth century. Robert Bellah, a sociologist of religion, believes that liberal Protestantism has been eclipsed in numbers because it has been so successful with its social-cultural agenda!

11. Putnam and Campbell, *American Grace*, 537.

Brief Christian Histories

Most everyone has an Aunt Susan, "a saint" but of a faith tradition not one's own. Aunt Susan's piety, her practices, her grace-full way of being in the world inspire admiration and create acceptance of difference in religious affiliation. Behavior matters. It is as though Constantine's 312-CE Edict of Toleration finally has come to fruition via saintly persons.

For this period, match

contemporary practices	*faith history happenings*
a. saying grace at meals	1. social gospel movement
b. being ecological	2. Vatican II
c. speaking in tongues	3. rise of science
d. witnessing to a neighbor	4. Azusa Street revival
e. marching for civil rights	5. church-state separation
f. watching televangelists	6. Great Awakenings
g. walking an ecumenical labyrinth	7. Moravian pietism

(My answers to the above are a-7, b-3, c-4, d-5, e-1, f-6, and g-2.)

*

The Gospel of John ends with these words,

> There are also many other things that Jesus did;
> if every one of them were written down,
> I suppose that the world itself could not contain
> the books that would be written.

The *"many other things"* may be said about the varieties of religious expression in the Christian faith. We have mentioned some—**dance**, for example. Dancing to the Lord began in our faith story, at least, when "David danced" and continues to the present. Dan Crawford, a Brethren missionary arriving in Africa, watched a convert-lady dancing. As he watched, he grasped how great were the marvels he himself could hardly enter:

> To me, a newcomer, what a gazing-stock! The amazing, maddening mix-up of the prayer of the heart, and the prance of the feet! I asked her what it meant at all, and she quaintly replied, "Oh, it is only the prance getting out at the toes."[12]

12. Quoted in MacCulloch, *Christianity,* 881.

Practices and Pieties of The Pilgrimage

Drumming is the way of and to faith expression in some Pacific Rim cultures, as well as in Native American Christianity. **Chanting with staff pounding** is the way to be faithful in Armenian Christian circles. Some Protestant Christians **will lock themselves in their bathroom** to read the Bible and pray—for one, my mother, to whom this book is dedicated. Orthodox homes often **have a "bright/red/beautiful corner"** where icons are kept and candles burn. In Central America, as suggested in the opening of this chapter, **carrying a heavy bier bearing a Santos during Lent** is a way in holiness.

What else? Distributing tracts . . . aspersing water . . . snake handling . . . keeping silence. And on and on. (See the "Practices and Pieties List" in Appendix B.)

While Søren Kierkegaard says the knight of faith walks through Deer Park in Copenhagen giving no *outward* indication of holiness, it should be noted that *he*, Kierkegaard, expressed his faith in **much writing**. Others have been known to do the same.

Questions for Reflection and Discussion

1. If someone were to follow you around with a camera for a week, how would they "catch you" being a Christian?

2. Do you think more Christian practices come from the Bible or from church history? Or the culture? Illustrate for each source.

3. Is there a practice or piety that is sine qua non—absolutely essential—in the Christian life? What might it be? Praying? Attending mass? Charitable giving? What?

4. Of central events in the history of our faith, which events most shaped/shapes Christian practice and piety: the exodus, prophetic utterance, Jesus' teaching, the Edict of Toleration, monastic *Rules*, Franciscan spirituality, Protestant pietism, science and reason, or the current culture wars?

5. Who do you feel is the faith figure most shaping Christian practices and piety today? Moses? Isaiah? Jesus? St. Paul? Augustine? Pope Innocent III of the 4th Lateran Council? John Wesley? Aunt Susan?

Chapter 4

Christ and Culture Interacting
Societal Settings, Dynamics, and Formations of the Faith

A wandering Aramean was my ancestor; he went down into Egypt and lived there as an alien, few in number, and there he became a great nation, mighty and populous. When the Egyptians treated us harshly . . . we cried to Yahweh. . . . Yahweh brought us out . . . into this place and gave us this land, a land flowing with milk and honey.

—Deuteronomy 26:5b–9

What indeed has Athens to do with Jerusalem? What concord is there between the Academy and the Church? What between heretics and Christians? Our instruction comes from "the porch of Solomon," who had himself taught that "the Lord should be sought in simplicity of heart."

—Tertullian (160–230 CE), *Against Heretics*

If history lasts long enough for archaeologists some five hundred or a thousand years hence, say, to dig back into our age, I predict they will be stunned by what they discover. I picture them in their beards with pith helmets unearthing the movies and plays and television we watched, pouring over the books we read, the art we created, the kind of black comedy we laughed at, and the kinds of horrors that fascinated us on the evening news, violence without motive. Darkness without escape. Sex without love or beauty. The criminal, the monstrous, the demonic. I picture them staggered to discover how obsessed we were with the very madness that destroyed us. I picture them unearthing the steam tables in our church kitchens and wondering, for all the world, what kind of sacrifices we offered.

—Frederick Buechner, *A Room Called Remember*

Though Jesus instructed his disciples—and us—to be "*in* but not *of* this world,"[1] we know we've been *in* many cultures and societies and, oftentimes, *of* them. H. Richard Niebuhr, in his book *Christ and Culture*,[2] offers five typologies suggesting the dynamic relationship the Christian religion has had with the world. He speaks of

> Christ against culture
>
> Christ of culture
>
> Christ above culture
>
> Christ and culture in paradox
>
> Christ the transformer of culture

"Christ," of course, means, "Christianity," and, in this book, Christ or Christianity means to include configurations of the faith both of the last two thousand years (110 CE–present) *and* during biblical times (1800 BCE to 110 CE). "Culture" in these pages suggests prevailing sociopolitical-ideological systems in which our faith-parents were involved, CE and BCE.

Societies/culture/"the times" have shaped our faith in numerous ways, positive and negative, sometimes giving distinctive new character and form to our religion. On the other hand, this lively historic faith of ours has also influenced those societies, cultures, and times. In this chapter, then, we (1) look at the cultural settings in which our religion has lived, (2) see what

---

1. Actually this phrase is *not* in the Bible but is, in essence, contained in John 17:15–16. See also Romans 12:2, "Do not be conformed to this world, but be transformed by the renewing of your mind."

2. Niebuhr, *Christ and Culture*, 39–44, for an overview.

religious institutionalizations emerged in response, and (3) say how the faith has likewise influenced the world(s) of which it has been a part. For the purpose of highlighting various aspects, I bold **religious formations, institutionalizations, and features** that came to be in various historical settings. When using H. Richard Niebuhr's "Christ and culture" method of considering religious-societal interaction, I italicize prepositions like *over, under, of,* and so on.

For better or worse, culture is the water in which people, as fish, swim. To change the imagery, culture is the encapsulating bubble that we live in and see *through*. Seldom, though, do we see it—that is, the culture. In reviewing various historical cultural settings of our faith, however, we could begin to see our water, our bubble, a little better. At least, that is the hope. Familiarity with Christ and culture dynamics of the past four thousand years might give clues to help us live, work, and worship *in* our time. And who knows . . . Christians might influence our contemporary social setting a bit, even positively! In the last section of this chapter, we'll come back to present-day cultural analysis.

PRE-MONARCHIC MILLENNIUM (2000–1000 BCE)

Our faith story with cultic shape and culture begins with Abram and Sarai. Their time was about 1800 BCE. Living in Ur of the Chaldeans, today's southern Iraq, theirs was a Mesopotamian culture, built on an older Sumerian-Akkadian civilization. The Sumerians had been dominant in the third millennium BCE. When Abram and Sarai wandered from Ur up the Euphrates Valley to Haran, in today's southern Turkey, it is possible they brought some prevalent narrative legends (e.g., *The Epic of Gilgamesh*) and culture with them. Conceivably our **foundational biblical stories**—garden of Eden, great flood, and tower of Babel—had origin from such ancient source. Let me hasten to say that, these stories might have been picked up fourteen hundred years later, when our faith-parents were tied into another, later culture, the Babylonian. The point is that something of early-second-millennium Mesopotamian culture doubtless shaped the religion of our earliest religious ancestors.

One interpretation of the move of Abram and Sarai is that it was *against* culture; that is, they could not live comfortably in the urban setting of Chaldea and so fled from it, inspired to travel to a new land to which God would lead them. Settled life and Babylonian religion were not for them. They were, I believe, basically nomads. If so, the culture of this period most noticeably shaping ancestral faith was desert nomadic. James Kirk, world religions professor at the University of Denver, contends that physical environment gives considerable contour to people's religious sensibilities. So those who live near great rivers, experiencing the regular rise and fall of the waters, come to a more cyclical understanding of God, as in India. Persons who live in a tropical forest, with abundant, lush vegetation and multiple shapes and sounds, could be inclined toward belief in many gods.

Our religious ancestors were "wandering Arameans," that is, they were Semites, desert tribesmen and tribeswomen—bedouins, if you will—living on the edge of the Fertile Crescent of the Middle East. Under a vast sky and a sparse landscape, the religious imagination could run toward a more unitary image of God, even of one God. Moreover, since life on the desert is fragile, such life could dictate that, under God and to survive, "we need to treat one another in hospitable ways." The tribal people who came to be known as Israel, responding to their environmental setting, tilted toward **monotheistic religion** with significant **ethics**.

In this regard, the greatest, specific human influence on the faith was the Kenite tribe of the Sinai Peninsula. The Kenites were the people to whom Moses fled when he had to leave Egypt. This was about the year 1250 BCE. In the tribe the influencer most significant was his father-in-law, Jethro, a priest. Jethro's desert religious seems to have been monotheistic. It deepened Moses and opened him to the burning-bush religious experience described in the book of Exodus, chapter 3. From that religious experience, Moses learned the name of the Lord, *Yahweh*, and received orders to lead the People of Israel out of their slavery in Egypt.

Egypt/Egyptian culture is the next great faith-shaping social reality. Contrary to the above theory of the *desert* origins of monotheism, belief in one God might have been insight appropriated from the Egyptian pharaoh Akhenaten. Akhenaten had notions of a unitive god, a sun god, called Aten. Certainly Sigmund Freud suggests that is where Moses got the notion of one God.[3] What we most want to understand about Egyptian culture, though, is how Israel understood itself to have been born out of the experience of living under Egyptian rule. According to the Bible, our nomadic ancestors went down to live in Egypt and there resided for 450 years, perhaps 1700

---

3. Cf. Freud, *Moses and Monotheism*, 27.

to 1250 BCE. They lived there as slaves under a dominative power. The experience gave them greater **empathy for the dispossessed**, the poor, the least, and the lost. Such empathy is a major ongoing ethical characteristic of our faith. Forever after, right to the present, when the faithful remember their Egyptian experience, they/we will call for a doing right by the "wretched of the earth." The usual descriptive formula is "remember the widow, the orphan, and the stranger at your gate." Why? Because "you were once strangers in the land of Egypt" (Deuteronomy 10:19).

Living *under* Egyptian hegemony gave way to being *against* that culture and eventually to leaving it, just as Abram and Sarai left Chaldea. God through Moses, the Bible asserts, led the children of Israel out of bondage. This is the exodus to the wilderness. Then for forty years our ancestors wandered in the desert, honing their faith. On Mount Sinai, Moses received ten crucial commandments, specifying duties toward Yahweh and one another. The former slaves entered into a **covenant community**. This self-understanding, of being in a social-contract-plus relationship with (1) God and (2) each other, is the most important institutionalization to emerge from the exodus and desert wandering. So our faith-parents became the **People of God**.

Concrete artifacts symbolizing the emerging religion were the stone tablets of the Ten Commandments, stored in a portable wooden box called the Ark of the Covenant. One can well imagine a caravan in procession moving along the eastern ridges of the lower Jordan Rift, periodically pitching camp and laying out a special tabernacle or area for the placement of the Ark. This is a people and religion in the making.

Two other religious formations entered into the patriarchs' and matriarchs' experience from being in Egypt. One is the idea of **priesthood**, something major in Egyptian culture. Early on, Moses' brother Aaron came to fulfill this role. It would be a major feature of our religion in time. Secondly, an understanding of **kingship** and how a monarch operates certainly entered Israelite consciousness. Though the institution of having a king for the incipient nation was resisted, it did come to pass.

If Moses left Egypt around 1250 BCE, by the next century the People of Israel were entering Palestine with its Canaanite culture. Joshua was their leader onto "the promised land." While our faith narrative (the Bible) has it that entry into the land was just by Joshua and his people, in actuality some kin may have already been in the area. Perhaps they never left Palestine. However it was, our nomadic ancestors came to dwell amid the more settled native Canaanites. The Canaanites practiced a fertility religion, cyclical in nature, involving a male storm deity called Ba'al, symbolized by a bull; the religion had a female goddess, Astarte. In the Canaanite myth, Astarte went underground in the fall; then in the spring Ba'al brought her back to restart the growing season. In addition to those principle deities, Canaanites had small household gods, statue figurines. The whole mix was polytheistic. As our Israelite ancestors became a settled people, elements of Canaanite fertility worship entered into monotheistic Yahwism. The **first-fruits harvest festival**, for example, indicates a bowing to agrarian cultural ways. In addition, as the Canaanites placed their temples in "high places," so did the Israelites, and the bull became a sometimes-symbol in Yahwist observance. Still, Israelite monotheism pushed back against polytheism, sometimes superseding it.

Other desert people competed with the Israelites for control of Canaan. The Midianites, for one, had to be fought off. As nomads, the Midianites came into Palestine looking for grazing land, much as the desert-wandering Israelites themselves may have done.

Even so, the Israelites' major adversary was the Philistines. A seafaring people, perhaps from Mycenaean Greece, the Philistines came ashore on the southeast Mediterranean coast (roughly, today's Gaza) and settled. By *iron* sword—better than any bronze weapon—they began to cut their way north and east into lands of the Israelites. Fearing the threat of takeover, the loose federation of Israelite tribes began to come together. Samson the judge, for example, fought *against* the Philistines. Later in time, Saul and David, each separately crowned king by the prophet Samuel, joined the fight. David prevailed and out of the conflict with the Philistines forged a **united kingdom of Israel**. That was about the year 1000 BCE.

TIME OF THE KINGS AND PROPHETS (1000–550 BCE)

David centered his government and our faith in our most holy city, Jerusalem. The wilderness-carried Ark of the Covenant with the Ten Commandments tablets came into Zion, David leading the procession, dancing. Now in essence nation and religion were one, each *of* the other. As nation-religion in tribal society, Israel was for a while relatively independent of other regional powers. What made such independence possible was that the perennial megapowers of the Middle East—Babylon to the east,

Assyria to the north, and Egypt in the south—were neither strong nor aggressive for a time. It was even possible for the kingdom of Israel to expand its borders, especially so during the reign of David's son Solomon. Most importantly, though, Solomon built a temple, *the* temple, **the temple of Solomon**. It became the center for religious life, functioning so for almost four hundred years, until 586 BCE.

The architectural model for Solomon's temple was provided by the Phoenicians, a people living north and west of Israel, in what is now Lebanon. They were craftsmen who used "the cedars of Lebanon"[4] to build boats *and* to construct temples. Equally important, the Phoenicians introduced the Israelites to writing with an alphabet that ultimately made our faith-parents a literate people and the first **people of the book**.

In this period, however, the Israelites were more nearly **people of the temple**. Our ancestors had the Aaronic/Levitical **priesthood**. The Levites, one of the historic twelve tribes of Israel, were set aside to serve the nation in Solomon's temple. In that society they stood—as priests everywhere do—between the people and God, offering sacrifices, prayers, music, and ritual to God.

The Jerusalem temple with its priests continued to function in this way for centuries, but not for all the tribes of the confederacy. After Solomon's reign, the political situation changed. The united kingdom split north and south. For the next two hundred years, then, we have a culture of parallel kingdoms. This meant a couple of things. One is that that the northern kingdom—often called Israel, sometimes Ephraim—forsook the temple in Jerusalem and developed alternative **worship centers**, notably in Shechem and Bethel. The northern kings sometimes allowed the old religions, such as that of Ba'al, to be practiced alongside Yahwism, placing the faith more *under* culture.

North and south also developed differing stories for their past. Scholars believe there was a J writer with a southern or **Judean** point of view. J speaks more easily about J*ahweh* or *Yahweh* and has a favorite ancestral person in Abraham. In the northern kingdom, aka Ephraim, the E author pulls together tales that lifted up the patriarch Israel/Jacob. E used the name *Elohim* for God. Both writers were developing our **sacred stories**.

---

4. It is held that the wooden pillars in Solomon's temple were *spiraled* . . . and so the baldachin altar canopy pillars in St. Peter's Cathedral in Rome, built in the fifteenth century CE, were modeled. The spiral tradition spread to Spain and ultimately to the American Southwest, so that to this day the entrance posts in many Native American adobe churches, from Texas to California, are the same.

Christ and Culture Interacting

Without doubt the most important response to the societal-cultural phenomenon of the two parallel kingdoms was the rise of the religious institution of **the prophets**. It is hard to say exactly how this establishment occurred, but we do know that Samuel, who anointed Saul, and then David, to be king, was called a prophet. As often as not, the prophets stood *over* and *against* the culture of the kings and their priests, seeking ways to *transform* religious and ethical life in a more godly direction. The prophets spoke **the Word of the Lord**, often interpreting the times as determined by obedience or disobedience to Yahweh. A most important early prophet was Elijah, confronting King Ahab and Queen Jezebel of the northern kingdom. The writing prophets of the eighth and seventh centuries include Amos, Hosea, Micah, Isaiah, and Jeremiah. They too sought to *transform* their societies. Prophetic utterance came to constitute a vital and long-important component in our faith.

The Word that the prophets spoke was always uttered to keep the nation, the society, the culture from absolutizing itself, from pretending that its way was the way and will of Yahweh. "Not so!" they insisted. The eighth-century prophets were able to speak so because they lived out a **radical monotheism** with a decidedly **ethical foundation**. The prophet Isaiah, for example, held that even the evil enemy Assyria was "the rod of *God's* anger" (Isaiah 10:5). God's favorable or unfavorable judgments, Isaiah believed, would be meted out on the basis of the people's faithfulness to Yahweh and the practice of moral righteousness. The prophets held, further, that even if the people proved faithless and destruction came—as it did—the mercy of God would finally be greater than God's wrath. God is faithful, they said, though all the world prove false.

In the southern kingdom, with its capital in Jerusalem, only loyal Yahwists, such as King Josiah, who instituted temple reform in 621 BCE, received good marks from those who oversaw Bible history. In truth, Josiah may have been responsible for the first tentative assembling of **the Bible**, subsidizing and directing writer(s) to interpret the nation's history and to re-present the Law.[5] Such re-presenting is especially seen in the book of Deuteronomy or Second Law. Deuteronomy, along with the books Joshua, Judges, Samuel, and Kings, is attributed to a D author.

Josiah's reign was one of those times when the faith/"Christ" was *transforming* culture.

---

5. Cf. Finkelstein and Silberman, *Bible Unearthed*, 1–3.

Brief Christian Histories

What was troubling Josiah in the late seventh century BCE was the continuation of invasions by then-active regional superpowers. Little Judah in the south and only slightly stronger Ephraim in the north long had been beset by the armies of Syria. Then came the more powerful Assyrians. Ephraim fell to them in 722 BCE and was simply dismantled. Northern kingdom leaders and many people of the land were carried away, never heard from again. Those who remained on the land intermarried with foreigners brought in by the Assyrians. So the inhabitants of the region become known as the Samaritans. So far as those living in Judah were concerned, the Samaritans practiced a "corrupt Yahwism."[6] The Judeans, meanwhile, survived the fate of their Ephraimite brothers by paying heavy tribute to the Assyrians.

The two parallel kingdoms were reduced to one.

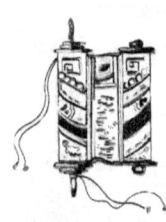

SECOND TEMPLE PERIOD (550–20 BCE)

Josiah's fear in 621, that little Judah might be overcome by a superpower, came to pass in 586 BCE. In a "year that will live in infamy," Jerusalem fell to Nebuchadnezzar, king of Babylon. Once again leading citizens were carried off into exile, this time to the Tigris and Euphrates Rivers area. Some citizens fled to Egypt, starting the *Diaspora*, a scattering of the faithful.

More may be said about the influence of Babylonian culture. For fifty years the primary leaders of old Jerusalem/Judah lived "by the waters of Babylon," longing for their Holy City and land six hundred miles away. A consuming problem for the exiles was how to respond faithfully in their captive circumstance. The prophet Jeremiah counseled the people, "Build houses and live in them; plant gardens and eat what they produce. Take wives and have sons and daughters . . . multiply there, and do not decrease. But **seek the welfare of the city** where I have sent you into exile, and pray to the Lord on its behalf, for in its welfare you will find your welfare" (Jeremiah 29:5–7). And pray to the Lord they did, much of their prayer being lamentation, as reflected in the verse, "O God, you have rejected us, broken our defenses; you have been angry; now restore us" (Psalm 60:1). They were adjusting to the new cultural setting.

---

6. Today, these semi-original inhabitants are the Druze, occupants of the mountainous area of northern Israel and southern Lebanon.

As they longed, they also listened. So at this time and in this culture—though *possibly* a millennium earlier—they heard **stories** of a seven-day creation, of a world flood, and of the building of the tower or ziggurat of Babel. Over time these stories went into the Bible.

Then came the year 539 BCE. In that year King Cyrus of Persia defeated the Babylonians. So now and for the next two hundred years, Persian culture was the dominating presence in our faith-parents' world. One of Cyrus's first acts was to allow captive peoples to return to their ancestral homes. In 538 BCE our people—increasingly called Jews (from *Je*rusalem, *Ju*dea)—went home. Some commentators say of the exiles, "They went out a nation and came back a religion."

Back home, the returnees quickly rebuilt **the temple.** (So we call this the Second Temple Period.) Though *under* the suzerainty of Persia, the Judeans were allowed to put a protective wall around Jerusalem. Somewhat secure, religious leaders then *began* to assemble **the Hebrew Bible**, our Older Testament, sometimes called *Tanakh*. The *Tanakh* finally had three major portions to it: the Law, the Prophets, and the Writings. Here's a quick overview of the parts:

Ta—Torah. The first five books of the Bible (Genesis, Exodus, Leviticus, Numbers, and Deuteronomy) constitute the Teachings, Law, or Torah, created from older sources previously mentioned (J, E, and D). Those most ancient writings were given final form by a P/priestly writer and by R/redactors during these centuries.

Na—Nevi'im. The scrolls of the Prophets were added to Torah, to include oracles of the eighth-century prophets and later writers, such as Second Isaiah and Ezekiel, concluding with the book of the prophet Malachi.

Kh—Ketuvim. Thirdly, to the Law and the Prophets, the Writings came in, books such as Psalms and Proverbs.

For Jews today there are twenty-four books in the *Tanakh*, but for most Christians there are thirty-nine, the difference being how the manuscripts are divided—for example, Samuel alone vs. 1 Samuel and 2 Samuel.

Dispersed throughout the Middle East, North Africa, and Mediterranean Europe, our ancestors always had this question before them: "How do we keep the faith while being strangers in a strange land?" Their answer was threefold.

First, they maintained themselves by adhering to **the Bible**. The Bible was a *portable* sacred referent to keep them religiously and ethically grounded. The second creative response in the scattered condition was to set aside persons to interpret the Law-Prophets-Writings for the community. Hence the office of **teacher** or **rabbi** came into being. Rabbis in the Diaspora replaced priests back in Jerusalem. Thirdly, since they were no longer able to worship and offer sacrifices at the Jerusalem temple, the Bible-centered, rabbi-led faithful gathered in a local **synagogue** to study, pray, and support one another. Thus the faith was kindled on distant shores and in different climes. A new Judaism, what we call **rabbinic Judaism**, was coming into being in the wider world of sundry cultures and societies.

Wherever they went and were, some of the faithful sensed that the world was too much with them. Many then tried to draw back from the Gentiles (non-Jews) and Gentile society. They tried **isolationism**, tried to be *separate from* the culture. The books of Ezra and Nehemiah, for example, show aversion to all things foreign. These leader-writers discouraged social interchange—especially cross-cultural marriage—with non-Jewish others, such as mixed-blood Samaritans. They urged Jewish men to divorce their non-Jewish wives.

Other leader-writers took a more universalistic—even evangelical— stance with regard to foreign nations and people. The books Ruth and Jonah make the case for drawing a bigger circle. They prescribed an **inclusive community**. The writer known as Third Isaiah, who wrote Isaiah 56–66 and lived under the Persians, was of such broad mind, saying of Jerusalem, "Nations/the Gentiles shall come to your light" (Isaiah 60:3).

So we see two different responses: withdrawal from surrounding culture and engagement with surrounding culture. We may say this was faith and culture *in paradox*.

Insofar as our ancestors did not just "hold on" but actually opened themselves to non-Jews, they were influenced in thought and practice. Certainly Persian/Zoroastrianism culture made a huge impact. Zoroastrianism suggested **dualistic theological concepts** to Hebrew imagination:

Good vs. Evil

Heaven vs. Hell

Angels vs. Demons.

Satan, unknown earlier to our faith-parents, shows up in the book of Job. The **notion of a resurrection** of the deceased, also not present in

Christ and Culture Interacting

Israel's earlier understanding, gets traction while Jews were living under Persian influence. By Jesus' time, questions about the resurrection shape debate between tradition-keeping, temple-centered Sadducees, who did not believe in the resurrection, and closer-to-the-people, synagogue-related Pharisees, who did.

In the late fourth century BCE, "Gentile" came mostly to mean "Greek." Alexander the Great of Macedonia defeated the Persians in 333 BCE, and so Greek or Hellenic culture became dominant in the eastern Mediterranean lands. That influence would hardly wane for the next almost-eighteen-hundred years. With over a million Jews living in Alexandria, our faith-parents were soon speaking Greek and thinking Greek. Greek philosophical thought stretched older concepts about God, humanity, and life. For one thing, they took to the Platonic idea of "soul" and "souls," and such notions have been around ever since. The Jewish scholar Philo of Alexandria attempted a serious synthesis of Hebrew and Hellenic thought. He suggested that God's ineffable *essence* (a Greek concept) was manifested in Sophia/**Wisdom** by which God created the world (a Jewish concept). Writers added ideas about "her" (that is, *Sophia*) into the Older Testament, saying, "The Lord by Sophia founded the earth" and "The Lord created me [Sophia] at the beginning of his work" (Proverbs 3:19 and 8:22). There is no way to overstate what powerful influence Greek and Hellenic culture had on our faith, BCE and CE. The Hebrew scripture was translated into Greek, that translation known as **the Septuagint** or **LXX**. It was read by Jews *and* by Greek-speaking people who became interested in our religion. It was the Bible known and used by writers of the Newer Testament.

Happy to say, (1) what our ancestors experienced over their then almost-two-thousand-year journey, (2) what they concluded in their scriptures, and (3) how they lived out their faith were attractive—yea, compelling—to some. **God-fearers**, persons from the wider world drawn to the faith, showed up in the synagogue. They were positively inclined. They liked two things in particular about our religion: (1) the notion of one supreme God, rather than many gods, and (2) the high ethical standards of the Bible and the Bible's people. It is by the God-fearers' coming around that the faith of Israel started to make inroads into wider societies of the Mediterranean world. Judaism was *transforming* culture, making an impact, at least.

Some Greeks, though, wanted to transform Judaism through Hellenizing it. One king of the Seleucid Greeks, Antiochus IV Epiphanes, among other affronts, placed a bust of a Greek god in the Jerusalem temple. To the faithful in Jerusalem, this brazen act was "the abomination that makes desolate" (Daniel 11:31). It precipitated an armed uprising, called the Maccabean revolt, *against* the Seleucids. The revolt began about the year 165 BCE, led by a Judas Maccabeus (aka as the Hammerer) and his brothers. After the Maccabees succeeded in ousting the Greeks, they rededicated the temple, the rededication now commemorated as **Hanukkah**. A century of relative independence for Judea under the Maccabean/Hasmonean families came with the ouster of the Greeks. It was a period of religious-political harmony, oneness, cultural *of*-ness.

Not for a minute dismissing ongoing Greek influence, now enter the Romans. In 63 BCE, Pompey came, saw, and conquered. All of Palestine, including Jerusalem, fell. The stage then was set for vassal kings, such as Herod the Great, to rule the country. With Roman approval, Herod reconstructed the Second Temple in BCE 20, which was an impressive redo. Now we might use the date of 20 BCE to bring the five-hundred-year period of religion-and-culture dynamics, which we've been considering, to a close.

Herod was king when two peasants, a Mary and a Joseph from Galilee (the northernmost section of Palestine), went south from Nazareth to Bethlehem in Judea to do their civic duty, be enrolled in a Roman census. While there, Mary bore a boy child. She and Joseph gave their son the name Jesus, meaning "God saves." He was *in* the world and by God's grace with God's people, come to save the world—so we affirm.

NEWER TESTAMENT PERIOD (20 BCE–110 CE)

By the time of the birth of Jesus, Palestine was in a **Judaism**-traditioned, **Aramaic**-speaking, **Greek**-influenced, **Roman**-controlled world. Roman governors or their surrogates enforced imperial law and kept the people pacified, requiring payment of taxes to support Rome's far-flung empire. In general, the ruling Romans were tolerant of native religions, but they certainly did not like Jewish infighting, especially when it caused difficulty for them. In Palestine there were

- the Zealots fomenting armed rebellion
- the escape-the-world Essenes at Qumran
- the keeping-themselves-pure, synagogue-related Pharisees and scribes
- the Roman-colluding Herodians
- the temple-supporting Sadducees

and, in time, a sect of Judaism whose people came to be called **Christians.** Christian adherents were most like the Pharisees, believing, among other things, in the resurrection of the dead.

How could these women and men *not* so believe?

It happened. Their rabbi, Jesus, executed by the Roman authorities, was raised to life from his burial tomb. He was the resurrection! Jesus' resurrection was—and is—the mind-boggling, foundational event for Christian faith. This man *of the world* became the Christ/Messiah/Anointed/Lord *of heaven*, the full announcement of God's love and forgiveness for the world. The resurrection, with its promise of new life, is why the earliest Christians-as-Christians proclaimed Good News/Gospel to all who would listen.

If the Gentiles could accept the resurrection—which they could, for overcoming death was *something a god might do*—they actually had more trouble believing that one-of-God could be crucified. Jesus' death on a cross was too ignoble a way for a deity to die. It was something reserved for base criminals. How plausibly to explain the crucifixion, then, was more a problem in the early church than explaining the resurrection.

Christians who reflected about Jesus' death, notably Paul of Tarsus, came to the conclusion that Jesus' crucifixion effected a reconciliation between God and humanity. The innocent one (Jesus, in whom God fully dwelt), Paul said, died on behalf of guilty men and women, who of themselves could not right-wise themselves with God. God's sacrificial offering of himself/herself in Christ effected that needed reconciliation. It brought about an "at-one-ment" between God and humanity.[7] Thus St. Paul interpreted Jesus' death for Gentile acceptance. It seemed to work, for many Gentiles came to be believers-in and followers-of Jesus as the Christ.

After (1) proclaiming the resurrection and (2) explaining the crucifixion, the third move that early Christians made was (3) lifting up the teachings of their Lord. Jesus was remembered as having spoken of God as *Abba*/"Daddy" and preaching about a **Basileia** or **Kingdom** or **Reign** or **Realm of God** beyond time and space, and yet in time and space. He prayed for it and gave his followers a prayer, our **Lord's Prayer,** asking that the Basileia "come on earth"—to *transform* culture. Bible scholar Walter Wink says that Jesus' proclamation was for "God's domination-free order."[8]

---

7. There are other theories of the atonement, to the effect that Christ's death (1) ransomed humanity from the devil, (2) satisfied requirements of divine justice, or (3) exemplified God's love/provided a saving model for the world. (I personally find the exemplar argument the most helpful.)

8. Wink, *The Powers That Be*, 64.

Into this new order, all persons were invited to live, practicing a nonviolent way of life in a violent Roman culture. Fourthly, following remembered words, Christians attributed specialness to incidents from Jesus' life: a transfiguration, a baptism, and, finally, his birth. These they recorded in writings about him, writings called the Gospels.

In sum, the early Christians concluded that this man Jesus—what he taught, what he did, how he lived, what he died for, and how he rose—was/is the

>Messiah
>
>One anointed of God
>
>God with us
>
>Son of God
>
>Christ
>
>Lord

and many titles more. This child of the peasant couple, this Jesus of Nazareth, we are wont to say, so influenced subsequent history that time itself divides through his godly name. Time became BC (Before Christ) and AD (*anno Domini*/"Year of Our Lord"). Scholarly circles today use BCE (Before the Common Era) and CE (Common Era) as a more inclusive way to date time, as I've been doing in this book. This decision about the dividing of time at the supposed-year of Jesus' birth came about in the year 527, when a monk, Dionysius Exiguus, suggested it. Jesus' most likely year of birth was 4 or 6 BCE.

For this BCE/CE cusp period, let us observe that the sect being created was known by the name of "the Way" and "Christian" (meaning "follower of Christ"). The sect became the **Christian church**, born out of an older-cultural Judaism, an everywhere-pervasive Greek society, and a then-dominant Roman Empire.[9] Christians took the name "church" from the Greek word *ecclesia*, meaning "called together." They saw themselves as called together to honor God through Jesus Christ, to break bread in a

---

9. Judaism of today, with its synagogue-based, Torah-focused, rabbi-led character, was also born during this same period, with the same cultural backdrop. The image I like for what happened is that of a river dividing, splitting in two, creating two of the world's great religions: Christianity and Judaism. In truth, there are such waterways. One, in Canada, sends water west to the Pacific Ocean *and* north to Hudson Bay. Another, the Casiquiare Canal in South America, sends water north through Venezuela to the Gulf of Mexico *and* east through Brazil to the Atlantic Ocean.

Christ and Culture Interacting

ritual known as the Lord's Supper, and to be a community (*koinonia*) of love (*agape*), service (*diakonia*), and worship (*leitourgia*). They arranged church offices—presbyter to bishop—as career grades, even as done in Roman civil service.

The early Christians were missionary-minded. They traveled on the good roads and open shipping lanes that the Romans created. Especially they went to the urban centers of the far-flung Greco-Roman world, proclaiming in those cities the Good News of God's love in Christ. These missionary-evangelists, wherever they went, usually spoke first in synagogues to Jewish coreligionists of the Diaspora. Their testimony, though listened-to by Jews, was received most warmly by God-fearers, mentioned earlier, that is, the Gentiles who were associated with synagogues. Soon then there were predominately **Gentile congregations**, worshiping on Sunday mornings, the day Christ arose, rather than on the Sabbath/seventh day, as prescribed in Torah.

Changes in thought and practice precipitated a split between those Christians who adhered more closely to traditional practices (e.g., insisting on dietary laws for believers) and those who were closer to Greco-Roman ways (e.g., taking meals over the graves of departed loved ones). Paul's letters to the Corinthians make it clear there were differences within the church, and the book of Acts acknowledges disagreements too. There were sects and subdivisions within the movement. The more traditional branch of the church, centered in Jerusalem, tried to set up governance under Jesus' brother James. It became known as the **Ebionite Church**, honoring the Law quite strongly. The Gentile church adhered more to the teaching outlined by the apostle Paul, who talked about "freedom in Christ." Church historian Mark Noll believes that the decisive moment creating Gentile Christianity came in 70 CE, when Jews and Christians, almost indistinguishable at that point, were both expelled from Jerusalem by the Romans.[10]

As Christianity spread, things about the emerging faith were written down. First came the letters or epistles of St. Paul. Then, in time, came a life sketch of Jesus by the author Mark, followed by Matthew and Luke and finally John, in the late first century. Luke also wrote the book of the Acts. Other letters and reflections were included, such as James and Revelation, the whole corpus becoming the **Newer Testament**. It was written in the lingua franca of the culture, Greek.

---

10. Noll, *Turning Points*, 17.

STRUGGLING CENTURIES OF THE CHURCH (110–500 CE)

During their time, the Romans were basically tolerant of conquered peoples' religions. So in the Greco-Roman world many cults existed, several coming from the east. The cult of Mithras from Persia, quite popular with soldiers, was one of the biggest. It had a dying-rising mythic god in its story—whose birthday was December 25! For a while Mithraism looked as if it would win the hearts and minds of the people widely. In addition, there were Greek mystery religions and revelry cults like that of Dionysius/Bacchus, god of wine. The Romans had their own imperial cult with remembrance of old gods; and often a reigning emperor would designate himself a god and demand veneration. These were some of the competitive religious groups around as Christianity came on the scene.

The main competitor to what became orthodox Christianity was **Gnosticism.** The Gnostics were folks with esoteric "knowledge" given for salvation. Gnosticism had adherents outside and inside the church. Such a special, inside-information group was hard to combat. Their *spirituality* was attractive. Ultimately, though, *incarnational*, ethical, and historically grounded Christianity prevailed. Fleshy narrative trumped spiritual mythology.

For one thing, the early Christians practiced a radical love ethic. Commanded to love all people, People of the Way were pacifists. They would kill no one, would not serve in the army, and would not attend coliseum/circus games or the theater, which were considered cruel and licentious. Our faith-parents opposed exposure of babies to the elements, and they refrained from engaging in trade, as it was too covetous, too acquisitive. Almost all Christians, when an emperor declared himself to be a god, would not put the pinch of incense on the coals before his bust. Fidelity was to Jesus Christ alone. "Jesus," they said, "and Jesus alone is Caesar!" To the Romans, this was "atheism," a rejection of or nonbelief in their gods. Increasingly the authorities became suspicious and began persecution of Christians. Christ and culture were in conflict; as H. Richard Niebuhr suggests, this was a time of Christ *against* culture. Harmonizing spirits—"apologists," such as Irenaeus, Clement of Alexandria, and Justin Martyr—tried to reconcile cultural differences, but the differences remained. When tensions fueled periodic persecution of Christians, a tradition of **martyrdom** developed.

Many Christians thought it better to die for the faith than to bow the knee to "the principalities and powers" of this world.

Things changed positively for the faithful in 313 CE. Then the Roman Empire's corulers, Constantine and Licinius, issued an Edict of Toleration for all religious groups. With that edict, Christianity was set on the road to becoming the empire's sole official religion—made so in 380 by Emperor Theodosius's edict.

Two things about Christianity especially appealed to Constantine. The first was that it was an organized **religion** with a program for helping the poor. He hoped the church, if he supported it, might be a meliorating, social-serving presence. Secondly, he liked that fact that this was a unitive **religion** with one God. Concerned about unity in the empire, he liked the idea of oneness in rule and thought. Seeing that Christianity was becoming a quite popular religion in the empire, he reasoned it might promote unity for him. He hoped, of course, that Christianity would be *of* Greco-Roman culture. Perhaps it was, for Christian clergy came to **dress** in Roman priestly style, including wearing a miter; organized themselves as **dioceses** under the leadership of deacons and bishops; took sacred **meals over grave sites**; and gathered for worship in governmental buildings called **basilicas**—all features quite Roman.

In seeking peace and cooperation with Christians, Constantine also started a thousand-plus-year tradition of temporal kings swearing allegiance to Christ as eternal King.[11] To help bring things together, in 325 CE Constantine convened a meeting of church bishops at Nicaea, near his soon-to-be capital, Constantinople. Thus began **conciliar Christianity,** which has never ceased to function. The Council of Nicaea established orthodoxy, that is, right belief, for our forebears, crafting a statement of faith for adherents to recite: the **Nicene Creed**. It echoes in churches to the present age.

Unity in thought was not, however, to be. Some Christians were not happy with the Council of Nicaea's formulations. Arius of Alexandria, whose thinking did not elevate the Son as highly as the Father, was a powerful dissenter. Against him, Athanasius, also of Alexandria, argued for the Nicene orthodox statement whereby the Father, Son, and Holy Spirit were presented as coequal and One. Over time Athanasius's view prevailed in both the Eastern/Greek and Western/Roman portions of the church, but **Arian Christianity** itself was a thousand years dying. It was the form of the

---

11. Noted in Pelikan, *Jesus through the Centuries*, 53.

faith with which some Germanic tribes/barbarians, across the Danube and Rhine Rivers, adopted.

Arianism was not the only problem with which the councils had to deal. There was a self-flagellating sect in the church, known as the Donatists, whose rigorousness was admired, but whose way could not be normative for more ordinary Christians. Also, there were the Pelagians, convinced of free will before God, whose views seemed to diminish the absolute sovereignty of God. In addition, there were the Coptic Christians of Egypt and the Nestorian Christians of Syria-Persia, whose views were rejected at the Council of Chalcedon in 451 CE. Concerned for unity, the early church made declarations about—really *against*—such groups, calling them "heretical."

Still working at unity, bishop-theologians—such as Clement of Alexandria, Athanasius, the great Cappadocians (brothers Basil of Caesarea, Gregory of Nazianzus, their sister Macrina, and Gregory of Nyssa), Ambrose of Milan, and John Chrysostom of Constantinople, to name a few—tried to define doctrine and order the church. Thus the church worked at unity within, for the empire and itself. What these men and women were doing was **theological reflection**, one of the ongoing institutional hallmarks of Christianity. The greatest of the ancient thinkers was Augustine of Hippo in North Africa; he helped define the church's understanding of sin and grace. When Rome fell to the Arian Visigoths in 410 CE, Augustine made that fall seem less cataclysmic by his book *The City of God*. In it he emphasized that God's domain is not identifiable with any earthly city or culture! Augustine helped position the church to be *above* culture.

When persecution of Christians ended and the era of tolerance emerged, some Christians felt that life "in the world" had become too soft. To suffer as Christ suffered—but voluntarily—seemed to be the most faithful thing to do. These men and women chose a self-denying path through **ascetic monasticism**. Some practiced solitary monasticism in the desert, while others gravitated toward a disciplined life in community. In the fourth century CE, Basil of Caesarea, known as "the Great," established a *Rule* for monks and nuns that has guided them even to the present day. In time, monasteries were located on Greek islands, in Turkish caves, upon a mountain in the Sinai, in Syrian and Egyptian deserts, and near important cities, such as Jericho. Monasticism developed more slowly in the West, but it came. In both East and West, it had enormous importance in our history, to be discussed in the next section. What might be underscored here is that while, at one level, there was a coming together of Christ *and* culture, there were simultaneously those who hued to a modality where Christ was *against*, beyond, or separated from culture.

As time passed in the East, with a Byzantine empire and culture developing, we discover a Christ *of* culture—or Christ *under* culture. The church-state accommodation that emerged, called **Caesaropapism**, suggests state and church living together as partners, the church praying for the state, the state protecting the church. In reality, the emperor usually had the upper hand, controlling religion. The oncoming Orthodox Church stayed under the watchful eye of ruling authorities, especially so after the capital of the empire moved to Constantinople, making that city "the second Rome." Something of the tension between Christ and culture can be seen when Emperor Constantius II (–361) wanted to call a church synod for the purpose of condemning one of his enemies. He was told by the patriarch of Constantinople he could not so order. Why? "Because the canons of the church do not allow it." He replied, "My will is also a canon of the church." So the Synod of Sirmium was held in 356 CE.

As suggested, the imperial will usually prevailed over that of church leaders. Christ was more *under* culture. If a church patriarch occasionally spoke against something that went on in the state and was not listened to, that patriarch retired to a monastic sanctuary. That is what John Chrysostom did when he criticized the decadence of Byzantine women. Such was the Christ and culture situation in the East.

In the West, the emerging Catholic or Latin Rites Church was freer of direct imperial interference. The pope in Rome and Western clergy had greater control over their own destiny and environs. The church could be *above* culture, more of a shaper thereof, but "in time."

AGE OF MONASTICISM (500–1100 CE)

In the East and the West, as bishops in cathedrals and emperors in palaces went about their business, all was not secure in this Greco-Roman-Christian world. New major outside influences were coming to change things for all.

Let us begin with the intrusions of the so-called barbarians, tribes of Germanic people who lived beyond the empire's northern frontier, across the Rhine and Danube Rivers. The names of Visigoth, Ostrogoth, Angle, Jute, Saxon, Frank, Vandal, Lombard, and, later in the millennium, Magyar/

Hun, can be mentioned. For years the tribes had been threatening to break inside the borders of "the civilized world." In the winter of 406 CE they did. Then the rivers of Europe froze over, enabling the barbarians to cross them at will, defeat outpost guards, and pour into the Roman Empire. In particular, the Visigoths, originally from the region of Poland, crossed over the Danube to enter the Balkans. Expelled by the Byzantine emperor's soldiers, they pushed on into Italy, where in 410 Alaric I and his tribesmen sacked Rome. They moved on to Spain, settled down, and eventually connected to Catholic/Nicene Christianity.

Invaders like the Visigoths, it should be noted, did not come conquering in order to attain spoils or slaves on behalf of a political center "up north." No. They entered for purposes of resettling. Their desire was to find more pleasant lands and to enjoy the physical comforts of southern Europe. As a rule, they were little interested in educational traditions, legal customs, or cultural achievements of the ancien régime. Nor were they given to the Nicene Christianity of southern Europe. As noted, the Visigoths were Arian Christians, at best heretics. Other German tribes were simply pagan. In rampaging through southern and western Europe, taking over in many places, they devastated much of Roman civilization and Catholic Christianity.

Western culture and Nicene-Creed Christianity, however, were preserved in that barbarian culture primarily by monasticism. When persecution ended, religious enthusiasm increasingly went into monastic life. Such life was communal. Among the activities of the monasteries and nunneries were the collection and copying of manuscripts both Christian and classical (for example, the works of Plato). When the monasteries with their libraries were threatened with burning by the invading armies, the abbots and abbesses sought a place to send books and manuscripts for safekeeping. One place was Ireland.

Ireland was the only country in western Europe that the barbarians did not overrun. Converted to the faith by St. Patrick in the fifth century, the Irish quickly took to Christianity. Irish culture and **ascetic monasticism** seemed a match. The Celtic monks were ready and happy to receive books and manuscripts from the Continent. Their monasteries became the repositories of Western learning, culture, and Christianity. The manuscripts then were copied, awaiting opportune time to be brought back to earlier homes.

Christ and Culture Interacting

In 564 CE a Celtic monk named Columba, "the Dove," sailed east from Ireland with twelve other monks to the island of Iona, there beginning **missionary activity**. Columba's work eventuated in strong Christian reestablishment in Europe. He himself had success among the Picts in Scotland. His followers made inroads in northern and western England, the isle of Lindisfarne becoming an important religious outpost. The Irish monks then went to the continental lowlands and on to France, Switzerland, and Italy. In time they went as far as Russia and North Africa. They came Christianizing and "culturizing," if you will. Historian Thomas Cahill contends that "the Irish saved civilization."[12] These Celtic monks, with their Holy Spirit symbol of the wild goose (see the icon of this section) moving out, suggest what Frankish and Byzantine monks also were doing for the faith during the Middle Ages.

Germanic tribal culture, into which Christianity reintroduced itself, was governed by what is known as customary law. This was a no-tolerance kind of rule whereby all persons in the society were expected to think, believe, and act in accord with the one-way mentality of the chieftain. Under customary law, if the chieftain converted to Christianity, then the people were to follow. That very thing happened via King Clovis the Frank in 496. If there was any escape from all-or-nothing customary law, it was through monasteries and nunneries. These institutions offered sanctuary and, more important, presented an **alternative lifestyle**. They were countercultural outlets that in the long run became *transformative* for Europe. First the Celtic monasteries and later the French Cluniac monks provided positive models of life. The monks and nuns built societies on *ora et labora* ("prayer and work"), their convents and monasteries being islands of piety, industry, and learning in an otherwise harsh sea. The religious

taught children	copied manuscripts	carried on scholarship
cultivated gardens	did animal husbandry	kept worshiping
wrote and sang songs	provided hospitality	cared for the poor
practiced nonviolence	lived ascetically	maintained contact

and did other "civilized" things. Christian monks and nuns served as slow-working leaven in the coarse world about them. **Cenobetic**—that is, communal—**orders** were a major Christian response to the Germanic tribal onslaught.

---

12. Cahill, *How the Irish Saved Civilization*, 193–96.

Reinvigorated Christianity took hold in western Europe with its first stronghold in the land of the Franks/France. Resurgence there was brought about by alignment of the Franks' palace in Aachen with the Vatican cathedral in Rome. So in the year 800 CE, Pope Leo III crowned Charles the Great (Charlemagne) king of the Franks, in essence, *emperor* of the empire. The action infuriated the Byzantines in the East, but they could do nothing to change the new close relationship of state and church in the West. In a Frankish culture the **Roman Catholic Church** came to clearer definition.

Via the Franks, other things happened in Christian formation. For one, Charlemagne organized the first **parishes** for local communities. Through his palace school, serious scholarship was renewed, and Latin was established as the language for church and state—in part, because Charlemagne thought God understood only Latin! Charlemagne also encouraged use of the phrase *filioque* (Latin for "and the Son") when reciting the Nicene Creed. People saying "the Spirit proceeds from the Father *and the Son*" contributed to the Eastern Church separating from the Western in 1054.

All the while, in the Eastern part of the empire, an identifiable and distinct **Greek Orthodox Church** took shape. A patriarch (not called a pope) ruled in Constantinople while metropolitans (perhaps distinguishable from archbishops) presided in sees/jurisdictions in the East, such as Antioch and Alexandria. Church buildings in the shape of equal-arm crosses went up; this was distinct from the long-nave basilicas of Western architecture. In the seventh century the Emperor Justinian in Constantinople saw to the construction of the great Hagia Sophia church, still standing (although for centuries a mosque and now a museum) and the model for Orthodox Christianities everywhere.

Something of the tension between Byzantine rulers and Orthodox prelates is revealed during the eighth and ninth centuries CE in the iconoclastic controversy. Emperor Leo III in Constantinople became convinced that the visual arts, especially sculpted depictions of Christ, amounted to idol worship, something prohibited in the Ten Commandments and scrupulously not practiced in Islam—which had risen so rapidly in the seventh century. Thinking to win back God's favor, Leo called a council to condemn icons. He got his way. The monks, the people, even the pope resisted, but could not prevail. Much destruction of Christian art, especially statuary art, happened. A century after Leo, a pro-icon ruler, Empress Theodora, empowered another council, and the popular images—at least, two-dimensional icons—were restored. In the case of both Leo and Theodora, the state, rather than the church, was the primary decider.

When today people question Orthodox Christianity's limited independence and engagement beyond its doors, they need to remember that domination by state has been the norm for the Orthodox. They had to "keep their head down," their nose clean—filled only with incense. More than "right belief," *Ortho-doxy* means "right worship." An **otherworldliness**, a heaven-focused gaze, developed early. Looking centuries ahead, as Orthodoxy developed in Russia, it too was subservient to the czars, preaching to believers "the holiness of obedience." The Romanov czar Peter the Great in 1722, in deciding not to appoint a patriarch, became the de facto head of the church, and the czars functioned so till 1917, when a patriarch was reinstalled.

Christianity came to Russia when Prince Vladimir of Kiev—actually a Swedish Viking—was baptized in 988. He then ordered the baptism of all of the people of Kievan Rus. A century earlier the brothers Cyril and Methodius had prepared the way by translating the liturgy, the scriptures, and the lives of the saints into Slavonic with an alphabet they created. Thus the Eastern Orthodox Church had its birth among the Slavs. Across the centuries the **Russian Orthodox Church** became a powerful force in shaping Russian culture, becoming one of the largest national churches in the world. Indebted to the Greek monks who tutored the Kievan Rus, Muscovite or northern Russia culture eventually put its unique stamp on iconography, church music, and architecture—especially signaled by the "onion" or beet-root shape of the many domes on Russian churches, designed to *shed snow* in northern clime. Monasticism also had a profound effect on Russian spirituality, especially through wandering hesychast monks who practiced the **Jesus Prayer**. (Such solitary "holy fools" date back to the fourth century.) The colorful/fantastic Cathedral of St. Basil on Red Square in Moscow is named after such a "fool" who even taunted Czar Ivan the Terrible in the sixteenth century. There were also those extraordinary characters like the notorious Rasputin in the early twentieth century, who under the guise of religion brought death to the family of Czar Nicholas II and, ultimately, tragedy for all of the Russian people.

Staying with the East, let me say a word about Arab culture. In Arabia during the early seventh century Islam was born, created by the spiritual insights of the prophet Muhammad. After Muhammad's death, his Arabian followers came streaming out of the desert, conquering in the name of

Allah. Within a century they took over the Middle East, including Persia. They moved across North Africa and extended their power into Spain. Of the five historic Eastern centers of Christian faith—Alexandria, Jerusalem, Antioch, Ephesus, and Constantinople—only the last was not overrun. Interestingly enough, some Middle Eastern Christians, such as those in Syria, Egypt, and North Africa, positively welcomed an overlord other than the Byzantine. Over time, of course, these Christians found themselves in an attenuated position. In North Africa, Christianity disappeared entirely.

The great conquering sweep of Islam isolated or cut off various Christian bodies, one from another, creating even more **distinct eastern Christianities**, such as those in Armenia, Ethiopia (Abyssinian), Sudan (Coptic), Turkey/Iraq/Persia (Church of the East/Nestorian), and India/Sri Lanka (St. Thomas and Malabar). These churches evolved with varying forms of liturgical expression, clerical dress, primary symbolism, even church architecture. In Ethiopia, Christians chiseled churches out of red volcanic rock! Some sense of Middle Eastern church distinctions may be observed in Jerusalem's Church of the Holy Sepulchre. On a Sunday morning today African Copts in black robes chant in deep guttural voice, while in the same sacred space highly bejeweled Armenian priests stomp staffs, each as part of their distinct worship tradition.

Let me lift up one branch of the several eastern Christianities for consideration. That is the **Church of the East**, aka the **Nestorian**, almost forgotten. At one time it was the largest geographical communion in the world. Beyond the borders of the Roman Empire, it lived in Mesopotamian and Persian cultures from the fourth through the fourteenth centuries in strength. In faith the Nestorians were not quite orthodox, believing as they did that the two persons of Christ were more distinct (dyophysitic) and that emphasis on Mary as the *Theotokos*/Mother of God was too great. Their theological take set them apart from the dominant Byzantine church, but that very distinctiveness made them more acceptable to anti-Byzantine rulers of Persia. Nestorian Christianity thrived for several centuries with their metropolitan based in Edessa. In nearby Nisibis they had what may be the first university. With zeal the Nestorians took the faith eastward to China and southward to India. Katholicos or Patriarch Timothy I even established a bishopric in Tibet! In time the Church of the East, as it may now be called, was reduced under long-lasting Ottoman Turk domination. For a while it made inroads among the Mongols on the steppes of Asia, but not enough to

Christ and Culture Interacting

last. Today, as they are found, say, in Baghdad, they may be best described as a **remnant faith community**.

Islam, historically, was not aggressively hostile toward Christianity or Judaism. From 712 to 1492, for example, Jews and Christians were amicably tolerated in Andalusia/Spain. Even so, the dominant Muslim culture, whether Moorish, Arabic, Persian, Seljuk, Mongol, or Ottoman, functioned through the centuries as a stifling overlord. The Christianities surviving in Muslim lands became extremely withdrawn, conservative, and, sociopolitically disengaged from the dominant culture, basically *under* it, subservient.

Though the Byzantine Empire was losing ground and the Greek Church losing membership, both state and church in the East were in some ways better off than Western Europe and the Roman Church during the Middle Ages. The story is told that in the year 800 CE, Charlemagne, just crowned emperor, in returning to France, visited the Italian city of Ravenna. In Ravenna he saw mosaics of Eastern monarchs and churchmen from two centuries before. By the finery of their wear, shown in the mosaics, Charlemagne sensed how superior that culture was. He resolved to make his new empire and its church as good or better. In the reigns of Charlemagne and subsequent Carolingian monarchs, improvements began. Among other things, scholarly monks from all over Europe were brought to Aachen (on the French-German border) to lead a renaissance in arts and letters. Moreover, the Franks sent missionaries in outreach to Saxon and Norse people.

Right arm to Carolingian culture advance was **Cluniac monasticism**. Following Benedict's *Rule,* the Cluniacs kept worship and communal life alive through a thousand chartered houses set in France, Spain, England, and other locales. Cluniacs encouraged reform in the church generally and for their motherhouse in Cluny, France, erected what was then the largest cathedral in the world.

The West and Western Christianity were coming back—even into a Christendom.

HIGH CHRISTENDOM YEARS (1100–1450 CE)

During the last half of the first millennium, the church in the Eastern part of the empire (rich in culture but now Islam-beset) and the church in West (poorer but barbarian-overcoming) grew further and further apart. In the year 1054 the patriarch in

Constantinople and the pope in Rome issued mutual anathemas against each other. From this point on, we must speak of a distinct **Greek/Eastern Orthodox Church** and a **Roman/Western Catholic Church**. The first was in the Byzantine world, while the latter now was in a *new* Holy Roman Empire, called that since Otto the Great crowned himself emperor of it in 962. In the centuries now under consideration, the Orthodox Church—with one exception—became confined to southeastern Europe around Constantinople. It hewed ever more tightly to its Byzantine past. That one exception is that Orthodoxy expanded into Russia, so much so that, after "second Rome" Constantinople fell to the Ottoman Turks in 1453, the Russian prelates in the late fifteenth century proclaimed Moscow "**the Third Rome**." What we need to say here is that Slavic culture now had a shaping hand on the Orthodox churches in eastern Europe. At least Slavic languages provided the **vernacular tongue** of liturgies.

In spite of the Orthodox-Catholic mutual anathemas in 1054, relations between East and West were not totally severed. In 1095 the emperor in Constantinople requested help of the pope in Rome to help combat the Seljuk Muslim Turks, whose armies were moving into Byzantium territory. The pope responded by calling for a **holy crusade** against "the infidels." The First Crusade succeeded in capturing Jerusalem, setting up a fluid Western presence in the Holy Land for the next two hundred years. Peasant pilgrims, kings, knights (Templar, Hospitaller, and regular), monks, even children from western Europe marched and sailed eastward into futile battles, giving up in 1291, when the last crusaders left Acre.

By their presence in the Middle East and by contending in Spain with Islamic Moors, Western European Christians were exposed to Byzantine and Islamic cultures. In the process, they/we received much. Here are some of gifts to the Western world from Islamic-Byzantine-Moorish society and libraries:

paper	rhyming poetry	rhythmic music
table setting	desserts	Arabic numbers 0–9
Turkish towels	coffee, oranges	steel hardening
calligraphy		bagpipes, guitars

plus the academic disciplines of astronomy, optics, architecture, engineering, chemistry, anatomy, biology, botany, physics, algebra, and meteorology. Especially there was a reopening of the intellectual and aesthetic treasures

Christ and Culture Interacting

from classical antiquity. Ancient Greece's Aristotle, whose writings had been lost to the West for almost a thousand years, was found. Jewish and Christian scholars struggled to appropriate that philosopher's thought. In time, Thomas Aquinas, a Dominican friar, worked out a great new synthesis of classic philosophy and Christian theology. This was in the thirteenth century. By the sixteenth century **Thomistic philosophy**, with its proofs for the existence of God and its understanding of natural law, was formally adopted as definitive in the Catholic Church. It prevails to the present.

In due course, Western Europe began to renew itself. With intellectual achievements, such as Aquinas's, and with strong leadership, provided by popes like Innocent III (1198–1216), the Roman Catholic Church reached an apex of power and prestige unmatched before or since. Innocent III convened the society-shaping Fourth Lateran Council of 1215. Among many things, the Ccouncil put forth regulations on marriage, making it a sacrament of the church, which effected ordinary people. It also made marriage a sacrament of the church. That was different. It made celibacy normative for regular clergy, not just monks. So—on the books, at least—priests could no longer have wives or children, as they had had for centuries before. Christendom, essentially a culture, came to be what Niebuhr calls "Christ *above* culture," with popes being power brokers, anointing kings, and commanding armies. In 1302 Pope Boniface VIII issued a bull or declaration called *Unam Sanctam*. It held in essence that a bishop's miter is taller than any king's crown, that the pastoral staff reaches higher than the sword. "Temporal authority," the bull said, "must be subjected to spiritual."[13] In and for feudal culture, the popes established **"peace of God" days** on which no fighting could take place. We are witnessing something close to Christ *over* culture—or maybe more. Diarmaid MacCulloch says of Pope Innocent III: "Few Christian leaders have had such a *transforming* effect on their world."[14]

Introduction of classical art and learning generated a renaissance in society and church. **Gothic cathedrals**, such as those in Reims and York, sprang up; such cathedrals housed incredibly beautiful stained-glass windows, sculpture, and art. Painting flourished, with religious subjects a dominant theme. Leonardo da Vinci's *Last Supper* was painted on the wall of a convent refectory. Learning-as-learning advanced too. From embryonic cathedral schools great **universities** grew: at Salerno (strong in medicine),

---

13. Quoted in González, *Changing Shape of Church History*, 113.
14. McCulloch, *Christianity*, 403 (italics added).

Bologna (specializing in law), Paris (in theology), and Oxford (emphasizing letters). These are but a few of the eighty universities in Europe functioning at the close of the Middle Ages. Literary achievements came in Dante's poem *The Divine Comedy*, Plutarch's *Parallel Lives*, Boccaccio's *The Decameron*, and Chaucer's *Canterbury Tales*.

Feudal society had a clearly hierarchical understanding of the world. People were classified into three estates: (1) the nobility, (2) the clergy, and (3) serfs. Artisans and tradespeople came in at the head of the third estate. Everybody was in relation, up and down, one to another. Such thinking in society reinforced ideas in the **orders of church hierarchy**:

the pope

cardinals

archbishops/abbots/abbesses

bishops/priors/prioresses

priests/monks/nuns

deacons (novitiates)

the laity.

Each rank was to be obedient to the religious office above. The "religious," especially monks and nuns, were to maintain the practices of "chastity, poverty, and obedience."

The creation of **parish churches**, begun in the ninth century by Charlemagne, now became widespread, alongside the presence of **guild churches**, supported, for example, by cloth workers, wheelwrights, and stonemasons. The guilds often sponsored morality plays or outfitted wagons with tableaus depicting biblical stories. The ironworkers guild might present the crucifixion, as Jesus' hands and feet were fixed to the cross by *iron* nails! The waterworks guild created their tableau around Jesus' baptism.

The best sign of church vitality in medieval Christendom was the new **mendicant orders**, notably those of the Dominicans and Franciscans. The friars or brothers in these orders came begging, preaching, serving the poor, advancing learning (Aquinas was a Dominican), and living out a New Testament ethic, as few had for centuries. The Franciscan brothers had their counterpart sisters in the Poor Clares, Clare being "Sister Moon" to "Brother Sun" Francis. These mendicant orders and militant orders, such as the Knights Templar and Hospitallers, had to be approved by the Vatican, ever so strong.

In medieval Christendom, however, all was not tranquil. There was trouble. How could it be otherwise? There was tension between church and state regarding the question of *lay investiture*, for example. Did civil rulers have the right to appoint bishops? Kings said yes, and popes said no. This was the church's prerogative, Rome said. On this issue Pope Gregory VII excommunicated King Henry IV and in 1077 drove Henry to concede. Henry stood barefoot and penitent in the snow at Canossa until forgiven. Later, Henry returned to capture Rome, sending Gregory into exile, where he died. A *French* bishop friendly to King Henry was put on the usually-Italian papal throne. Two centuries later, in a similar church-state conflict, another French prelate was set up as pope, this time in Avignon, France, by King Philip IV. So began the almost seventy-year "Babylonian captivity of the papacy," as Dante aptly described it. Making matters more complex, for a while there were *three* different reigning pontiffs, each beholden to a different European monarch, and each in a different locale! These popes controlled territory, people, money, and armies, as did most bishops.

Dismayed by the infighting and excesses, some **dissenting groups** of Christians appeared in the late fourteenth and early fifteenth centuries, trying to remodel the faith closer to simpler, biblical ideals, that is, away from indolent, complex Catholic Christendom. Consider, for example, the Lollards in England. They began to teach that personal faith was more important than obeying church law, contending that every person had the right to read and interpret scripture as he or she saw fit. Lollard John Wycliffe translated the Bible from Latin into English. These dissenters were against obligatory oral confession of sin, against monasticism, and even against pilgrimages to holy sites. They denied the doctrine of transubstantiation, the belief that bread and wine in communion became the real body and blood of Christ. Eventually their movement was put down by church and civil authorities—as were the reform efforts of John Hus and Girolamo Savonarola. Physical extinction, however, did not destroy ideas. Lollard agitation prepared the English soul to receive Protestant thought in the sixteenth century and the Puritan revolution in the seventeenth.

REFORMATIONS/NEW WORLDS ERA (1450–1650 CE)

People sometimes talk as if sixteenth-century Protestant Christianity succeeded because of the thought and witness of one man, Martin Luther. He was singularly important, for sure, and the case for charismatic, individual leadership can be made; however, it would be an error to overlook the larger cultural factors that enabled Luther's witness to prevail. A key element is simply that Luther lived in an emerging technological culture, to be more precise, in a print culture. In that culture, the printing press made all the difference. Luther's posting of ninety-five theses for debate caused a stir *because* his debate points were put on paper—also sheepskin—to be quickly duplicated, widely distributed, eagerly read, and responded to. The printing press made Protestants a **people of the book**, with sacral authority now vested in the Bible. (Note the icon for this section.)

A second cultural factor that aided Protestantism in general and Luther in particular was the rise of regionalism or nationalism, or what church historian Diarmaid MacCulloch calls "magisterialism," where magistrates/princes/kings decided issues for their subjects. . In Luther's case, before Holy Roman Emperor Charles V of Spain and Holland could muster forces to capture him, *German* princes put up a protective shield—and kept it there. Luther, in turn, affirmed the princes as legitimate, while at the same time also affirming separate loyalty to Christ. So, Niebuhr contends, an understanding of Christ and culture *in paradox* came to characterize Lutheranism.

In England, growing nationalism helped King Henry VIII successfully take the churches of his country away from Rome and create an autonomous English church, eventually called Anglican. The importance of one Holy Roman Empire under one emperor and one pope seemed not self-evident anymore, either to the British or others on the Continent. The center did not hold. Things fell apart. Language, ethnicity, geography, nationalism, and so on shaped events. Protestantism arose. Initially Protestantism took four major forms, with strength in various countries:

- Lutheran in Germany, Denmark, Norway, Sweden
- Reformed in Switzerland, France, Holland, Scotland, Hungary

Christ and Culture Interacting

- Anglican in England (and, in time, the British colonies)
- Anabaptist in districts of Germany, Holland, Moravia, Poland

None of this should be taken to suggest that theology and doctrines were unimportant. They were important. For sure, Protestant thought appealed to people moving *away* from top-down, medieval, dogmatic ways. Some of Protestantism's attractive ideas were salvation by faith alone, the centrality of the scriptures, the priesthood of all believers, and, from the Anabaptists' perspective, the right of individual conscience. **Worship in the vernacular** especially may be seen as a response to the growing sense of national identity.

The Anabaptist branch of Protestantism also helped shape a distinct new polity or form of governance for churches called **congregationalism**. They said *local* Christian churches should make decisions about their life, who will be their minister, how money will be spent, and so forth, and nobody higher up should dictate to local churches. Congregationalism was different from the traditional episcopal (bishop-centered) structure or the Reformed branch's presbyterial (collected churches decide) polity. The Anabaptist idea of **adult believers' baptism** also was a new (though ancient and biblical) idea that, among other things—such as their pacifism, their refusing to take oaths, and their practice of communitarianism—put them at odds with magistrate culture. They ended up being *against* magistrate-prince-king rule, seeing all such as an abomination.

Given new theological emphases and differences in governance, Protestant Christianity began to vary from Catholic and Orthodox Christianity in practices too. **Preaching**, especially, became a major and ongoing characteristic of this emerging Christianity. Reformers of whatever brand made preaching tantamount to a sacrament, implying that that is how God is mediated. Protestantism brought on still additional changes, such as congregational hymn singing, not just chant or plainsong. With Luther marrying and having children, **the Christian family** was given shape.

The Catholic Church reacted to Protestantism with a **Counter-Reformation**. A zealous new religious order, the Jesuits, engaged Protestantism in several countries and extended Roman Catholic influence worldwide. In addition, a special council, the Council of Trent, was called and met from 1545 to 1563 to shore up doctrine and discipline in the church. Protestant interpretations of the faith were repudiated, while some of the Catholic Church's own worst practices, such as the sale of indulgences, were vacated.

The council officially adopted the thought of Aquinas as normative and fixed the number of sacraments for the church at seven.

Unable to break from medieval thinking completely, the *major* religious parties—Catholic, Lutheran, and Calvinist—held tightly to the idea that there could be only one right way and one church. Consequently, conflict went on for a century, including the bloody Thirty Years' War of central Europe. Finally, in 1648 the Peace of Westphalia reaffirmed the principle of *cuius regio, eius religio* ("the religion of the region shall be that of the ruler," literally "whose region, his/her religion"). It was a settlement by overlords, not by any principle of tolerance—**"magisterial" Christianity**, in that magistrates/princes/kings decided people's religion.

Magisterial decisions of the Westphalia formula worked fairly well for the religious groups who had connection to secular powers, but for Anabaptists and other lesser groups, the formula failed. Often they were driven off, if not hunted down and killed—by all sides. Poland-Lithuania, however, proved a short exception. There, happily, an assembly of the region's delegates said that a new king, to serve, had to agree that theirs would be "a state without stakes"! Unfortunately, tolerance in Poland was only short lived. A later Polish king allied himself with Roman Catholicism . . . and so the country and the populace.

*

One solution, other than war, emerged for the competing faith groups. It came about by nautical culture. Ocean exploration led to the "discovery" of new worlds and, with that, the opportunity for faith adherents to direct energy outward, rather than at one another. Sailing ships enabled all faith groups eventually—but especially the Catholic Church early on—to spread throughout the understood-now-to-be-round world. A new **missionary movement** came about because of nautical culture. Missionaries were part of the exploratory, flag-planting, commercial, and colonial expeditions. Jesuits went with Portuguese sailors around Africa to the Far East. St. Francis Xavier introduced Christianity in Japan. Other Jesuit missionaries did so in China, showing great respect for that ancient Asian culture, as suggested in this review:

> Alessandro Valignano... insisted in the first place on knowledge of the Chinese language. Therefore he called a few Jesuits to Macao in 1579, ordering them to focus their attention entirely on the study of language.... Two years later Michele Ruggieri (1543–1607) entered China through the south, and Matteo Ricci (1552–1610) followed one year later.... [T]hey dressed like Buddhist monks ... [and] adapted themselves to the life-style and etiquette of the Confucian elite of literati and officials.[15]

Dominicans and Franciscans accompanied Spanish explorers to America. They found Mayan, Aztec, and Incan civilizations in Central and South America. The Spanish conquistadors perceived themselves superior to and "by right" entitled to be *over* indigenous cultures. Illustrative of that self-perception is what happened on May 26, 1521. That date could, conceivably, be remembered by Protestants as the day Martin Luther proclaimed, "Here I stand," at the Diet of Worms. More significantly, for the indigenous peoples of the Western Hemisphere, it was the day Hernándo Cortés massacred Chief Montezuma and the Aztec warriors in Mexico City. Aztec/aboriginal culture was changed, almost extinguished. Other native cultures and tribes suffered similar tragedies in the centuries ahead. **Conquistador Christianity** had a long and bloody run.

Spanish violence was *somewhat* ameliorated by Dominican Friar Bartolomé de Las Casas. Appalled by what he saw going on in the Indies, he got the pope to rule that native Americans were fully human beings with human rights. Recognition of such humanity, however, was not given to men and women captured in Africa and forced into slavery. Black Africans would have to win acceptance of their humanity through struggle and the abolition of slavery, which did not come until the nineteenth century.

While accompanying explorers and conquistadors, Catholic missionaries themselves worked nonviolently and constructively among native peoples. They traveled far to preach and practice the faith, establish mission stations, and build churches. Before the Pilgrims ever landed at Plymouth Rock, for example, a Franciscan church was ringing a tower bell in Santa Fe, in what is now New Mexico. In the eighteenth century, Padre Junípero Serra lived and worked with Indian people along the *Camino Real* of California, setting up a Christian presence that endured long after the conquistadors pulled back. What eventually happened in these areas was

---

15. From a paper by the Dutch scholar Nicolas Standaert, "Matteo Ricci: Shaped by the Chinese," written in 2010 on the 400th anniversary of the death of Matteo Ricci. Found by Google search.

cultural syncretism, a joining of imported faith and indigenous culture. Christ came to be *of* native complexion. Syncretism happened, in part, because an Indian peasant, Juan Carlos, had a vision of a holy woman, the Virgin, who looked very Indian. She became the still-venerated Our Lady of Guadalupe.

As a part of the nautical-missionary dynamic, Jesuits went with the French into Canada and traveled deeply inland with explorers. Reaching out to First Nation people, the missionaries were sometimes welcomed and sometimes martyred. Eventually, in Canada and other places in the Western Hemisphere, **Native American churches** came to be. Drums were heard in worship, rather than organ pipes. Circle dance replaced linear processionals.

Beyond exploring, conquering, and converting, there was escape and settling-in by Europeans. By 1607 an Anglican clergyman was in Virginia; by 1620 a lay-led congregation of Pilgrims was present in New England. Both were positioned on the edge of the North American wilderness.. The Pilgrims and soon-to-follow Puritans were motivated in strong measure to escape the religious turmoil in England and to settle where they were free to build their version of a New Jerusalem. The names *New* Bedford, *New* Haven, *New* Hampshire, *New* Salem, and *New*port suggest their hope. Other faithful believers of other communions followed. Dutch Reformed people came to New Amsterdam/New York, as did some German Lutherans. Scottish Presbyterians went to America's middle colonies. French Huguenots (Protestants) ventured into what would be the state of Tennessee. That's to name just four groups coming to resettle in this New World. All would contribute to an emerging American culture. One feature in the church for this setting—at least in New England—was an election day sermon, appropriate and expected in a more democratic society, where elections happened.

ECUMENICAL/GLOBAL AGE (1650 CE–PRESENT)

While the sixteenth- and seventeenth-century missionaries invariably were Catholic, those of the nineteenth included Protestants. Nautical culture ever-continuing enabled a **Protestant missionary movement.** The names of William Carey in India, Adoniram Judson in Burma, and David Livingstone in Africa come to mind. To these, the names of thousands of others from various missionary societies should be added.

Christ and Culture Interacting

They went out to take the Good News around the world. Most never returned to their place of birth but were buried in the land beside the people with whom they served and whom they came to love. For the Catholics, Charles Lavigerie was one of the White Fathers who worked from Algeria into Saharan Africa. Good seeds were being planted widely.

Certainly missionaries went with honorable intention and overall did exemplary work with the people to whom they reached out on behalf of Christ. That they sometimes were myopic about their own cultural baggage and less than sensitive regarding the customs of native people must be admitted. A Norwegian missionary, for example, thought that the wearing of trousers and a hat was a basic characteristic of a Christian, and missionaries in South Sea Islands insisted that female converts wear high-neck Mother Hubbard dresses!

Foibles, excesses, and travesties of Christian missions notwithstanding, the net effect of half a millennium of mission efforts, made possible by nautical culture, is the establishment of **indigenous Christianities** and enormous growth. During the twentieth century the Christianized became Christianizers. In Africa today 95 percent of evangelism is by Africans to Africans. South Korean Christians now *send* missionaries, as to South America. Worldwide Christian numbers have grown. One way to comprehend this growth is to know there are 220 million Christians in North America today, but in the Orient and South Pacific, there are more than 300 million. Every twenty-four hours there are 16,000 Christian converts in sub-Sahara Africa alone. By comparison, each day there are 3,000 *fewer* baptized Christians in Europe and North America.

It may be asked, "How was Christianity able to have such effect in basically colonial cultures?" The answer may be because of the Bible. Wherever missionaries went, they translated scripture into native languages. Often enough a translation was the first *written* literature for a people, as my wife and I discovered was the case with one island people of an Indonesian archipelago. The Bible could be read, read aloud, and preached from. There is no way to underestimate the positive effect of "hearing the Good News in one's own sweet tongue," as missions historian Lamin Sanneh puts it.[16] Moreover, since the Bible is generally about tribal-agrarian-marginalized people, Third-World people "get it" sooner than most in the First. Moreover, they find things in scripture of great value: stories of a captive tribe

---

16. Lamin Sanneh, speaking at the History of the Missionary Movement and World Christianity Conference in Edinburgh, Scotland, June of 1996, which I attended.

breaking the bonds of slavery, prophets who declare on behalf of the poor, and Jesus proclaiming an inclusive Reign of God. These things speak to and for people under systems of oppression, whether they be colonial cultures, caste systems, oligarchic dictatorships, various apartheids, or multinational corporations. Folk in such situations, inspired by the Bible, have worked to change the structures that held them down. Many of the shackle-breaking leaders in South Africa, for example, have been Christians, notably Albert Luthuli, Desmond Tutu, and Nelson Mandela. The impact of Christ on culture has been immense, even *transformative*.

Missionary societies sent their emissaries—women more often than men—all over the world. Work was done in the South Pacific from the Cook Islands (Hawaii) to Australia, bringing Polynesian, Melanesian, Micronesian, Maori, Aboriginal, and other Pacific Ocean peoples into Christian acquaintance. Southeast Asia (China, Korea, Japan, etc.) and India were entered for witness too, as was Africa, where Christianity, as noted, took off almost on its own. Everywhere **new-name churches** emerged. In Transvaal a Methodist minister founded a denomination he called "Ethiopian," noting that such a name was in the Bible, whereas "Methodist" (his denomination), "Anglican," and "Catholic" were not. By the start of the twenty-first century, more Christians were living in the Southern Hemisphere than the Northern.

As the faith was growing on several continents, diminution occurred in Europe. Most pointedly, loss of allegiance for Christianity happened in western Europe. The primary reason for that pulling away was the mid-eighteenth-century culture of the Enlightenment or Age of Reason. Such was a game-changing force. Rationalism emerged out of French, German, and English sources. Writing in England, John Locke presented ideas of social contract in government, which critically undermined the idea of sacred monarchy. Enlightenment thinking cast doubt on other traditional Christian "givens," metaphysics, miracles, mysticism, and the authority of scripture. These were rejected in favor of human reason, nature, and Nature's God. Theology in the Age of Reason went to deism, the notion of God winding up the world like a clock and then stepping away.

Keeping more to the historic Christian baseline, **liberal Protestantism** came into being. For it Friedrich Schleiermacher defined religion as

Christ and Culture Interacting

closer to feeling and emotion, not divine revelation or hallowed tradition. As Protestants began to think this way, Catholics and Orthodox mostly worked hard not to be moved by Age of Reason influence. To the point, in the nineteenth century a Catholic council affirmed some non-Enlightenment ideas: papal infallibility and, later, the bodily assumption of Mary into heaven. Likewise, it is not imaginable that the Orthodox ecumenical patriarch in Istanbul spent time reading much Locke and Diderot. Adjustment to modernity for those traditions had to come later—or maybe is still to come.

Early on, however, Enlightenment thought was attractive to the authors of the United States *Constitution*. When it came to writing a Bill of Rights for that constitution, James Madison and Thomas Jefferson saw no need to allow a national "establishment of religion," though such establishments were present in nine of the thirteen colonies. They opted for governmental neutrality in matters religious, calling for a **separation of church and state**, the first such separation since Constantine's uniting the two in the fourth century. Separation freed all churches from both governmental support *and* governmental interference. Thereafter, religious institutions had to make it on their own.

It was not until the twentieth century—and around the years of the First World War—that most European countries disestablished religion, separating religion from monarchy. It happened first in Russia, when the Bolsheviks killed the czar, who controlled the Russian church; next in Germany, when Kaiser Wilhelm, head of the Prussian church, was defeated. With his defeat came also the fall of Charles I/IV of Austria-Hungary, emperor of the remnant of the Holy Roman (Catholic) Empire.[17] Thus Orthodox, Protestant, and Catholic Christendoms, so long running, disappeared. A fifteen-hundred-year way of church-state togetherness was undone. Only in England did the monarch remain head of the church (Anglican) but, in reality, not even there. Separation of religion from government, involving Islam, occurred also in Turkey shortly after World War I. That is when the Muslim sultan of the Ottoman Empire was deposed.

Now, back to America of Enlightenment-shaped, increasingly secular culture. Here **modern Protestant Christianity** came to be. Disestablished Christian leaders in the United States started reaching out to the

---

17. In 2004 Charles was beatified by the Catholic Church and has become commonly known as Blessed Charles of Austria.

unchurched and staying closely attuned to the needs of people. Seemingly, it worked. A highly religious America came about. It is estimated that at the beginning of the nineteenth century only 7 percent of the population was church-affiliated, a residual number from the Great Awakening of the mid-eighteenth century. In the early decades of the nineteenth century, the Second Great Awakening began. **Revivalism** reinvigorated the churches and continued into the next century. By 1955 some 65 percent of the population in the United States indicated church membership; 80 percent *think* they belong to some religious group. Affiliation has stayed near this level for half a century. Christianity proved able to warm hearts toward God, win converts, inspire social service, influence politics, and do some shaping of the American social landscape. It probably was *not* what the deist founders envisioned happening when they inserted the disestablishment clause.

In the freedom of the new United States of America culture, division within Protestantism grew. Denominationalism happened. Having no "big tent" to stay under, as Roman Catholics did, Protestants split many ways. What happened is suggested by seeing how one limb of a church branched:

    Anglican
        Episcopal
            Methodist
                Salvation Army
                    Holiness
                        Wesleyan
                            Church of God
                                Assembly of God
                                    Four-Square Gospel

Other forks came off several of these splinter denominations. This is simply illustrative of the diversification that took place in the cultural milieu of America. From the original four major branches of Protestantism of the sixteenth century, dozens, then hundreds, now thousands of denominations have emerged. Protestantism opened the floodgates for sect proliferation. H. Richard Niebuhr says in *The Social Sources of Denominationalism* that divisions are about many things: doctrine, nationality, race, ethnicity, economics, deprivation, class, language, lifestyle, and so on. One can imagine that in some place a Korean-American Country Club Charismatic Snake-Handling Lutheran Church exists. In the Yellow Pages of the Atlanta,

Georgia, phone book, "churches" are listed between "chiropractors" and "cigars." Some intriguing names appear:

- Saint Stephens Overcoming Church of God
- For Christ's Sake Christian Center
- God's First Breakthrough Ministries, Inc.
- Polite Ministries, Inc.
- Whosoever Will COGIC Ministry
- The Interdenominational True Church of Christ
- First Apostolic Church of the PAW
- Church in the NOW
- It's Jesus Anyhow Holiness Church
- Free for All Baptist Church
- Kidist Mariam Ethiopian Orthodox Church
- St. Martins in the Field Episcopal Church
- Druid Hills United Presbyterian Church
- Millennium Training Church
- Prayer Warriors in Motion for Christ Church
- New Rising Star Missionary Baptist Church
- Just Jesus Word of God Church
- Sweet Honey in the Rock Restoration Church
- Tabernacle of David Church of the Apostles
- Thankful Apostolic Deliverance Temple

and, for the longest title of all: The Ministers of Jesus Christ Church of the Lord Jesus Christ Assemblies of Apostolic Faith.

Everywhere in the world, sects and denominations have cropped up. Church historian Martin Marty says there are over 25,000 identifiable denominations.[18]

*

---

18. Marty, *The Christian Story*, tape six. I've also seen a 38,000 number for denominations worldwide.

The modern era has also been the Age of Science. Western—usually northern—people learned to think in terms of objective truth, physical matter, mathematics, empirically replicable investigation, and things quantifiable and measurable. Such thinking called into question earlier assumptions about the way the world is and, especially, the way the Bible explained things. The Bible suggests that the world is flat and surrounded by water, that the sun could stand still, and that the man Jesus walked on water. Scientific understandings, though, caused doubt—or outright rejection—of such things. As a consequence, many modern folk turned away from Christianity, seeing our faith as hopelessly lost in superstition and irredeemably soft-headed.

There were, though, those modernist Christians working to reconcile science and religion, the faithful who have stayed open to science and education, believing that, "as we proceed in learning, we are thinking God's thoughts after him/her." Biblical scholars, especially in Germany and England, positively welcomed scientific literary investigation into the scriptures and church history. In the last century one positive response to the scientific culture was **process theology**. This theology sees (1) the world, (2) humanity, and (3) God in dynamic relation, aimed toward a fulfillment of world-humanity-God, even as intended from the beginning. In this dynamic, the resurrected Jesus becomes the Cosmic Lover, calling persons into an open future. Such a faith stance fits with an emerging whole-earth consciousness.

Modernist Christianity, by and large, has subscribed to a progressive and evolutionary understanding of history. Liberal Christians believe that women and men may have a strong hand in shaping the future for Christ, even of building the Kingdom of God. Liberals birthed the **social gospel movement**, which sought to redress inequalities and wrongs in society by applying social scientific insights with the teaching of Jesus. Jesus became primarily a teacher. **Liberal-progressive-Enlightenment Christianity** went forward to significantly shape American society, influencing education, tolerance, internationalism, liberty, egalitarianism, women's rights, and much more. Some have been so bold as to suggest that "mainline Protestants won the cultural war"[19]—at least the war of fifty years ago.

---

19. The Rev. Dr. Benjamin Broadbent in a sermon, September 8, 2013, First Congregational United Church of Christ, Colorado Springs, Colorado. Broadbent had been reading Robert Bellah, American sociologist of religion, on this point.

Christ and Culture Interacting

Against the scientific worldview and liberal Christianity, two reactions set in. One reaction goes by the name of **fundamentalism**. In 1910 and the years immediately thereafter some *Fundamentalist Papers* were issued by conservative theologians at Princeton Seminary. The *Papers* set forth the principle tenets that "true believers" ought to have, such as the inerrancy of scripture—first and foremost—but also Jesus' virgin birth, his bodily resurrection, vicarious atonement for sin, and the miracles of Jesus. Liberal preacher Harry Emerson Fosdick wondered aloud at mid-century whether fundamentalism would not soon die out, but it did not. In fact, **fundamentalist**—now usually called **evangelical**—**Christianity** grew in the last third of the twentieth century. Such Christianity (except regarding the select social issues of abortion and homosexuality) seems quite content in contemporary American culture. Evangelical Christians—not unlike mainline Protestants and Catholics—are *of* the culture in materialism and flag flying.

Another Christian response to modernity, not nearly so academically resistant or socially conservative, was **neo-orthodox theology**. Birthed in the early twentieth century, neo-orthodoxy questioned liberals' assumptions about the nature of humans, the inevitability of progress, and wishy-washy talk about God and Christ. Karl Barth, a German theologian, issued a call to take the Bible, sin, and Christ much more seriously than nineteenth-century Protestants had. What Barth said resonated positively with many recovering liberals and penitent social gospelers. From a position of historic theological grounding, the adherents to neo-orthodoxy in Germany critiqued the rise of National Socialism (Nazism) during the 1930s. They called those in the church who did *not* go along with Hitler the **Confessing Church**. It was *against* Nazi culture.

Beside German National Socialism in the last century, another secular ideology grew up and became a veritable culture, Soviet Communism. Through a violent revolution, Communism found a home in czarist Russia—now without a czar. The Soviet Union was created. By Marxist-Leninist dogma, the U.S.S.R. was antireligion generally, specifically against the Orthodox Church. Father Vladimir of St. Prince Vladimir's Cathedral in St. Petersburg says that in the last century 150,000 church leaders were tortured.[20] During the years of Joseph Stalin, tens of thousands of priests were murdered. The number of monasteries went from 1,025 to not many

---

20. October 1, 2013, in conversation with group on tour of Russia led by the Rev. Dr. Bruce Rigdon.

more than three. More than 50,000 churches were shut down, especially during the Nikita Khrushchev years (1958–1964). For centuries under the czars, the church had been *of* the culture, valued and protected, expected to be compliant, which it usually was.

During most of the twentieth century, the Russian Church was *under* a new rule, a hostile rule. To survive, it tried to accommodate, but the main response of the faithful was to become an **underground church**, waiting for the state to "wither away." The withering happened quickly—in 1991, three years after the thousandth anniversary of the founding of the church at Kiev. In St. Petersburg more than four hundred churches functioned in 1917. Under the Soviets that number was reduced to just fourteen. Now more than two hundred celebrate Holy Communion weekly.. Monasteries and seminaries once closed are reopening. My wife and I visited several on a recent trip to Russia. Today, when governmental officials sign laws, priests in black cassocks and jeweled pectoral crosses often stand in the background of the photos taken. That church is somewhat more *of* culture again, though, as in the United States, *not* supported by the government per se.

In the United States, where Christians were freer to criticize wrongs in the society, some did. Clergy and lay people, on the basis of their ownmost values—such as justice—have, at times, taken to the streets to change the order of things. Against the culture of slavery, **Abolitionists** of Quaker, Methodist, Congregational, and other denominational persuasion worked. Abolitionist efforts were aided by the **black churches**, South and North, churches that slaves and former slaves brought into being. Forcibly separated from Africa and tribal religions there, slaves in America accepted Christianity and thereby availed themselves of a separate worshiping niche for their lives. In church, with strong sermons, great music, and much prayer, they sustained and encouraged one another. Black and white Christians together challenged and changed that slave culture in the 1860s, and via an uncivil Civil War finally threw off the official shackles of oppression. A century later, spearheaded by black Christian leadership, still-persisting segregation was outlawed, especially through national civil rights legislation passed in 1964. In 2008 a black Christian was elected president of the United States.

Slavery was one issue, but not the only one, to which progressive Christians in America directed attention. Prohibition, women's suffrage, the rights of the unborn, and other issues were front-and-center issues. In the past fifty years, a **peace movement** arose in the church, Christians protesting several wars, most notably the one in Vietnam and two in Iraq. The cultural backdrop for this movement is the military-industrial complex so strong in the United States.

So we have reviewed some of the Christ and culture interaction in North America.

In Central and South America, faith vs. society dynamics were different. Most of the countries of Latin America have been two-class cultures, with wealthy ruling elites and poor campesinos. For the most part the established Roman Catholic Church has aligned itself with the ruling elites, but there have been clergy-with-campesinos studying scripture and analyzing society, a work called *conscientization*. The working and worshiping together has happened in **base communities**. In Brazil there are 70,000 base communities functioning today. Guided by liberation theology, which posits that God has a "preferential option for the poor," the bottom-up efforts of the base communities have brought about some positive changes in political, social, and economic structures. Nicaragua and Venezuela, for example, are more democratic today because Christ, *the transformer* of culture, has been at work through communities of conscientization.

In keeping with liberation movements of Christianity, we must also note worldwide variations of the same, not the least of which has been a **women's liberation movement**. It comes in reaction to almost-universal male chauvinist culture generally, and church male-gender practices in particular. In the long run, women's Christian liberation aims to break stained-glass ceilings! Who knows, maybe one day there will be a female pope.

*

Culture, as I said at the beginning of this chapter, is the water in which we swim, the invisible clear-glass bubble we are in. It is difficult to see the world in which we exist. Below is a "list of suspects" to be considered as the dominant culture of our day, especially in the United States. Our culture, our society is . . . what?

education valuing

individual indulging

capitalistic

scientific-technological

Brief Christian Histories

> family/child centered
>
> psychologized
>
> sex-drugs-rock 'n' roll-ed
>
> eco-conscious
>
> military-industrial-academic
>
> multinational corporationist
>
> racist . . . sexist . . . classist
>
> open, tolerant, permissive
>
> consumerist
>
> secular

It is difficult, if not impossible, to know just what items on the list above are most descriptive of our social setting. Old Testament scholar Walter Brueggemann in his book *Mandate to Difference*—unbeknownst to him and me—pulls together some of the above possible suspects into a composite profile. We have been inculcated, he says, to and by a "script":

> *The dominant scripture of both selves and communities in our society, for both liberals and conservatives, is the script of therapeutic, technological, consumer militarism that permeates every dimension of our common life.*

What he says certainly rings accurate in my estimation. Other commentators offer supportive analyses.

Harvard political scientist Robert Putnam contends that we are a people in a wired world. He observes that all generations—especially the young—are losing social connectedness.[21] Bowling leagues, PTAs, labor unions, service clubs, bridge groups, and so on all have fewer participants now than just a few decades ago. Historically such associations generated "social capital" or trust, Putnam says. Trust in social institutions (government, schools, church, press) and in public figures (politicians, businesspeople, doctors) is down. He hypothesizes that the drop in trust and in social capital is attributable to the enormous amount of television watching, computer concentrating, and Facebooking that individuals do. People do not have time for bowling-league participation and face-to-face relating. Something like a media culture could be the bubble we live in.

21. Putnam, *Bowling Alone*, 283–84.

Christ and Culture Interacting

If that is so, it can account for one religious formation in recent decades: the **megachurch**. Supersized churches seem to fit with a media culture, attracting people via a kind of entertainment evangelism. Winsome preachers preach with authority, and attractive vocalists sing with microphone to the mouth. Rock bands, rather than an organ, provide the music. All the presenter-performers are wired and show up on giant television screens in the modern sanctuaries. Also, in keeping with the society of shopping malls, megachurches offer smorgasbord programs: Bible study, barista coffee, basketball. Such for people of all ages. These churches are a major *of*-culture response.

Yet another response to modernity must be noted. This one is worldwide and of immense consequence. It is **Pentecostalism.** Beginning in a small way in the early nineteen-hundreds, this spiritual movement went viral with emotional, ecstatic, faith-healing, miracle-working, and speaking-in-tongues components. Pentecostalism swept through the world, making it a gargantuan expression of Christian faith. If we could count the number of charismatics in disparate constituencies, that number would be just behind the Roman Catholic Church in affiliation. Pentecostalism has had its greatest success in the Southern Hemisphere.

"What," we might ask, "is going on culturally to so facilitate this rapid and enormous expression of the Spirit?"

In part, it may be a reaction to the modern scientific-rational world into which much of Western—really *Northern* Hemisphere—Christianity has fallen (of which this book is illustrative). Pentecostal Christianity fills a need for things having to do with feelings and emotions. No dry-dust religion here! Pentecostalism, often allied with fundamentalist-evangelicalism, has appeal, however differing with other/older/northern formations of the faith. Philip Jenkins, professor of history and religious studies at Penn State University, provides this telling story:

> Neatly illustrating the cultural gulf that separates Northern and Southern churches is Moses Tay, the Anglican archbishop of Southeast Asia, whose see is based in Singapore. In the early 1990s, Tay traveled to the Canadian city of Vancouver. When he visited that city's Stanley Park, he encountered the totem poles

that are a local tourist attraction. To him, they [the totem poles] were idols possessed by evil spirits, which required handling by prayer and exorcism. This horrified the local Anglican church, which was committed to building good relations with local native communities, and which regarded exorcism as absurd superstition. Considering his own standards, though, it is difficult not to feel some sympathy for the archbishop. He was quite correct to see the totems as authentic religious symbols, rather than merely tourist kitsch. Considering the long span of Christian writings on exorcism and possession, he could also summon many literary witnesses to support his position, far more than the Canadian church could produce in favor of tolerant multiculturalism. On that occasion Tay personified the global Christian confrontation.[22]

It is a confrontation likely to repeat itself. Jenkins suggests that Southern Christianity—not Islam— may be the "problem religion" of the twenty-first century.

At their best moments, Christians north and south, east and west are aware that they/we exist in an interdependent, one-world context. In response there has been and is in Christianity an **ecumenical movement**. A World Missionary Conference was held in Edinburgh, Scotland, in 1910. The delegates came to this conference, it was said, speaking about "the churches," but they left speaking about "the Church."[23] By fits and starts, that speaking has gone on for a century. Occasionally aware that "we are one" and occasionally remembering that Christ wants us to be so (see John 17:21), ecumenical Christianity has been building cooperation and understanding among previously divided faith groups. Some success has been seen. In 1948 Protestants and Orthodox of many communions and nationalities joined together in a **World Council of Churches**. Some 350 Christian communions today are full members or associates in the WCC. Leaders of the council helped write the United Nations' Universal Declaration of Human Rights, a positive, potentially *transforming* contribution, if ever there was one.

Ecumenicity has proceeded apace in other communions too. In 1963–1965 the Roman Catholic Church had an *ecumenical* council called **Vatican II**. One of the council's door-openings was to the Greek Orthodox Church, enabling the rescinding of the mutual anathemas hurled in 1054. Diarmaid

---

22. Jenkins, *Next Christendom*, 130–31. See also his article, "Next Christianity," *Atlantic Monthly*, 64.

23. Mullin, *Short World Christianity*, 227.

MacCulloch observes that today "modern Christianities are more closely in touch than they have been since the first generation of Christians in the first-century Middle East."[24]

"Ecumenical" comes from the Greek word *oikoumene*, meaning "the whole inhabited world." (See the boat symbol at the start of this section.) In its future, ecumenical Christianity is likely to become more dialogical with other world religions *and* with the societies and cultures in which this faith of ours swims.

*

CONCLUDING THOUGHT ON CHRIST AND CULTURE

Our ancestral nomadic ancestors under the desert sky came to believe that "the Lord our God is One God." The Lord they surmised under that blue sky then and the Lord of the blue-orbed earth that astronauts view from space now are one and the same, the Holy One inviting faithful response from his/her people. It is an exciting time to be alive, responding to culture, world, people, and God, through the church. Though this institution of ours *seems* at times to be fragile, it is not ephemeral. A verse of an old hymn says it well:

> O where are kings and empires now
> Of old that went and came?
> But, Lord, thy church is praying yet,
> A thousand years the same.

Praying "*yet the same*"? Perhaps. Differently too. Because we are influenced. Yes. We are that. But we are also, we pray, influencing kings and empires.

*

---

24. MacCulloch, *Christianity*, 4.

Brief Christian Histories

Questions for Reflection and Discussion

1. How much do you think nature and geography shape faith? And what does the natural world, as we understand it, call for in the way of Christian response and formation today?

2. In which of the nine time periods (Pre-Monarchic to Ecumenical/Global Age) do you think our faith-parents were at their best, the most godly? When did we come closest to losing it? Can cultural/societal/civil circumstances be so severe as ultimately to destroy Christianity? Conversely, what were the best climates or cultures for Christianity?

3. Much Christian history shows our religious ancestors "keeping the faith" when they were under a dominant hostile power. Recount the occasions when this was true. Now ask, where is persecution happening today? Of whom? By whom? What about *on our part*?

4. In the text just above is a "list of suspects" as the main culture forces operating in America today. Which one or two of these seem most pervasive?

5. How might Christians be working to transform the world/culture/nation/neighborhood? Suggest a particular positive tension *for Christ's sake* for you and your church.

Conclusion
Looking Back, Looking Forward

Let me begin this concluding section with a question put by the seventeenth-century mystic Angelus Silesius (1624–1677 CE) to an archangel:

> Of what use, Gabriel,
> Your message to Maria
> Unless you now give
> The same message to me?

What might that message be? Well, first, foremost, and always, "Fear not!" And then, perhaps, "Know whom you carry." Christians of every time and place need to hear the "Fear not" and then go forward carrying the message of God's great love in Christ Jesus for them and all the world.

Whether you have read only one "history" in this book or all four, I hope you have a *feel* for the long historic Christian pilgrimage. Possibly/hopefully, the reading did more: it enriched understanding—even appreciation—of this faith. The best outcome of all, of course, would be that the book deepened the reader in this hoary-yet-ever-fresh faith of ours, and stimulated ideas on how to carry the story forward with resolve to do so. As we come to the end, I have questions:

> Was there a person in the chapter 1 narrative who intrigued you, made you want to know more about him/her, even stimulated thoughts of emulation?

> Did you receive any clarification in the Christians' ethics chapter that helps you recognize your own ethical stance and, perchance, encourages action for the good?
>
> How about learnings from the practices and piety pages? Did you recognize deportments of the past that operate today, even in you? Most assuredly you heard about some things only worth forgetting! How about discovering "behaviors of old" worth resurrecting?
>
> Finally, in consideration of Christ and culture, did those pages activate consideration of where the church and society today should be going? Is there now any new "tension for Christ's sake"?

At the end of these histories, it is "meet and right" to consider where our long story may be heading. Given the endurance of religions generally and of Christianity in particular, it seems fair to believe there will be no "withering away" of religion in the years to come. Christianity, Judaism, Islam, Buddhism, Hinduism, Shintoism, and others will all be around to comfort and to afflict. Of the six million people on earth, probably 99 percent are religious, with the great majority connected to one of the major world religions. Christianity has by far the largest number of adherents, 2.3 billion. What will happen with these two-plus billion remains to be seen. Robert Bruce Mullin quotes church historian Sydney Ahlstrom to the effect that "history has no future." Still, Mullin speculates along three lines involving overlapping trends: there will be (1) a Northern-Southern-Hemispheres split in Christianity, (2) continued vigor in the Western evangelistic churches (and, I would say, especially through Pentecostalism), and (3) positive developments in Roman Catholicism.[1] Mullin adds, "[I]f the long story of Christianity shows one thing, it is that surprise is the stuff of history."[2] Another world Christian historian, Philip Jenkins, also sees continued growth in Southern Christianity and that it may be "the problem religion" of the twenty-first century. He also thinks there is no way to avoid Christian vs. Islam competition, perhaps conflict. Finally, though, he says,

> If there is one overarching lesson from this record of changing fortunes, it is that (to adapt the famous adage about Russia) Christianity is never as weak as it appears, nor as strong as it appears. And whether we look backward or forward in history, we can see that

---

1. Mullin, *Short World Christianity*, 279–81.
2. Ibid., 282.

time and again, Christianity demonstrates a breathtaking ability to transform weakness into strength.[3]

Yet a third analysis of the foreseeable religious scene—one for America, anyway—comes from Robert Putnam, political scientist and professor of public policy at Harvard. He observes that, though "the nones" (meaning people who check "none" when asked about their religious affiliation) are growing in number in the United States, according to his and other studies, these "nones" are still open to faith involvement and will be reached by "religious entrepreneurship," which is still alive and well in Christianity.[4]

However things take shape for Christianity in the future, I believe we can have a share in keeping the story alive. One of the keeping-alive ways is to continue telling the story in fresh ways. To the four histories plus the people timeline laid out in this book, let other holistic biblical-ecclesial trajectories be given. I know I have taught and drafted "in kind" possibilities. For this book, I considered doing something with the theme "Geo-Movements of the Faith(ful)—Pilgrims' Treks on/to 'Thin' and 'Hard Rock' Places." That theme would take our story from the time of Abram and Sarai's journey along the Fertile Crescent in the eighteenth century BCE to Pentecostalism's sweep through the Southern Hemisphere during the last one hundred years. It would say definitely that we have been a people "on the move"—and a people moved.

There are other possible themes, for example, worship through the centuries, earth spirituality, women's work done, our story in architecture-music-art-literature. Such histories need not be traced just by this author. I would encourage pastors and teachers to identify important motifs and line them out historically . . . like, word of the Lord, justice and love's story, and teachers in the tradition. Parishioners and students may be grateful for topical-yet-whole-cloth presentations. Then too students could write essays on the Christian long story by themes of interest: children and youth through the years, apocalypses then till now, animals on the ride, and so on. Let historical-possibility imaginations run. Topics and venues for presentation are virtually endless. Go for it, dear reader-teacher-pilgrims!

To go, you may want to get beyond *Brief Christian Histories* and peruse other shorter books on Bible narrative and church history—which, please remember, are never joined. Still, look at books in both genres as you can. Consider too a good *un*brief history. There are some great ones,

3. Jenkins, *The Next Christianity*, 220.
4. Putnam, *American Grace*, 119.

as the bibliography of this book reveals. The thicker volumes do not, sad to say, combine biblical story with post-Jesus ecclesial history either, as I've done here, but one notable and commendable exception stands: Diarmaid MacCulloch's *Christianity the First Three Thousand Years*. It's a really, really big read of 1184 pages, in which he, at least, traces a millennium of our pre-Jesus story. I commend such an unbrief publication to readers who want to review our long history in greater depth and to gain appreciation for the breadth of Christianities. In the meantime, hopefully, this book of four concise whole-narrative trajectories has gotten the inquirer well started.

Thank you for journeying with me.

Appendix A
A Listing of Some Biblical and Ecclesial Roles, Offices, Titles, and Functions

Abba/e/ess/ot
Abun (Ethiopia)
Acolyte
Activist
Administrator
Advocate
Agnostic
Altarboy/girl
Anabaptist
Anchorite/ess
Angel
Anointed
Anti-Christ
Antiquarian
Apologist
Apostate
Apostle
Archbishop
Archimandrite
Architect
Archpriest/deacon
Artist (in . . .)
Atheist
Author

Baptizer/ed/ist
Believer
Bishop
Brother
Builder

Canon
Cantor
Cardinal
Caregiver
Catholic
Celebrant
Celibate
Cellarer
Cenobite
Chairperson
Chaplain
Charismatic
Choir director
Choir member
Chorister
Chosen
Christian +
Clergyperson
Clerk
Coadjutor
Comforter
Committee member
Composer
Confessor
Confirmand
Conservative
Contemplative
Copyist
Counselor
Crusader
Cupbearer

Curate

Deacon/ess
Dean
Defender
Deist
Delegate
Deliverer
Director of . . .
Disciple
Dissenter
Divine
Doctor of . . .

Editor
Educator
Elder
Emperor
Eremite
Ethicist
Evangelical
Evangelist
Exarch (Bulgaria)
Exile or Exilic

Faith Healer
Father
Follower
Founder
Freedom fighter
Friar or Fray

201

Appendix A

God-fearer
Governor
Greeter
Guest Master

Healer
Heretic
Hermit
Hesychast
Historian
Holy helper
Holy man
Holy Roller
Homiletician
Hospitaller
Hymnist

Innocent, Holy
Inquirer
Inquisitor
Intercessor
Jacobean/ite
Jesuit
Judaizer
Judge
Jurist

King
Knight Templar

Lawyer
Layperson
Leader
Lector
Legate/delegate
Levite
Liberal
Liberator
Librarian

Martyr
Medium
Mendicant
Mentor
Messenger
Messiah
Metropolitan
Minister of . . .

Miracle worker
Missionary
Moderator
Monk
Monsignor
Mother superior
Mourner
Musician
Mystic

Nazirite
Negus (king)
Novice
Nun

Oblate
Officiant
Organist
Orthodox
Pacifist
Padre
Pallbearer
Papist
Parson
Pastor
Patriarch
Patron
Penitent/e
Pentecostal
Pharisee
Pilgrim
Poet
Pope
Porter
Praise team leader
Pray-er
Preacher
Preacher's kid
Preacher's wife
Prebend
Prelate
Presbyter
President
Priest/ess
Primate
Prince
Prior/ess
Professor

Prophet/ess
Protector
Psalmist
Puritan

Queen

Rabbi
Rationalist
Rector
Redactor
Reformer
Religious
Repairer
Restorationist
Reverend
Revivalist
Ruling elder

Sadducee
Saint
Satanist
Scholar
Scooter
Scribe
Secretary of . . .
Seer
Sexton
Singer
Sinner
Sister
Soldier
Spiritual director
Sponsor
Steward
Student
Sub-prior
Superintendent

Teacher
Theologian
Timothy
Translator
Treasurer
Trustee

Usher

A Listing of Some Biblical and Ecclesial Roles, Offices, Titles, and Functions

Vardapet	Visionary	Writer
Verger		
Vestryperson	Widow	YMCA secretary
Vicar, vicar general	Witness	Youth pastor
Virgin	Wonder worker	
Virgin-Martyr	Worshiper	Zealot

*There are hundreds more categories that could be added, especially were we to put down the names for certain movements, orders, or denominations to which people are adherents. For the letter "M," consider: Manichean, Marcionite, Marianist, Maronite, Melchiorite, Melchite, Melitianite, Mennonite, Mercedarian, Methodist, Miaphysite, Millennialist, Molokan, Monarchist, Monophysite, Monothelete, Montanist, Moravian, and Mormon. But no!

Appendix B
Christian Practices and Pieties through the Years

(A Partial List, of Ccourse)

Acolyting
Art (many kinds), doing of
Ashes, imposing/wearing
Aspersing holy water
Ashes, imposing/wearing

Baptizing children and adults
Bell tolling, stone ringing
Bible reading/studying
Blogging for the faith
Bowing one's head for . . .
Bright corner keeping
Bulletin typing and reading
Bumper sticker messaging

Candle lighting
Canvassing for stewardship, etc.
Caring for . . .
Castrating oneself / breast removal
Catechetical learning
Chair stacking, setting up tables
Chanting
Choir singing
Christ-mass attending
Christening one's child
Church attending, weekly/daily
Committee work (!)
Communion-taking
Confirming the faith
Conscientious objecting

Contemplative praying/living
Cross/angel/pin wearing
Crossing oneself at . . .

Dancing liturgically
Devotional reading
Dressing up for church

Easter worshiping
Ejaculating praise
Evangelizing

Fasting
"Faith alone" living
Fasting
Flagellating oneself
Forty-day Lent observing

"God bless you" saying
Good deeds doing
Gourd calabash rattling
"Grace" saying at meals

"Hate-hymns" singing
Healing acts
Hospitality, offering of

Incense burning
"Intentions" offering
Invoking divine intervention

Appendix B

Jesus Prayer reciting
Jewelry/ring wearing

Keeping holy days/seasons
Killing for Christ

Labyrinth walking
Laying on of hands
Learning/studying

Listening to Christian radio
Living simply
Lord's Prayer reciting

Marching in/for . . .
Marriage and other vows keeping
Martyrdom accepting
Meditating
Miracle working
Mission trip, going on
Monstrance showing
Music playing, singing, writing

Not cooking a hot-meal
Not doing _____, _____
Not going to _____, _____
Not playing _____, _____
Not pledging allegiance to flag
Not saying _____, _____

Offering tithes and gifts
Ora et labora routine following
Oath taking on Bible, bell, relic

Painting, sculpting, carving, etc.
Paying Peter's Pence (to Rome)
Pilgrimage taking
Playing the organ or other instrument
Pledging allegiance to flag
Poster drawing and distributing
Potluck supper dish preparing
Poverty-chastity-obedience keeping
"PPM" (Peter-Paul-Mary) scribbling
Prayer group participating
Prayer mat praying
Prayer shawl knitting
Praying anywhere, anytime
   at church, in a closet
   before a meal
   hands folded, raised, on lap, etc.
   seated, knelling, prostate
Profanity-avoiding

Rain- entreating/making
Reciting a psalm or prayer
Recycling
Responding antiphonally
Retreat, going on
Roadside shrine building
Rosary saying

Sabbath or Sunday keeping
Sacraments and ordinances keeping
Seancing
Serving as usher, reader, janitor, etc.
Silence observing
Shrine visiting
Singing
   in choir, at home, solos, etc.
   Sanctus, refrains, hymns
Small Group praying/studying
Snake handling
Solo fide living
Speaking in tongues/*glossolalia*
Spiritual counseling, taking, giving
Spiritual living
Staff (tall cross) bearing
Studying the scriptures or a book
Suffering voluntarily
Sweat lodge purging

Taizé-style worshiping
Taking Communion
Tattooing (Ethiopia, Maori)
Teaching a class on/for . . .
Teetotaling
Theological reading/teaching
Tracts distributing
Trusting the wind in a boat
Tithing/giving
T-shirt messaging
Ushering

Venerating Mary, relics, a saint, icon
Visiting the sick, shut-ins, prisoners
Vow taking and keeping

Christian Practices and Pieties through the Years

Wearing religious apparel
Weeping over one's sins
Welcoming guests
Witnessing for Christ
Working (as one's vocation)
Worshiping at church
   listening, singing, note taking
   praying, passing peace, giving
   responding "Amen"/"Alelluia"
   barking, dancing, etc.
Writing politician on an issue

Yoga, Qigong, etc., practicing

Appendix C
Author's History with These Histories

(A Thirty-nine-year Record)

MOST AMAZING TO ME is how many years I have been working on this book. Some parts of it as early as 1976! When I first taught classes on any of the themes of this book, I talked from a one-page outline. Many of those outlines I kept. They've reminded me of when and where and for whom I've made presentations. In the 1990s, I started to turn those scratchy notes into prose sentences for hand-out papers, and I began to think about compiling these documents for a book. All along the way I recorded when and where I wrote and who helped by listening, reading, and responding.

In 2006 *Christianity 101: Tracing Basic Beliefs* was published.

I considered a sequel to that book, for I had some chapters roughly completed. But no, that seemed the end of writing Christian history for me. I was more interested in doing a fishing book, and I did: *Round Boys Great Adventures: Fish-a-logues through Rocky Mountain Trout Waters*, published in 2010 by Whitefish Press.

Through the last decade, however, I did several interim ministries and taught courses in those churches that I served, using the themes of the '06 book *and* other themes for conveying "sense of our whole faith story." I compiled considerable written material. Finally, in 2012, came the thought, "Instead of a sequel, how about a fresh book on faith history?" It started to take shape. Inquiries were made and an offer to publish was tendered by Wipf and Stock (thank you, Christian Amondson!). Focused reading and writing started anew. Eventually, the *Brief Christian Histories* manuscript emerged.

Appendix C

The records below recall dates of work, important people who helped with reads and critiques, as well as notes about settings for writing, some of it decades ago, some quite recent. The notations also reveal a variety of titles for the talks and chapters—and great differences in abbreviations.

Thanks, dear reader-friends, for your red pencils. Many of your names are shown below, And thank you, providers of space for reading and composition—but again, especially, thanks, Patti, wife nonpareil, for your patience and support. Once, when I came home from a long fly-fishing trip, you surprised me with a totally remodeled study. The built-to-order oak desk has been an inspirational work station! And, there was/is an attached fly-tying bench! The main desk makes for productive work, the bench for satisfying distraction!

Hoping the abbreviations used below are semi-self-explanatory, here, are the records:

INTRODUCTION

Writing/Rewriting Mar to May into Aug, 2013 . . . Critiques by Tom Stella & Deb Saxon . . . Then, changes via reading MacCulloch's *Christianity* . . . Shortening at Carol Malkin's suggestion . . . Clean-up by Patti White, 22 August 2013 . . . Incorporating Lucy Bell's suggestions Sep 7, 2013 . . . Supposed finishing second week of Sep, 2013 . . . Fall 2013 content- and copy-editing by Hermann Weinlick's revising and polishing.

PEOPLE OF GOD

Teaching Occasions

First taught from outline "Persons and Roles," October 10, 1977, First Plymouth UCC, Denver . . . Again at FP2C, April 23, 1978 and November 13, 1979 as "Persons and Literature" . . . March 16, 1988, First Cong'l UCC, Westfield, NJ, as "Faith Models—Principle Figures" with accompanying sermon entitled "The Fulcrum of History: One Solitary Life") . . . September 26, 1989, First Cong'l UCC, Colorado Springs, "Faith Models—Holy Figures" . . . March 22, 1995 as "Our Faith's Main Characters and Evolving Roles" . . . February 19, 2002, First Cong'l UCC, Colorado Springs . . . Again, March 12, 2003 . . . University Cong'l Church in Wichita, June 17, 2008 . . . Bukit Doa Protestant Church of Bali, January, 2012 . . . Taught at

FCC/UCC and Pillar Adult Learning Center, Colorado Springs, Feb & Mar 2013

Written Drafts

Sentence outline, 7pp, 1977 . . . First draft November 6–8, Taos, NM & December 9, 2000, Colorado Springs . . . Draft, November 21–December 2, 2001, Columbia Seminary, Decatur, GA . . . Revising, December 2, 4, 5, 6, 9, 10, 11, 12, 13, 16, 17, 18, 19, 20, 24, 2002, Colorado Springs, CO . . . Incorporating reads by John Saxon and Kay Branine, March 22 & 23, 2003 . . . Revising May 28–29, 2003 . . . Editing, August 15, 2004 . . . Redrafted June 19, 2006 . . . Start rewrite in Bali Jan 2012, followed in Colorado Springs, off & on till November 2012 . . . More work from Jan until Mar 18, 2013 from read by Professor David McCracken . . . Rework after reading MacCulloch's *Christianity*, Aug & Sep, 2013 . . . Supposed finishing 2nd Week of September, 2013 . . . Fall 2013 content- and copy-editing by Hermann Weinlick =s revising and polishing.

PEOPLE TIMELINE

Nov 12, 2012 . . . Jan 29 . . . Feb 14 . . . Apr 7 . . . Jul 30 . . . Aug 9–Sep 10, 2013 . . . Supposed finishing 2nd Week of September, 2013 . . . Fall 2013 content- and copy-editing by Hermann Weinlick =s revising and polishing.

CHRISTIANS' ETHICS

Teaching Occasions

November 7, 1976, First Plymouth, Denver as "Theology & Ethics" . . . May 7, 1978, First Plymouth, Denver as "Belief and Behavior" . . . March 15 & 20, 1988, Westfield, NJ as "Ethics: Faith in Action" . . . March 19, 1991, FCC CS as "Evolution of Ethics" . . . March 6, 1996, FCC CS as "What Was/Is Sin & Evil?" . . . February 12, 2003, FCC CS as "ETHICS" . . . April 20, 2008—University Cong'l Church, Wichita . . . January 8, 2012 in Bali as "Christians' Ethics" . . . Feb & Mar 2013 at Pillar and FCC, C/S

Appendix C

Written Drafts

March, 1996, FCC CS as "Whence Sin/Evil?" . . . February 19, 1997, from teaching First Cong UCC, Colorado Springs Class . . . Corrected: March 5–8, 1997, CS as "ETHICS/SIN/EVIL" . . . Reworked August 21–23, 2000 as "Not an Oxymoron: Christian Ethics" . . . Reworked December 7–14, 2001, Decatur, GA with comments from Walter Brueggemann, Mark Douglas, and Justo Gonzalez . . . Minor reworking February 11, 2002 . . . Thorough rewriting April 29–30, May 1–8, 2003 . . . Final final [I was wrong] revising June 5, 2003 [Thought *eight* chapters were going into a *BC 101*] . . . Updating, April 2008 . . . Revising with hope for Publication, January and July 2012 . . . Further work Jul 1–28, 2012, then Feb 22–Mar 5, Aug 11–20, 2013 . . . Reworking after Reading MacCulloch's *Christianity*, August 8ff, 2013 . . . Supposed finishing 2nd Week of September, 2013 . . . Fall 2013 content- and copy-editing by Hermann Weinlick =s revising and polishing.

PRACTICES AND PIETIES

Teaching Occasions

First Class, First Cong'l UCC, Colorado Springs: March 10, 1997 . . . FP2C (Denver) Retreat: September 13, 1997 . . . FCC/CS Men's Retreat, October 25, 1997 . . . . . . "Basic Xnty 102" Class, FCC CS, April 27, 2008 . . . Bali Church Class, January 15, 2012 . . . FCC CS Class, March 24, 2013

Written Drafts

First Draft @ Taos, NM: March 8–9, 1997 . . . Rewriting September 7–12, 1997 . . . Bali, Indonesia, January, 2012 . . . Colorado Springs, Aug & Sep, 2012 . . . Work on 24 Aug, 2012 . . . Reworking, Colo Sprgs, March into Apr 9–16, 2013 . . . San Juan River Writing, Apr 24–25, 2013 . . . Reads by Tom Stella and Deb Saxon for critiques, May & Jul, 2013 . . . Fixing after reading MacCulloch's *Christianity*, Aug 11–30, 2013 . . . Supposed finishing 2nd Week of September, 2013 . . . Fall 2013 content- and copy-editing by Hermann Weinlick =s revising and polishing.

CHRIST AND CULTURES INTERACTING

Teaching Occasions

First Plymouth, Denver, November 7, 1976 as "Cultures & Cultus"... FP2C, Denver, May 14, 1977 as "Ecclesiology/Cults & Roles" . . . FP2C, Denver, April 30, 1978 as "Cultures & Faith Shaping" . . . FP2C, Denver, December 11, 1979 as "Cultures/Faith/Art"... First Cong, Colo Sprgs, March 19, 1997 as "Cultures and Created Cults" . . . Sept 13, 1997—FP2C (Denver) Men's Retreat as "Cultures Faith Has Lived *In* / Lives *In*." . . Oct 25, 1997—FCC (Colo Spgs) Men's Retreat as "Cultures Faith Has Lived *In* / Lives *In*." . . January 22, 2012 (Bali) as "Cultural & Social Interactions" . . . Pillar Adult Educaton Center & FCC CS, March 12 & 17, 2013

Written Drafts

April 5, 1995, FCC CS as "Cultures and Created Cults" . . . March 27, 1996, FCC CS as "Religious Formations" . . . 10/27ff/97 & 2/2–5/98 as "Culture and Faith" . . . February 24–27, 2002 in Taos, New Mexico . . . July 1–6, 2002 — Arrowhead Ranch, Fairplay, CO . . . February 12–22, 2003, Reworking, Colorado Springs . . . June 3–7, 2003, Revising a la John Saxon's read . . . In prep for class, January 2012, Bali, Indonesia . . . Start rewrite, post-Bali, Colorado Springs, 2012 . . . Continued reworking, given to Jim Matson for editing March, 2013, then reworking using Matson's critiques April 6–8, 2013 . . . Day of work on it, Aug 11, 2013 . . . Rework after reading MacCulloch's *Christianity*, Aug 29–Sep 7, 2013 . . . Supposed finishing 2nd Week of September, 2013 . . . Fall 2013 content- and copy-editing by Hermann Weinlick =s revising and polishing.

CONCLUSION: LOOKING BACK, LOOKING FORWARD

Collection of "Possible Material," late 2012 into 2013 . . . Worked on Mar 7, 2013 . . . Serious composition and revising 21 August 2013 . . . More work on conclusion, September 7, 2013 . . . Supposed finishing 2nd Week of September, 2013 . . . Fall 2013 content- and copy-editing by Hermann Weinlick =s revising and polishing.

Appendix C

BIBIOGRAPHY

[Bibliographies *had* been attached to individual chapters.]

First Collection/Compilation, C/S, July 22, 2012 . . . February 22, 2013 work. . . off and on through the summer, 2013 . . . Supposed finishing 2nd Week of September, 2013 . . . Fall 2013 content- and copy-editing by Hermann Weinlick =s revising and polishing.

Bibliography

Alighieri, Dante. *The Divine Comedy.* Translated by John Ciardi. New York: New American Library, 2003.
Anderson, Bernhard W. *The Unfolding Drama of the Bible: Eight Studies Introducing the Bible as a Whole.* Philadelphia: Fortress, 1990.
Aristotle. *Nicomachean Ethics.* Translated by J. A. K. Thomson. *The Ethics of Aristotle.* Baltimore: Penguin, 1953.
Armstrong, Dorsey. *The Medieval World.* Great Courses CD Lectures and Guidebook. Chantilly, VA: The Teaching Company, 2009.
———. *Turning Points in Medieval History.* Great Courses CD Lectures and Guidebook. Chantilly, VA: The Teaching Company, 2012.
Atlas of the Christian Church. Edited by Henry Chadwick and G. R. Evans. New York: Facts on File, 1987.
Bailie, Gil. *Violence Unveiled: Humanity at the Crossroads.* New York: Crossroads, 1999.
Bainton, Roland. *The Church of Our Fathers.* New York: Charles Scribner's Sons, 1978.
Bangley, Bernard, editor. *Butler's Lives of the Saints.* Brewster, MA: Paraclete Press, 2005.
Baur, John. *2000 Years of Christianity in Africa: An African Church History.* Nairobi: Paulines Publications Africa, 2001.
Brown, Robert McAfee. *The Bible Speaks to You.* Philadelphia: Westminster, 1955.
Brueggemann, Walter. *An Introduction to the Old Testament: The Canon and Christian Imagination.* Louisville, KY: Westminster John Knox, 2003.
———. *Mandate to Difference: An Invitation to the Contemporary Church.* Louisville: Westminster John Knox, 2007.
Buechner, Frederick. *Peculiar Treasures: A Biblical Who's Who.* San Francisco: Harper & Row, 1979.
Cahill, Thomas. *How the Irish Saved Civilization: The Untold Story of Ireland's Heroic Role from the Fall of Rome to the Rise of Medieval Europe.* New York: Doubleday, 1995.
———. *The Gifts of the Jews: How a Tribe of Desert Nomads Changed the Way Everyone Thinks and Feels.* New York: Nan A. Talese/Anchor Books, 1998.
Campbell, Alexander. *The Covenant Story of the Bible.* New York: Pilgrim, 1986.
Chidester, David. *Christianity: A Global History.* New York: HarperSanFrancisco, 2000.
Chittister, Joan. *In Search of Belief.* Liguori, MO: Triumph, 1999.
Christianity: The First Thousand Years. Video program. A&E Television Network, 1999.
Cook, William R. *The Lives of Great Christians.* Great Courses CD Lectures and Guidebook. Chantilly, VA: The Teaching Company, 2007.

Bibliography

Culver, Elsie Thomas. *Women in the World of Religion: From Pagan Priestesses to Ecumenical Delegates.* Garden City, NY: Doubleday, 1967.

Cunningham, Lawrence S. *A Brief History of Saints.* Victoria, Australia: Blackwell, 2005.

Daileader, Philip. *The Early Middle Ages.* Great Courses CD Lectures and Guidebook. Chantilly, VA: The Great Courses, 2004.

Dowley, Tim. *The Story of Christianity.* Herts, England: Lion, 1981.

Edwards, David L. *Christianity: The First Two Thousand Years.* Maryknoll, NY: Orbis, 1997.

Eerdmans Dictionary of the Bible. Edited by David Noel Freedman. Grand Rapids: William B. Eerdmans, 2000.

Fant, Clyde E., Donald W. Musser, and Mitchell G. Reddish. *An Introduction to the Bible,* Revised Edition. Nashville: Abingdon, 2001.

Farmer, David Hugh. *The Oxford Dictionary of Saints.* Oxford: Oxford University Press, 1997.

Fedler, Kyle D. *Exploring Christian Ethics: Biblical Foundations for Morality.* Louisville, KY: Westminster John Knox, 2006.

Feiler, Bruce. *Walking the Bible: A Journey by Land through the Five Books of Moses.* New York: HarperCollins, 2002.

Finkelstein, Israel, and Neil Asher Silberman. *The Bible Unearthed: Archaeology's New Vision of Ancient Israel and the Origin of Its Sacred Texts.* New York: Simon & Schuster, 2001.

Fosdick, Harry Emerson. *A Guide to Understanding the Bible: The Development of Ideas within the Old and New Testaments.* New York: Harper & Bros., 1938.

Foster, Richard J. *Streams of Living Water: Celebrating the Great Traditions of Christian Faith.* New York: HarperSanFrancisco, 1998.

Freud, Sigmund. *Moses and Monotheism.* New York: Vintage Books, 1967.

George, Timothy. *History of Christianity*, Video Lectures. Samford University, 1998.

Girard, René. *The Girard Reader.* Edited by James G. Williams. New York: Crossroads, 2000.

González, Justo L. *The Changing Shape of Church History.* St. Louis: Chalice, 2002.

———. *Church History: An Essential Guide.* Nashville: Abingdon, 1996.

———. *The Story of Christianity.* Volume 1: *The Early Church to the Dawn of the Reformation,* and Volume 2: *The Reformation to the Present Day.* San Francisco: Harper, 1984.

Great People of the Bible and How They Lived. G. Ernest Wright, advisor and consultant. Pleasantville, NY: Reader's Digest Association, 1974.

Hart, Michael H. *The 100: A Ranking of the Most Influential Persons in History.* New York: Citadel, 1992.

Howell, James C. *Exploring Christianity: The Bible, Faith, and Life.* Harrisburg, PA: Trinity Press, 2001.

Ignatius of Loyola. *The Spiritual Exercises.* Preface by Avery Dulles. New York: Random House, 2000.

Internet, The. Google, Yahoo, and other search engines.

Introduction to the History of Christianity. Edited by Tim Dowley et al. Minneapolis: Fortress, 1995.

Jenkins, Philip. *The Next Christendom: The Coming of Global Christianity.* New York: Oxford University Press, 2002.

———. "The Next Christianity," *The Atlantic Monthly.* October 2002.

Bibliography

John of Damascus. *The Precious Pearl: The Lives of Saints Barlaam and Joasaph*. Quoted and referenced in a larger Christian history, MacCulloch's *Christianity*.

Johnston, George. *Opening the Scriptures: A Journey through the Stories and Symbols of the Bible*. Toronto: United Church of Canada, 1992.

Kempis, Thomas à. *The Imitation of Christ*. Garden City, NY: Image Books, 1958.

Lawrence, Jim. "The Great Story of Your Faith: Defining Moments in Christian History," an interactive media course, Pacific School of Religion, Berkeley, CA, August 6–12, 2013.

Lester, Toby. "Oh, Gods." *Atlantic Monthly*. February, 2002. Pages 37–45.

Lovin, Robin W. *Christian Ethics: An Essential Guide*. Nashville: Abingdon, 2000.

Lynch, Joseph H. *The Medieval Church: A Brief History*. London: Longman, 1992.

Marty, Martin E. *A Short History of Christianity*. Minneapolis: Fortress, 1987.

———. *The Christian Story*, six videos. Minneapolis: Tabgha Foundation, 2002.

MacCulloch, Diarmaid. *Christianity: The First Three Thousand Years*. London: Penguin, 2011.

McBrien, Richard P. *Lives of the Saints: From Mary and Francis of Assisi to John XXIII and Mother Teresa*. San Francisco: HarperSanFrancisco, 2001.

McManners, John. *The Oxford Illustrated History of Christianity*. Oxford: Oxford University Press, 1990.

Mullin, Robert Bruce. *A Short World History of Christianity*. Louisville, KY: Westminster John Knox, 2008.

New Encyclopedia of Christian Martyrs, The. Compiled by Mark Water. Grand Rapids: Baker, 2001.

Niebuhr, H. Richard. *Christ and Culture*. New York: Harper & Row, 1951.

———. *The Responsible Self: An Essay in Christian Moral Philosophy*. New York: Harper & Row, 1963.

Niebuhr, Reinhold. *Moral Man and Immoral Society: A Study in Ethics and Politics*. New York: Charles Scribner's Sons, 1932; Louisville, KY: Westminster John Knox, 2013.

Noll, Mark A. *Turning Points: Decisive Moments in the History of Christianity*. Grand Rapids: Baker Academic, 2012.

Oxford Dictionary of the Christian Church, The. Edited by F. L. Cross and E. A. Livingstone. Oxford: Oxford University Press, 1997.

Pelikan, Jaroslav. *Jesus through the Centuries: His Place in the History of Culture*. New Haven, CT: Yale University Press, 1985.

Prothero, Stephen. *Religious Literacy: What Every American Needs to Know—and Doesn't*. New York: HarperCollins, 2007.

Putnam, Robert D. *Bowling Alone: The Collapse and Revival of American Community*. New York: Simon & Schuster, 2000.

———, and David E. Campbell. *American Grace: How Religion Divides and Unites Us*. New York: Simon & Schuster, 2010.

Robinson, James M. *Trajectories through Early Christianity*. Philadelphia: Fortress, 1971.

Rosenwein, Barbara H. *A Short History of the Middle Ages*. Toronto: University of Toronto Press, 2009.

Sanneh, Lamin. *Translating the Message: The Missionary Impact on Culture*. Maryknoll, NY: Orbis, 1995.

Schleiermacher, Friedrich. *The Christian Faith*. Edinburgh: T. & T. Clark, 1956.

Sedgwick, Timothy F. *The Christian Moral Life: Practices of Piety*. Grand Rapids: Eerdmans, 2008.

Bibliography

Shelley, Bruce L. *Church History in Plain Language*. Dallas: Word, 1995.
Sundry Professors of The Teaching Company. *Great Authors of the Western Literary Tradition*, 2nd Edition. Chantilly, VA: The Teaching Company, 2004.
Tillich, Paul. *Theology of Culture*. New York: Oxford University Press, 1959.
Twain, Mark. *The Adventures of Huckleberry Finn*. New York: Bantam, 1989.
Volf, Miroslav. *A Public Faith: How Followers of Christ Should Serve the Common Good*. Grand Rapids: Brazos, 2011.
Westminster Dictionary of Church History. Philadelphia: Westminster, 1971.
White, James W. *Christianity 101: Tracing Basic Beliefs*. Louisville, KY: Westminster John Knox, 2006.
Who's Who in Christian History. Edited by J. D. Douglas and Philip W. Comfort. Wheaton, IL: Tyndale Publishers, 1992.
Wink, Walter. *Engaging the Powers: Discernment and Resistance in a World of Domination*. Minneapolis: Fortress, 1992.
———. *The Powers that Be: Theology for a New Millennium*. New York: Doubleday, 1998.
Wogaman, J. Philip. *Christian Ethics: A Historical Introduction*. Louisville, KY: Westminster John Knox, 1993.
———, and Douglas M. Strong, editors. *Readings in Christian Ethics: A Historical Sourcebook*. Louisville, KY: Westminster John Knox, 1996.
Wright, G. Ernest, and Reginald H. Fuller. *The Book of the Acts of God: Contemporary Scholarship Interprets the Bible*. Garden City, NY: Anchor, 1960.
Wright, N. T. *After You Believe: Why Christian Character Matters*. New York: HarperCollins, 2010.
Yearbook of American and Canadian Churches 2003. Edited by Eileen W. Lindner. Nashville: Abingdon, 2003.
There are any number of movies, made both by major film companies and religious media houses, about biblical and ecclesial figures: *Becket, Bonhoeffer, David, Francis of Assisi, Jesus, Joan of Arc, Hus, Luther, Michelangelo, Moses, Paul, Romero, Teresa of Lisieux, Thomas More, Wycliffe*, etc. Nexflix, Gateway Films (info@visionvideo.com), and Christian Videos are three excellent sources for these.

People Index

Persons mentioned two-plus times with some singular exceptions)
(Also, see People Timeline, pp. 51–64)

Abram/Abraham (and Sarai/Sarah), 10, 52, 69, 71, 100, 106, 110, 150, 152, 154, 199
Adam and Eve, 10, 52, 68, 108, 115, 117
Aaron, 12, 49, 152, 154
Ahab, King, and Queen Jezebel, 13, 111, 155
Alaric the Visigoth, 23, 25, 55, 168
Amos, 14, 49, 53, 74, 155
Anskar, Saint, 28, 50, 57
Arius, 23, 165
Athanasius, 23, 55, 122, 165, 166
Antony/Anthony, Saint, 14, 24, 55, 87, 111, 137
Augustine of Canterbury, 26, 56
Augustine of Hippo, 23, 32, 55, 70n, 85–86, 89, 92, 123, 166

Barth, Karl, 46, 63, 100, 189
Bartolomé de las Casas, 38, 60, 98
Basil of Caesarea, 23, 24, 86, 124, 166
Beecher, Henry Ward, 44, 100
Benedict of Nursia, 2, 25, 50, 51, 56, 86
Benedict XVI, Pope, 4, 7, 64
Bernard of Clairvaux, Saint, 58, 131
Bonhoeffer, Dietrich, 46, 64, 101
Boniface/Wynfrith, 26, 30, 56, 129
Boniface VIII, Pope, 59, 175
Brown, Robert McAfee, 9

Brueggemann, Walter, 72, 192

Charlemagne, 29–30, 57, 87, 129, 170, 172, 175
Chaucer, Geoffrey, 33, 126, 176
Chittister, Joan, 8, 215
Chrysostom, John, 49, 111, 166
Coffin, William Sloane, 46
Columba, 25, 56, 86, 169
Cranmer, Thomas, 35, 61, 135
Cromwell, Oliver, 35, 62
Cyril and Methodius, 26, 57, 120, 171
Cyrus the Persian, 15, 53, 76, 113, 157

"D"/Deuteronomist, 13, 16, 73, 74
Daniel, 114
Dante Alighieri, xi, 33, 59, 76, 92, 176, 177, 215
Darwin, Charles, 42, 43, 63, 97, 140
David, King, 12–13, 16, 52, 72–73, 109–110, 113, 126, 146, 153–155, 218
Deborah, 12, 52, 72, 109
Descartes, René, 42, 62, 97, 140
Dominic, Saint, 32, 58

"E"/Elohist, 13, 154
Edwards, Jonathan, 40, 141
Elijah, 13, 14, 53, 107, 111, 155
Esther, 16, 54, 116

219

People Index

Ezra, 15, 53, 78, 158

Francis of Assisi, 31, 59, 91, 119, 120, 137, 176, 218
Francis Xavier, 37, 61, 96, 180
Franklin, Benjamin, 42

Girard, René, 19n
Grebel, Conrad, 2, 35, 60, 135
Gregory I, Pope, 26, 56
Gregory VII, Pope, 30, 58, 177
Gutenberg, Johann, 60, 136

Henry IV, King, 30, 58, 127
Henry VIII, King, 35, 63, 94, 95, 135, 178
Henry the Navigator, King, 37, 60
Herod the Great, 17–18, 53–54, 160

Ignatius Loyola, 36
Isaiah(s), 14, 16, 53, 74, 75, 78, 112, 155, 156–157

"J"/Yahwist, 13, 16, 154
James, The Apostle, 18, 49, 82, 119, 163
Jeremiah, 14, 53, 75, 155, 156
Joseph (father of Jesus), 160
Joseph (OT patriarch), 11, 52
Judas Iscariot, 18
Innocent III, Pope, 31, 58, 175
Jefferson, Thomas, 40, 42, 62, 185
Jenkins, Philip, 193, 194, 198
Jesus Christ, 2, 8–11, 17–19, 22–23, 42, 46, 54, 78–84, 107, 118–122, 135, 146, 160–165n; Crucifixion, 19, 161, 120, 176; Resurrection, 18, 80, 118, 161, 189; Sermon on the Mount, 79, 84, 93, 119, 136
Joan d'Arc, 60, 218
John, The Apostle, 54, 80, 82, 120
John XXIII, Pope, 49
John Paul II, Pope, 49
Joshua, 12, 52, 72, 109, 152
Josiah, 13, 53, 155, 156
Justinian and Theodora, 56, 170

Kierkegaard, Søren, 42, 135, 147
King, Martin Luther, Jr., 68, 74
Knox, John, 35, 61, 135
Küng, Hans, 134

Leo I, Pope, 56
Leo III, Emperor, 57, 90, 127, 170–171
Leo III, Pope, 30, 87, 170
Leo IX, Pope, 29
Livingstone, David, 44, 63, 182
Locke, John 42
Louis IX, King, 31, 90
Luther, Martin, 34, 60, 68, 93–95, 135, 178

Maccabee, Judas 17, 53, 160
MacCulloch, Diarmaid, 36, 178, 200
Macrina, 23, 122, 166
Madison, James, 40, 42, 62, 185
Mann, Thomas, 10, 68
Mary (mother of Jesus), 56, 63, 105, 110, 127, 132, 138, 160, 185
Mary Magdalene, 18, 20, 82, 119
Micah, 53, 65, 75, 155
Michelangelo, 33, 60, 218
Miriam, 4, 12, 49
More, Thomas, 95, 218
Moses, 2, 11–12, 16–17, 23, 50, 52, 69–70, 107–109, 151–152
Mullin, Bruce, 5, 198
Mott, John, 44, 48, 63

Napoleon Bonaparte, 45n, 63, 140, 142
Nebuchadnezzar, 15, 53, 156
Newton, Isaac, 42–43, 62, 97, 140
Niebuhr, H. Richard, 4, 66–67, 79, 149–150, 164, 175, 178, 186, 217
Niebuhr, Reinhold, 46, 64, 100, 217
Noah, 2, 10, 107, 108

Odoacer, King, 56, 86
Origen, 21, 55, 85

"P"/Priestly writer, 16, 157
Pachomius, 24, 55
Patrick, Saint, 25, 56, 168
Pascal, Blaise, 142
Paul/Saul of Tarsus, 19–20, 54, 80–82, 118–125, 141, 161
Paula, Saint, 22, 32

People Index

Perpetua and Felicity, Saints, 21–22, 54
Peter, Simon, 18, 19, 54, 82, 119, 141
Peter the Great, 62, 62, 171
"Prester John," 37, 58, 60
Putnam, Robert, 141, 145, 192

Ricci, Matteo, 37, 61, 97, 181
Richard the Lionheart, 31, 90
Romulus Augustus, Emperor, 56, 86

Samson, 12, 52, 109, 153
Samuel, 12, 52, 109, 126, 155
Saul, King, 12, 52, 72, 109, 126, 153, 155
Schleiermacher, Friedrich, 42, 63, 184, 217
Scopes, John, 64
Sennacherib, 14, 15
Serra, Junipero, 38, 181
Simons, Menno, 35, 111, 135
Solomon, 13, 16, 52, 72–73, 110, 148, 154
Spong, John, 134
Stephen, 19, 54

Stowe, Harriet Beecher, 44, 100

Tertullian, 21, 54, 148
Thecla, Saint, 20, 54
Thomas the Apostle, 18, 20, 50, 82
Thomas Aquinas, 32, 36, 85, 91–92, 130, 132, 137, 175, 180
Thomas à Kempis, 33, 60, 134, 217
Thomas Becket, 58
Tillich, Paul, 43, 218

Vladimir, Prince, 26, 57, 129

Wesley, John and Charles, 40, 62, 99, 100, 104, 109, 142
White, James W., 6, 19n, 218
White, Loree, v, 147
Williams, Roger, 39, 61
Woolsey, Thomas, 35

Xavier, Francis, 37, 61, 96, 180

Zerubbabel, 15, 53

Subject Index

abuses (church)
   indulgences, 33, 34, 91, 133, 135, 137, 179
   inquisition, 36, 61, 95
   sexual, 93, 133
   simony, selling offices, 92–93, 133
art, 29, 127, 130–131, 170, 175
   architecture/cathedrals, 59, 120, 131, 165, 171, 175
   artists, 33, 59, 60, 175
      icons/iconography, 110, 127, 133, 139, 147
      iconoclastic controversy, 29, 57, 170–171
Armenian Christianity, 27, 55, 56, 63, 88, 123, 138, 146, 172
atheist/atheism, 43, 83, 164

"Babylonian Captivity of the Church," 59, 133, 177
base communities/conscientization, 144, 191

Caesaropapism, 45, 98, 167
Cappadocians, 23, 55, 122, 166
cardinal virtues/deadly sins, 91–92
Celtic Christianity, 25, 56, 86, 89, 125, 168, 169
Catholic Christianity, 29, 49, 61, 95, 110, 130, 133, 136, 137, 138, 167, 168, 170, 174, 175, 185, 191, 194, 198
church life/structure/practices, 20, 34, 125, 136, 139, 170
   communion (see Communion)

   language, 29, 34, 49, 129, 135, 179
   liturgy, 106, 118, 135, 137, 163, 174, 179
   music (see music below)
   parishes, 30, 129, 170, 176
   roles/titles/offices (see appendix A)
   sermons, preaching, 136, 141, 179, 190
   services, 35, 123
   worship life, 82, 112, 118, 122, 133
Communion (Holy)/Eucharist/Lord's Supper, 12, 81, 118, 107, 116, 118, 122, 163, 190 (see sacraments)
   controversies around, 3, 94, 97
   "both kinds," 33, 34, 134, 136
   first communion, 122, 139
   transubstantiation, 58, 177
Confessing Church, 64, 100, 189
Coptic Christianity, 24, 27, 56, 88, 123, 138, 166, 172
Councils (Church), 57, 93, 95, 133, 142, 166, 185
   Chalcedon, 24, 123, 166, 168
   Council of Trent, 36, 61, 138, 179–180
   First Ecumenical (Nicaea), 55, 57, 122, 127, 165
   Fourth Lateran, 175
   Last of the seven Ecumenical, 57
   Vatican I, 63
   Vatican II, 49, 57, 64, 145, 194
Counter-Reformation, 36, 95, 137 (see Council of Trent)
creed(s), 112
   Apostles, 54
   Nicene, 23, 165

Subject Index

Chalcedon, 24, 56, 122
crusades, 31, 58, 59, 90, 131, 174
cuius regio, eius religio, 36, 180
cultures/empires/societies
   Akkadian/Sumerian/Mesopotamian, 52, 150
   Arab/Muslim, 27, 56, 58, 88, 127, 131, 171–175
   Assyrian, 13, 14, 15, 153, 75, 112, 154, 155, 156
   Babylonian, 53, 75–76, 112, 113, 150, 156
   Barbarian/Germanic, 24, 55, 86–87, 123, 166–168
   Byzantine, 60, 127, 167, 173
   Colonial, 38, 62, 180, 183–184
   Contemporary/modern, 91, 98, 188–189, 193, 195, 198
   Enlightenment/Age of Reason, 42–43, 46, 61, 97–98, 140, 184–185, 188
   feudal, 57, 175–176
   Frankish, 24, 56–57, 89, 131, 170, 173
   global, 38, 48, 62, 64, 101, 126, 143, 145, 180, 183, 193–195
   Greek, 17, 19, 21, 22, 53, 55, 64, 67, 77–78, 81, 84, 114, 115, 121, 159–160, 162, 163
   Italian Renaissance, 33, 59, 114, 175
   magisterial, 36, 60, 178, 180
   nation-state, 62, 178, 190
   nautical, 60, 96, 180, 182–183
   nomadic/tribal, 52, 71, 151, 153, 195
   Nordic/Viking, 28, 57, 87, 129, 171
   Ottoman Turk, 31, 45, 60, 63, 88, 138, 172–174, 185
   Persian, 15, 24, 27, 53, 56, 76, 77, 113–115, 157–159, 172
   Philistine, 12, 52, 153
   Roman, 20, 23, 24, 25, 55, 83, 84, 86, 89, 92, 120, 122, 160–163, 165, 168 (see Holy Roman Empire)
   scientific, 42–43, 62, 97, 98, 143, 145, 188, 189, 191, 193
   Slavic/Russian, 26, 57, 129, 139, 174
   technological, 60, 178, 191, 192
   united kingdoms (twelve tribes), 13
   wired, 64, 192, 193

denomination(s)/denominationalism, 39–40, 41–42, 144, 186, 187
dyophysite(s)/ism, 56, 123, 172
dissenters
   Albigenses/Cathari, 32
   Hussites, 60, 93, 134
   Lollards, 134, 177
   Savonarola, 33
   Waldensians, 33, 93, 134
Dominicans (see mendicant orders)
Donation of Constantine, 57

ecumenical/ecumenicity, 49, 64, 143, 194–195
empires (see cultures)
ethics, 3, 4, 66–67, 82, 102
   ends/telos, 67, 69, 75, 84, 89, 90, 91, 94, 96, 97, 98, 99, 100, 102
   response, 67, 69, 70, 71, 75, 77, 78, 80, 81, 85, 91, 94, 97, 98, 101
   rule/command, 67, 70, 72, 75, 77, 80, 83, 86, 87, 88, 89, 92, 96, 98, 99, 100, 101
   triadic, 69
   virtue, 67, 71, 75, 78, 85, 88, 91, 99, 100, 103
Ethiopian/Abyssinian Christianity, 24, 55, 56, 59, 88, 138, 171
exodus event, 69, 107, 108, 152

filioque, 28, 29, 49, 170
fly-fishing, xiii–xv, 210
Franciscans (see mendicant orders)
fulcrum of Christian history, 8–11, 16, 17, 18, 19
fundamentalism/evangelicalism, 47, 143, 144, 189, 193

glossolalia (see Pentecostalism)
Gospel(s), 1–2, 80, 107, 162
   writers, 17, 19, 54, 81
   as good news proclaimed, 20, 85, 120
Great East-West Papal Schism (with anathemas), 29, 58, 59, 90, 170, 173, 174, 194

heresy, 36, 134

Subject Index

heretic(s), 21, 23, 33, 54, 60, 91, 148, 168
heretical, 32, 122, 166
hesychasm/hesychasts, 26, 88, 133, 139, 171
holidays/observances, 16, 77, 116
    Christmas, 94; Easter, 107, 118; First Communion, 139; First Fruits, 110, 153; Hanukkah, 160; Passover, 107, 118; Lent, 105, 107, 114; Maundy Thursday, 116; Pentecost/Shavuot/Weeks, 11; Purim, 116; Sunday, 18, 81, 94, 117, 129, 141, 163; Yom Kippur, 77
"holy fools"/"athletes of God," 24, 87, 124–125, 171
Holy Roman Empire, 29, 36, 45, 63, 140, 173, 178, 185

imago Dei, 10, 68, 69, 96
investiture controversy, 177
Islam/Muslim, 8, 27, 31, 41, 56, 57, 58, 59, 60, 64, 74, 77, 88, 90, 107, 112, 138, 173, 174, 185, 198

Jesuits/Society of Jesus, 36, 38, 61, 62, 137, 181, 182
Jesus Prayer, 26, 88, 133, 171, 179
"Jesus is Lord,"/Caesar/Führer, 46, 100, 164
Judaism, 8, 60, 74, 77, 83, 112, 114, 159, 173, 198
    rabbinic Judaism, 9, 114, 116, 121, 158, 162

Marian devotion/elevation/appearances, 56, 58, 63, 105, 110, 125, 127, 132, 138, 185
medieval thinking (hierarchical), 91–92, 95, 132, 176
mendicant orders, 31–32, 92, 132, 137, 176, 181
    Dominican, 33, 36, 38, 91, 96, 130, 175
    Franciscan, 31, 42, 46, 60, 91, 93, 181
miaphysite(s)/ism, 24, 56, 123
missions/evangelism, 183–184
    African to African, 37, 60, 183, 184
    Byzantines to Russia, 129, 169
    Catholic, 27, 63, 128 (see missionaries and Catholic Christianity)
    Celts to Europe, 25, 56, 86, 128, 169
    Copts to Sudan, 128
    Disciples to Empire+, 19, 54, 163
    English to Australia, other places, 137, 184
    Franks to Saxons, 26, 30, 56, 129, 173
    French to Canada, 38–39, 137
    Koreans to America, 129, 183
    Nestorians to China/Tibet, 26, 56, 88, 128, 172
    Orthodox to Slavs and Rus, 26, 129, 171
    Portuguese to Far East/Brazil, 37, 38, 60, 61, 96
    person to person, 75, 119, 141, 146
    Protestant, 43–44, 96, 137
    Russian Orthodox to North America, 62, 96
    Spanish to America, 38, 60, 96, 181
    Syrians to India/Ethiopia, 20, 82, 128
missionaries, 62
    disciples of Jesus, 20, 82, 119
    Catholic, 27, 37, 63, 96, 180, 183
    foibles of, 183
    Protestant, 54, 182
monasticism, 24, 27, 124, 168, 169
    Augustinian, 33, 58, 93
    Benedictine, 25, 30, 56, 86
    cenobitic, 44, 55, 124, 169
    Celtic (see missions and Celtic Christianity)
    Cistercian, 30, 58, 93, 131
    Cluniac, 30, 57, 62, 87, 129, 173
    disestablished, anti-, closed, 35, 47, 177, 189
    eremitic/hermit/solitary, 24, 55, 87, 88, 124, 133, 166
    Orthodox, 87, 88, 129
    Russian, 59, 171 (see Hesychasm/ts)
music, 22, 27, 125, 136, 137, 142, 174, 190, 199
    musicians, 4, 12, 33, 49, 62
    instruments, 94, 125, 128, 137, 174, 181, 182

Subject Index

Nestorian/Church of the East, 26, 27, 56, 88, 123, 128, 138, 166, 172
Norbertines, 32
office(s) in the church (see Appendix A)
ora et labora, 27, 86, 87, 125, 169
Orthodox(y), 27, 41, 42, 48, 49, 90, 127, 139, 167, 171, 174, 185, 195
    Eastern/Greek, 23, 29, 70n, 86, 88, 129, 138–139, 170
    monasteries/lavra at
    Athos, 59, 139; Cappadocia, 87; desert, 166; Kiev, 26; Sinai/Catherine, 23
    Russian, 45, 47–48, 86, 88, 115, 126, 129, 139, 142, 171, 174, 189
    Ruthenian, 26, 61
    "Triumph of Orthodoxy," 29, 57
    Ukrainian, 26, 47, 139
orthodoxy (right belief), 23, 24, 55, 164, 165, 172
Other Writings/*Ketuvim*, 16, 77, 78, 115, 116, 157, 158

patriarch and pope, 26, 29, 47, 49, 90, 167, 170, 176, 185
Pentecostalism/*glossolalia*/speaking-in-tongues, 48, 63, 82, 88, 119, 143, 193, 198, 199
pieties observed over time (see Appendix B)
pietism, 99, 142, 143
practices of Christians over time (see Appendix B)
preaching, 34, 58, 62, 75, 91, 132, 134, 136, 161, 171, 176, 179, 181
preacher(s), 12, 16, 17, 31, 32, 39, 40, 48, 58, 79, 131, 141, 189, 193
prayer(s), 29, 99, 104, 128, 135, 146, 154, 156, 190, 195
    Book of Common Prayer, 35, 61, 136
    Jesus Prayer (see same above)
    Lord's Prayer, 16, 132, 144, 161
    ora et labora (see same above)
    Rules for, 86, 125
    types: baptismal, 29, 129; lamentation, 156; written, 94
    ways in/to, 29, 89, 94, 106, 111, 114, 119, 126, 138, 146

Prophets, The/*Nevi'im*, 16, 53, 77, 115, 116, 157, 158
prophets, 9, 13, 75, 84
    eighth century BCE, 14, 74, 112, 155
    contemporary, 46, 134, 143, 184

Reformation/Protestant, 34–38, 60, 92–95, 135–137, 141, 178–179
relics, 89, 93, 106, 110, 126
renaissance(s)
    Carolingian, 29, 57, 87, 173
    Italian, 33, 59, 175
revivals/revivalism/awakenings, 40, 41, 48, 62, 63, 99, 141, 143, 146, 186
roles (see Appendix A)
roles, fourfold (from Moses), 11–12, 17, 20
Rome
    First, 23, 29, 53, 56, 123, 166, 168
    Second (Constantinople), 23 29, 58, 138, 165, 167, 170
    Third (Moscow), 60, 129, 139, 174
Russian Christianity, 26, 45, 47, 48, 62, 64, 88, 129, 139, 142, 171, 174, 185, 189, 190 (see Orthodoxy/Russian)

Sacraments, 94, 131, 136
    baptism, 129; believer's, 35–36, 95, 136, 179
    communion, 33, 34, 118, 122 (see same above)
    confirmation, 136
    confession, 58, 89, 90, 92, 95, 128, 177
    marriage, 34, 58, 115, 144 (gay), 175
    ordination, 125
    last rites, 131, 214
saints, 22, 46, 57, 93, 126–128, 132, 146
slavery, 184
    Biblical, 11, 15, 81, 83, 151
    African-American, 40, 44, 65, 96, 100, 181, 190
social gospel, 45, 63, 100, 144
southern/third world Christianity, 38, 44, 48, 143, 184, 193–194, 198, 199
"spirituality," 142, 199
Sermon on the Mount, 79, 84, 91, 119, 136

Subject Index

Syrian Christianity, 24, 55, 56, 88, 123, 138, 172

Tanakh, 9n, 53, 77, 116, 157 (see Torah, The Prophets, and Other Writings)
temple(s)
    Solomon's, 13, 52, 72, 73, 100, 111, 112, 154
    Second, 17, 18, 157, 160
    Herod's, 54, 80, 120
Ten Commandments, 4, 12, 13, 23, 70, 71, 72, 84, 103, 108, 110, 152, 153, 170
theology, 46, 55, 58, 142, 143, 179, 184
    liberation, 47, 64, 101, 102, 191
    neo-orthodox, 4, 46, 101, 189
    process, 43, 102, 188
    Thomistic, 91, 95, 101, 175
theologians
    of antiquity, 21, 22, 23, 24, 55, 86, 122, 166, 172
    medieval, 29, 32, 36, 58, 59, 85, 91, 93, 95, 130, 137
    reform, 34, 35, 42, 94, 135
    recent, 8, 46, 63, 100, 101, 189
Theotokos, 56, 123, 172
titles for Christians (see Appendix A)
Torah/Law, 5, 16, 76, 77, 115, 157, 163
"trial by ordeal," 89

Unam Sanctum bull, 59, 175
universities, 32, 91, 92, 142, 172, 175–176

war (just, holy), 31, 37, 63, 90, 174
World Council of Churches, 48, 64, 101, 194
World Missionary Conference (Edinburgh), 48, 63, 194

"Year to live in infamy" (586 BCE), 15, 112, 156

Zoroastrianism (see Cultures/Persian)

Bible and Literature Index

(Also, see the Bibliography, pp. 215–218)

BIBLE

Old Testament

Genesis, 1, 10–11, 42, 68–69, 71, 102, 106, 110, 115
Exodus, 1, 11, 12, 29, 70, 71, 89, 151
Leviticus, 71–72, 77
Deuteronomy, 70, 148, 152, 155
Joshua, 72
Ruth, 16, 158
Samuel(s), 72–73, 110, 157
Kings, 115, 155
Ezra and Nehemiah, 158
Esther, 16
Job, 74, 76, 115, 158
Psalms, 15, 16, 17, 77, 104, 112, 126, 156
Proverbs, 16, 77, 78, 159
Ecclesiastes, 78
Song of Solomon, 16
Isaiah, 14n, 16, 53, 74, 75, 78, 155, 158
Jeremiah, 14, 75
Ezekiel, 16, 75
Daniel, 16, 17, 114, 160
Hosea, 14, 53, 74, 75
Amos, 14, 53, 74
Jonah, 78
Malachi, 16, 110

New Testament

Matthew, 2, 54, 80, 88, 96, 163
Mark, 17, 18, 120, 163
Luke, 17, 54, 80, 102, 120, 163
John, 54, 80, 81, 120, 146, 163
Acts, 19, 82, 119, 120, 163
Romans, 149
Corinthians, 82, 83, 90, 92, 125
Timothy, 20
Hebrews, 10
Epistle of John, 81
Revelation, 54, 81, 163

Apocrypha

Sirach, 7

OTHER WORKS BY TITLE

Adventures of Huckleberry Finn, Twain, 65
Against the Iconoclasts, John of Damascus, 29
Apologies, Clement of Alexandria, 54
"As Kingfishers . . ." Hopkins, 8

Bible and Literature Index

Book of Common Prayer, Cranmer, 35, 61
Canterbury Tales, Chaucer, 33, 136, 176
Christian Faith, Schleiermacher, 63
Christianity 101, White, 4, 19n, 209
Christianity and the Social Crisis, Rauschenbusch, 45
Christianity, the First Three Thousand Years, MacCulloch, 200
City of God, Augustine, 55, 166
Cloud of Unknowing, unknown author, 59
Commentary on Romans, Barth, 46, 63
Communist Manifesto, Marx, 63
Confessions, Augustine, 23, 124
Cur Deus Homo, Anselm, 58
David Copperfield, Dickens, 1
Divine Comedy/Inferno, Dante, xi, 33, 76
English Church History, Bede, 57
Epic of Gilgamesh, 52, 150
Evangelization of the World in One Generation, Mott, 44
Fundamentalist Papers, Warfield, 6, 143, 189
"I am the coracle ... " Johnson, 128
Iliad, Homer, 52
Imitation of Christ, Thomas à Kempis, 33, 60
In Search of Belief, Chittister, 6
Institutes of the Christian Religion, John Calvin, 61, 84
Liberation Theology, Gutierrez, 47
Moral Man and Immoral Society, Niebuhr, 45, 64
Nicomachean Ethics, Aristotle, 65
"Of what use ... ?" Angelus Silesius, 197
On Prayer, Origen, 21
On the Origin of the Species, Darwin, 63
"Once to every man and ..." Gladden, 45
Pilgrim's Progress, Bunyan, 36
Rule of Benedict/Scholastica, 25, 86, 125, 139, 173
Rule of Basil, and *Pachomius*, 24, 55
Short World History of Christianity, Mullin, 5, 6, 194n, 198n
Showings of Divine Love, Julian, 59
Spiritual Exercises, Ignatius of Loyola, 36
Summa Theologia, Thomas Aquinas, 32, 59
The 100: A Ranking of the Most Influential Persons in the World, 43
"The Assyrian came down ..." Lord Byron, 14–15
Women's Bible, Stanton, 44
World Christian Encyclopedia, 42

www.ingramcontent.com/pod-product-compliance
Lightning Source LLC
Chambersburg PA
CBHW062016220426
43662CB00010B/1347